Say YES! to Own Your Success

Twelve Principles to Catapult a Career You Love…at Any Stage of Life

Ron Stein

Raven + Grace

Raven + Grace Press

Dedication

To my children: Casey (#1), Kyle, Dylan, and Erin (DG4E) and my loyal companions: Brooklyn and Daisy Duke (Bluetick & Redbone Coonhounds),

This book is for you.

Throughout my life's journey, you've endured the long hours and hard work I've poured into my passions and pursuits. From coaching countless games, attending your events, sharing unforgettable trips, and long walks together, we've built bonds that mean the world to me.

Still, I know there were moments when my time was spent elsewhere. By capturing these ideas and experiences in this book, I hope you'll gain insight into the lessons I've learned—and maybe even understand me a little better.

After all, we both know kids don't always listen to their dad's advice...but maybe you'll read it now and learn from it.

I LOVE YOU MORE THAN WORDS CAN SAY.

CONTENTS

Before We Begin

Before we begin, I want to give you an overview of how I perceive our life journey, which I have categorized into three volumes. Not tied to specific ages, because this book works for any stages, these volumes represent significant changes that impact our journeys. Each one will require planning and numerous adjustments throughout, and you can use this book to achieve where you want to be when you reach the end.

Volume I: Becoming an Adult encompasses the period from birth through college graduation or starting full-time work. It's the initial stage of self-discovery and independence.

Volume II: Post-College is the middle section of our life story, where we have become self-supporting, marked by pivotal decisions and responsibilities related to careers and relationships.

Volume III: Sunset Period encompasses retirement, the empty nest phase, and living out our remaining years. This marks a reflective period where accumulated experiences guide us through our remaining time on Earth.

As we progress through these volumes, we naturally grow older and, hopefully, wiser. We develop a deeper understanding of our likes, dislikes, and aspirations, armed with wisdom from the preceding experiences. Life's volumes offer a framework for self-reflection and a chance to create the road-map utilizing the companion workbook. Let's get started.

How to Use this Book

This book is based on 12 principles:

1. PASSION

2. CONFIDENCE

3. TIME MANAGEMENT

4. NETWORKING

5. PRIORITIZING

6. LISTENING AND LEARNING

7. WORKING HARD

8. ACT DECISIVELY

9. FOCUS

10. DOUBT MANAGEMENT

11. POSITIVE MINDSET

12. STRONG TEAM

Each principle will be explored in its own chapter, then in the final chapter, you will see how the 12 principals culminate all together.

This book also comes with a workbook to help you gain clarity and insight on how to use Say **Yes**! To Own Your Success. The workbook will guide your own successful plan and help you to make important life decisions to chart your direction. You will need to provide the Drive.

To get the most out of this experience, read the entire book first, then go back and fill out the workbook.

Download the free workbook here:
ownyoursuccessnow.com/workbook.

Welcome to My Story

I'm Ron, your guide to the transformative power of saying **YES**.

In the pages ahead, I will unveil the remarkable potential of embracing a **YES** attitude and navigating life's pivotal career decisions. Whether you're changing careers, choosing the right first job, figuring out a retirement strategy, or seizing life opportunities, this book is your road-map to unleash your fullest potential and give you the skills and structure to accomplish your goals by creating an achievable plan.

Before we dive in, let me ask you a few questions:
- Do you yearn for positive change in your life?
- Are you eager to learn effective strategies for career success?
- Do you crave richer, more fulfilling experiences?
- Are you striving to cultivate healthier relationships?
- Do you seek proven techniques to thrive in life and business?
- Do you wish to boost your self-confidence?
- Are you ready to take charge of your destiny and master your universe?
- Are you up for some laughter and fun along the way?

If you answered **YES** to any of these questions, then you're in the right place.

This isn't about blindly saying **YES** to everything. We're talking about effective strategies that propel you forward, enabling you to achieve your goals without compromising your values or endangering others. Common sense is vital.

My journey from a timid "no-guy" to someone with a more open and receptive mindset had its fair share of challenges. In fact, for the first eighteen years of my life, I moved through the world with a victim mentality—a place we've all found ourselves at times—drowning in a woe-is-me attitude. But once I discovered that dwelling in negativity only perpetuates it, I made a conscious effort to adopt a **YES** attitude. As a result, my life changed for the better and I want to share that approach with you.

In the chapters ahead, I'll share my triumphs and setbacks—from launching numerous (mostly) successful ventures in different areas to meeting fascinating people and embarking on unexpected adventures around the world. It wasn't always easy. I had to overcome some business failures and toxic relationships along the way.

Like my favorite movie, *The Good, the Bad, and the Ugly*, I have learned valuable lessons from every endeavor, including twelve Core Principles that will be highlighted in each chapter and repeated throughout the book. One or more of these Core Principles may be difficult for you to do or accomplish, but my examples may help you conquer and achieve them. These Core Principles have instilled in me resilience and perseverance, helping to shape me into the best version of myself—someone who takes calculated risks, rises above failures, focuses on gratitude, lives in the present, and is hopeful for the future.

Saying **YES** has ushered me into a realm of chance encounters, where seizing opportunities, cultivating optimism, and welcoming the unknown led to new discoveries and endless possibilities. Most importantly, it allowed me to navigate life as a creator rather than a victim.

But this isn't just my story; it's a blueprint for anyone seeking to unleash their potential.

In order to have direction and make decisions, you need to establish goals and a solid, achievable plan. Also, you must have the Drive (intestinal fortitude), desire, ***Focus***, and hunger needed to power through.

So, alongside my personal anecdotes and guidance, you'll discover lessons learned after each chapter. At the end of the book and within the workbook, these will culminate into ***Ronnie's Steps to Success***, the proven decision framework I honed through years of trial and error.

Now, take a moment to ensure that your seat-belt is securely fastened and your book is in the full and upright position, and join me on this incredible **YES**-adventure.

Our journey starts in the middle just months before my fortieth birthday, a life-changing **YES** propelled me onto an exciting new career path. And we're off...

CHAPTER 1

PASSION

WHEN ONE DOOR CLOSES, ANOTHER OPENS

May 2006

I sipped the fresh-steeped tea that my friend Tim handed to me, hoping the hot liquid would warm me up. Outside the big glass window of his office in Canary Wharf, I watched the rain tumble down from the gray sky. It hadn't stopped raining since my flight from New York to London landed an hour earlier.

"I'm sick of this shitty May weather. The never-ending rain and fog this time of year are depressing," I said, placing my cup of tea on Tim's desk. "I really wish I was in Cannes right now."

"Cannes? Isn't the film festival going on there?" Tim asked.

"Yeah, my buddy Mickey is there for his partner, Cheyenne Jackson's movie premiere of *United 93*."

"You should go," Tim suggested. "The weather is probably gorgeous in Cannes right now."

"I wish I could, but I'm supposed to meet with my former employees at the MPI office to hand over the accounts."

But images of parties, booze, beaches, and hot women prancing around in itty-bitty bikinis while sipping champagne flashed in my mind. That kind of fun seemed appealing right then, especially after months of grinding to close the deal on the sale of my company. As for the London office, I realized I could always help them remotely over the phone. Given that I always strive to surround myself with a *Strong Team*, I trusted that they could handle this without me.

Suddenly, I blurted out, "**YES!** You're right. I should go. I'm out of here." I stood up and reached out to shake Tim's hand. "Well, at least we got to see each other, even if just briefly."

Tim gave me a firm handshake. "Now, that's the Ron I know and everyone loves, spontaneous and always up for the next adventure," he said, nodding his head with a toothy grin. "Have some drinks for me."

Grabbing my rain-soaked suitcase, I said goodbye.

Tim and I go way back. He was my boss at my third job out of college when we worked at Lehman Brothers in the early nineties, and we have remained close friends ever since. We always have great discussions about the latest technology trends and how it applies to business, politics, and the world. Whenever I traveled to London for work, I enjoyed spending time with him, but at this point, I wasn't sure when I would be back there.

The Yiddish adage, "Man plans, and God laughs," proved accurate. Before I arrived in London, I had a full chock-a-block schedule, as the English say, with at least a dozen meetings planned over the next week that took hours and hours of preparation. But Tim's comment gave me a jolt and made me realize that I deserved a break in the South of France. Not to mention, I learned a while ago to follow the sun and good weather because people are genuinely happier in warmer climates (and you always have a nice tan).

Off to Cannes

I hopped in a classic English black taxi. On the way to the airport, I made three phone calls. I called Mickey, letting him know I was on my way to Cannes.

"Ron, no way!" Mickey exclaimed. "That's great. There's a big party this afternoon at Bâoli Beach Club. Cheyenne and I will take you as our guest."

"Thanks, man. Sounds like fun. Any idea what hotel I should book?"

Mickey laughed. "Dude, there's no way you'll find a decent room. It's packed here. Why don't you just crash in our suite? It's huge, so there's plenty of space for you."

"I appreciate that, but I'm sure I can find a room somewhere."

"Don't be ridiculous, Ron. Stay with us. We're at The Carlton Hotel. It's beautiful and quite the scene. A-list celebrities are everywhere. I'll leave a key for you at the front desk. We're in suite 725."

"Alright. Thanks, man. I'll see you soon."

Next, I called the London office and told them something came up, and I wasn't going to make it, but I promised to go over everything with them on the phone the next chance I got. "Good luck with the business. I know you chaps will kill it," I added before hanging up.

Since I had gone to Tim's office right after I landed early that morning, I never checked into the hotel I'd booked for my trip. My last call was to the front desk to cancel my reservation, not caring when they told me I would be charged for the night's room.

After arriving at London City Airport, I caught the next flight to Nice. Two hours later, I got off the plane to a world of brilliant sunshine that bathed my face and a few puffy clouds floating in the azure sky. It was incredible how much the weather affected my mood. Agreeing to bail on London had definitely been a good decision. I got into a cab, told the driver where I was headed, and rolled down the windows, breathing in the refreshing Mediterranean air. I flashed back to my first visit to Nice at eighteen, when I shed my insecure teenage self—more on that later.

The driver pulled up the driveway in front of the palatial hotel with its two-tone facade, wrought iron balcony railings, and giant domes pointing toward the infinite blue sky. My driver stopped behind a red Lamborghini, and a bellboy dressed in a crisp white shirt and dark gray vest ran to the door to let me out. He grabbed my suitcase from the trunk, and I told him Mickey's room number.

Inside the lobby, the elegance was breathtaking. The décor was filled with cream-colored grandeur, large pillars, shiny marble floors, and tall planters overflowing with fresh flowers and green shrubs. A man in a black tuxedo held hands with a stunning woman in a long, red silk gown, and they rushed past me. The smell of her rose-scented perfume made me sneeze. People were walking in all directions. Women in pastel sun-dresses, over-sized sun hats, large-framed sunglasses, and men wearing shorts, boat shoes, and linen button-downs were heading toward The Carlton Beach Club in the back of the hotel. A handful of others had donned evening wear.

Everyone's chic attire made me think I needed to go shopping, as the dark pants and blue button-downs I packed for London weren't the best fashion choice here. Before going to Mickey's room, I stopped in one of the hotel boutiques and bought a Vilebrequin bathing suit with a scattering of hot-pink turtles, a butter-yellow short-sleeved but-ton-down shirt, and white jeans. Purchasing clothes in fruity colors wasn't something I would normally do, but I suddenly found myself on vacation and wanted to fit in among all these stylish people.

After grabbing a key from the front desk, I rushed toward the elevator. Right before the door closed, two men jumped in next to me. One guy had perfectly coiffed brown hair and wore a pin-striped blazer over a pink Oxford shirt. His dark sunglasses covered his eyes. He looked familiar, and it seemed like he thought he was important.

Suddenly, it dawned on me that it was Tom Cruise. Acting composed, I didn't say anything or even glance his way. The freckle-faced, red-headed guy standing next to him had a strange expression. I got the feeling he wanted me to acknowledge who he was with.

"What floor?" I asked, about to press the button.

The redheaded man spoke out. "Eighteen, right, Mr. Cruise?"

Mr. Cruise didn't respond. He was holding a stack of white paper, his attention focused on the words on the page.

"Yo, Mr. Cruise? Is it eighteen?" I asked, annoyed that he was ignoring his sidekick assistant.

"Yeah," Mr. Cruise mumbled.

The door closed, and the redhead turned to me. "You know who this is, don't you?"

I shrugged my shoulders, not wanting to give the redhead the satisfaction.

Mr. Cruise stopped reading, took his shades off, and reached his hand in my direction. "Tom Cruise," he said.

"Ron Stein, damn glad to meet you," I responded, just like in the movie *Animal House*. Then, holding a blank look, I gave him a firm shake.

The elevator bell rang, and the door opened. "Have a nice day, Tom," I called out, stepping onto my floor. I smirked, imagining their dumbfounded faces after I didn't fawn all over one of Hollywood's most famous actors. I'm just not that starstruck. There was no way I was going to kiss some guy's ass to add to his huge ego simply because he was famous. Tom Cruise probably wasn't used to people like me. But guess what? I did the opposite of what was expected and acted as if I couldn't have cared less because I believe that it is important to be on the same playing field as others (even movie stars and I never want to feel inferior). When I got in front of Mickey room, I knocked loudly.

"Come in!" I heard Mickey yell. I slid my key card into the door lock and let myself in. "Ron, you made it. Great timing. We're leaving in about fifteen minutes," Mickey said, getting up from the tufted armchair facing the panoramic ocean view. He looked good with his five-o'clock shadow and gray beret.

"This room is unbelievable," I said while we embraced in a man hug, adding an extra pat on the back. "Thanks for letting me crash here." The one-bedroom suite was decorated in buttercream, with raised paneled walls, parquet floors, and French doors leading out to a terrace.

"Ron, what's up!" Cheyenne said in a sing-song voice as he walked out of the bathroom wearing a white robe. His dark hair looked freshly gelled in a messy, spiky style. He was a great-looking guy (my man crush). Women were constantly hitting on him, and I can only imagine their disappointment when they found out he was into men.

"I'm not sure I can stand next to you two with your golden tans," I said, only half-joking.

"Oh, Ron, you look handsome. A little pale but fine," Cheyenne said, smiling. "Why don't you hop in the shower and then get dressed? We've got to leave in about fifteen minutes for the party."

I got ready in record time, and then the three of us made our way toward one of the hottest parties in town, or so I was told. My face hadn't seen the sun in a long time, and the rays felt strong. I was hopeful I'd get some of my color back during my stay.

Party of a Lifetime

Entering the Bâoli Beach Club, we followed the loud techno music from the DJ out to the veranda. A server with long blonde hair who was wearing a skimpy one-piece bathing suit handed us each a glass of Dom Pérignon. The cool, bubbly drink quenched my thirst. While drinking a second glass, I took in the scene: a woman in a pink bikini top and short, cut-off jeans stood on a table, shaking her ass in some guy's face. Everyone was moving to the beat. Another woman, with an arm full of gold bangles, wobbled in her high-heeled shoes. I was concerned she was about to fall off the chair she was dancing on. Drunk people were grinding into each other—men into men, women into men, and I spotted a few women making out with each other.

Shot girls, in their skin-tight dresses, walked around with holsters wrapped around their waists. They had vodka on one side of their holster and a sugary beverage on the other. One of the women came up to me, signaling that she wanted me to take one. Another shot girl tipped my head back, so I watched on her sizable balloon-like chest while the other woman poured vodka and punch down my throat. With every shot after that, the day-to-night party became more blurred.

Finally, when the sun went down, the neon strobe lights began flashing while I moved my hips into the back of a curvy woman, inhaling her sweet, rose-scented, flowy hair. She was waving around a party sparkler. I heard her say something over the loud music, but I couldn't decipher the words. Then again, she might have been speaking in French, so I had no clue what she was trying to tell me. But who cared? Right now, this hottie and I were speaking the language of lust, and that was all that mattered. Just that morning, I was freezing my ass off in the dreary London weather, and here I was now, partying like a rock star.

Dancing with the sexy Frenchwoman was the last barely vivid memory from the night. I woke up early (I never sleep much, maybe four to five hours a night) on the pull-out couch in Mickey's suite with a throbbing headache and a mouth that felt as dry as the Sahara. I needed to brush my teeth. I needed diet soda. I needed an espresso. And I needed a greasy breakfast. I rolled out of bed and threw on my new Vilebrequin bathing suit, a linen button-down short-sleeved shirt, and aviator sunglasses. The door to Mickey and Cheyenne's bedroom was shut, so I quietly left without disturbing them.

Glancing at myself in the gold-plated mirror by the elevator, I noticed my face was sun-kissed, giving me a healthy glow. From that day forward, I vowed always to keep that color and follow the warm weather. Considering my hangover, I didn't look as bad as I felt and was ready to move forward with the day.

Another Life Chapter Begins With a Simple Question and One-Word Reply

In the lobby, I made my way toward the café for breakfast. The maître di sat me at a table overlooking the crystal-blue Mediterranean. I ordered a double espresso, diet soda, and eggs Benedict with bacon. Moments later, the server handed me my caffeinated hot beverage. I held the small cup, enjoying the view while watching large yachts floating in the sea.

"Hey, excuse me." The guy speaking to me appeared to be in his mid-thirties and was dressed casually in khaki shorts and a collared shirt. "I know you. You're a producer, right?" I wiped the runny eggs off the corner of my mouth with my napkin, and before I could respond, he said, "I've got this great script I want you to check out."

Why not, I thought. "I might be interested. What's the film about?"

He rambled about some action-packed sci-fi robot plot and all the famous actors and actresses who were interested and almost attached. And then he added, "I'm trying to get the last piece of financing secured. I promise you can't lose on this one, and it would be insane to pass up this golden opportunity. Can I leave you this teaser to look over?"

"Yeah, I'll read it." I grabbed the packet of pages from his hand. "Give me your number, and I'll be in touch."

I knew this guy was bullshitting me, and I also knew I could outsmart him. When I glanced at the other diners in the café, I felt this conversation was taking place at three different tables. This may have been my first time hearing these lines, but it wouldn't be the last. It made me wonder if they handed out a pamphlet in script-writing school, telling everyone exactly what to say to swindle money out of suckers.

After we exchanged contact information, the guy walked away. While perusing through the packet, a surge of energy pumped in my veins, and it wasn't the caffeine. Instead, a seed had just been planted in my mind. *Should I go into the movie business?* I knew it was a crazy thought. But why not? I had nothing to lose. After all, it was a creative endeavor and something I absolutely thought I would have **PASSION** for.

Then, the dark voice in my head emerged, and I couldn't help but wonder, *Am I nuts? Have I totally lost touch with reality? I had absolutely no experience in the film business whatsoever.*

But once I answered my inner critic and doubt, I realized I should follow my gut and go for it. Just like that, I said **YES** to trying a new career and making movies. But don't worry, I wasn't a total idiot. I knew I couldn't go into this blind; it would require enormous research, *Time Management*, and *Working Hard*. Since I didn't have any clue about the film industry, I racked my brain, trying to figure out which friends or acquaintances I knew who could help me learn anything and every-thing about making movies. In my experience, you can't accomplish big dreams if you're unwilling to take risks.

The bottom line is once a decision is made, start the process and try it out confidently. I applied **The Power of YES** philosophy and began the process of starting a new career. Again...

How Did This All Get Started?

That was a glimpse into the start of my life as a movie producer, and more will come later in the book. But before we dive into the crazier aspects of my Hollywood career, let's rewind to where it all began so you can see the progression, the moment that marked my first life transformation toward the end of my Life Volume I through the end of my Life Volume II.

Lessons Learned Chapter 1: Must Have PASSION

Discover Your Passion: The Spark That Changes Everything

They say finding your *Passion* is the secret sauce to happiness. Why? Because when you're doing what you love, it doesn't feel like work, it feels like living. As illustrated in this chapter, *Passion* doesn't knock politely; sometimes it bursts into your life when you least expect it.

Let's Recap:

Spontaneous Decision-Making

When I was sitting in the dreary London weather, my decision to fly to Cannes wasn't just about escaping the rain; it was about embracing adventure and following my gut instinct. This moment exemplifies how *Passion* often starts with a bold "**YES!**" to something unexpected.

Tapping into Curiosity

Meeting Mickey, experiencing the electric energy of Cannes, and observing the glamorous world of film sparked a dormant curiosity in me. It wasn't just about the champagne or the parties, it was about imagining myself as part of this vibrant, creative industry.

Exploring New Ideas

When approached by the guy pitching a sci-fi script, I could have brushed it off. Instead, I entertained the possibility, took the teaser script, and let the seed of a new career take root. My willingness to engage and explore an unfamiliar path demonstrates the first step toward discovering a *Passion*.

Acting on Inspiration

Rather than letting self-doubt hold me back, I took decisive action by researching and planning, leveraging my network to *Listen and Learn* the ropes of the film industry. This proactive approach turned a fleeting idea into a serious endeavor.

CHAPTER 2

CONFIDENCE

A SCRAWNY EIGHTEEN-YEAR-OLD

Spring 1985

Rachel's crimped blonde hair smelled like apples. The sweet scent lingered on my pillow for days after she snuck out of my house before my parents got home from work. When I wasn't with her, I couldn't get her off my mind; like sap on a tree, everything about her stuck to me. At football games, she was the only cheerleader I watched. Her slender figure bouncing up and down, her legs and hips jiggling, her full, frosted pink lips cheering, her hands shaking her blue-and-white pom-poms. I was sure all the guys in my high school fantasized about Rachel, but little did they know, I had memorized every detail of her naked body—her perky, round breasts, her innie belly button, the beauty mark on her collarbone.

Girls like Rachel didn't usually go for guys like me, a tall, scrawny eighteen-year-old. Instead, girls like Rachel tended to go for the football team's quarterback. We kept our relationship, if you could even call it that, a secret. I would've told the entire school about us if it were up to me. But Rachel didn't want anyone to know that she and I had been having sex most of our senior year. I guess I couldn't blame her. She could have any guy she wanted, and considering my lanky body wasn't that desirable, and my friends and I rarely attended any parties, I was the last guy whose hand she would like to hold in the school hallway or sit next to in the cafeteria.

Our secret sexual relationship happened by accident. In social studies class, Mr. Hammond assigned us the role of co-lawyers in a mock trial. Every day after school, we talked about nothing and everything in between taking notes and preparing for our court case. Then, one afternoon, it just happened. I don't remember who leaned in first, but somehow, we started kissing, our clothes came off, and we had sex on my living room's red-and-brown plaid couch. Afterward, she begged me not to tell anyone. I kept my mouth shut for months, not telling a soul about the two of us. I knew how embarrassed she would be if anyone found out that she was having sex with me, Ron, the geek. As much as I wanted to scream it over the loudspeaker, it wasn't worth the risk of losing Rachel.

A couple of days before graduation, Rachel called me on the phone and said, "Ron, listen, I don't think we should see each other anymore."

"What? Why? What do you mean?" My heart felt like it had a clamp on it.

"Well, I just, you know. I don't know." Her voice was squeezing the clamp.

"What? It's not like anyone even knows about us. So why do you want to end it? We have a good thing going."

"Remember Giancarlo?"

I knew where this was going. She put so much pressure on my imaginary heart clamp that I could hardly breathe. Giancarlo had graduated high school two years before me and had been recruited to Boston College for football. He was the big Italian stallion. I tuned Rachel out when she told me he was spending the summer at home, something about a knee injury ruining his football career, and Rachel was the only one he wanted, the only one who could help him through this challenging time. Every guy in Long Island wanted Rachel. I should've known better than to get involved with her and waste my time. (Later in life, I realized not to be so negative and realized there is no time wasted, just a series of moments to enjoy and learn from.)

At the time, Rachel was the best thing that had ever happened to me. The truth was, I felt like I would never get another Rachel again. For all I knew, I would never get another woman again. I would probably be single for the rest of my life. In another two months, I was going off to college to the University of Delaware. I didn't want to be the same loser in college that I was in high school, but maybe some people never change, and once a loser, always a loser. Boy, I disliked my life and desperately wanted to change it.

Sudden Change of Summer Plans

Skeeter kicked my bedroom door open and stormed inside, startling me.

"Ron-Bo, what's up?" Skeeter yelled. He wore a sleeveless shirt, and his overgrown hair was sticking out of his baseball cap. Skeeter grew up in West Virginia and was a poster boy for what I imagine most rednecks looked like from there. He and my older cousin, Jack, were college roommates and best friends. Skeeter was visiting for the weekend and they had stopped by my house as Jack often did.

I shrugged my shoulders.

"Yo, why so glum earlier, Ron-Bo?" I usually liked Skeeter, but I was not in the mood for him right now. "Are you having trouble with the ladies?" he asked with a smirk.

What was he? A fucking mind reader? How would he even know something like that?

"Jack and I are going to the mall. I need to buy some shit for our trip. Do you want to go shopping with us?"

"Nah, I don't feel like it."

"Ron-Bo, Ron-Bo. You're about to graduate high school. You should be psyched right now. You got any summer plans?"

"I'm just teaching tennis."

"That sounds boring. No other plans? No summer fun?"

"Nah."

"Lame, bro. Lame. Hey, I have a great idea. You should join Jack and me on our European backpacking trip. It's going to be fucking awesome."

"How am I going to do that?"

"Easy, bro, you've been working. You've got the cash. Get your ass out of bed, buy a plane ticket, buy a backpack, and go. It's that simple."

Skeeter did have a point. I had a lot of money saved from all my high school jobs. I supposed I could go. Getting out of town for the summer and getting Rachel off my mind would be nice.

"Jack!" Skeeter yelled into the paper-thin walls in our tiny split-level house. "Don't you think Ron should come with us to Europe?"

"Yeah, Ron. Come." I heard Jack yell back from the kitchen just down the hall.

Little did I know then that saying **YES** to this trip would alter my life trajectory.

European Backpacking Adventure: The Beginning of My Evolution

Two weeks later, Skeeter, Jack, and I were sitting in a booth in a dark, smoky London pub, drinking Guinness beer. We were reading a thick and heavy *Fodor's '85 Europe* book, trying to decide where to go next.

"What about Cannes? In the South of France. This place sounds so cool," Jack said. "And it might be nice to spend some time at the beach."

"Whatever you guys want," I replied, sipping the beer and not caring what we were doing. I was just happy to be on this adventure.

I did not realize I had a blank look on my face when Jack demanded, "Snap out of your funk, Ron. Since we arrived, you've been staring off into space like a zombie."

Jack was right. I was not taking advantage of this fantastic opportunity. Something kept holding me back. I thought going to Europe would help me forget Rachel, but it didn't. Every hot blonde girl I passed was another reminder of what I'd had . . . and lost. Even though I never really had her at all. I wasn't good enough for Rachel and probably would never be good enough for anyone. Before Rachel, I had no **CONFIDENCE** in myself, and after she dumped me, my self-esteem sank to its lowest level.

"Leave the kid alone, Jack. If he wants to be quiet and stay inside his head the entire trip, that's his choice." Skeeter chugged the rest of his beer and then released a loud belch.

The following day, we took the flight to Paris and checked into a nearby hostel. The plan was to spend three days here, wandering around museums, checking out the Arc de Triomphe and the Eiffel Tower, and then heading to the coast. We took in the sights, and I tried to fake a smile and feign interest, but I still felt this dark cloud following me.

Something changed in me when I visited the Rodin Museum by myself while Skeeter and Jack stayed in bed at our hostel, sleeping off their hangovers. Listening to ABBA's *Super Trouper* cassette on my Sony™ Walkman, I walked around the walled-off gardens with their tall hedges and blooming flower gardens. The song "The Winner Takes It All" came on when I stopped in front of *The Thinker*, the naked bronze sculpture of a hulking six-foot-tall man hunched over, his hand resting on his chin to show he was in deep thought.

I sat and stared at the iconic, melancholy statue in quiet contemplation. *Was I like him? Was this the kind of person I wanted to be? Did I want to be someone lost and dejected?*

But my thoughts were just thoughts. They were not who I was. *Could I become the man I wanted to be simply by reframing my perspective? Why did Rachel have so much power over how I felt about myself?* She did because I allowed her to, in my mind. That was it. No more. It was time to change the way I thought for good.

I realized that I needed time to think. Big ideas are in front of and inside every person, and we can all discover them. I stopped in a small café for some espresso and immersed myself in Parisian culture, people-watching (which would become a favorite pastime of mine) and lost in my thoughts. While sitting at a table, I noticed a mime with a white painted face, beret, and gray hair on the other side of the café. We stared at each other for an eternity until he finally blurted out, "Ouai!"

Strange. I didn't know mimes spoke. I always assumed they were physical mutes. After he left, I asked my server what that word meant, and he said, "It's a casual Parisian way of saying **YES**." I took that as the ultimate sign.

It was time to believe in my ability to shape my future and not be a victim of my circumstances, much like Rodin shaping art, by designing a better life for myself using the power of a ***Positive Mindset*** thoughts to guide me toward my dreams. Of course, embracing this new self-concept also meant I had to keep an open mind and practice saying YES to new experiences. But it wasn't enough to say and believe it; I needed to *just do it.*

Nothing Like the French Riviera

After this epiphany, I stood taller, held my head high, and moved with ***Confidence***. It was an incredible feeling, like a rush I never wanted to be without from that moment on. The next day, we took the train to Cannes, France, and found a hostel near the train station. We threw our backpacks into our room, put our bathing suits on, and went to the beach.

Everyone we passed seemed glamorous in their bright neon clothes and designer sunglasses. Jack and Skeeter stopped inside a pharmacy to buy tanning oil while I entered a high-end optical store next door. I bee-lined to the sunglass section and purchased a pair of black Vuarnets with mirrored lenses. I had never spent this much money on sunglasses (nearly twenty-five percent of the spending money I had brought on the trip), but I was empowered as soon as I put them on.

"Look at you, Ron. Nice shades," Skeeter said, whistling as I walked out of the store. "You've got swagger in your step now. You must have gotten some rest."

Skeeter was right. Wearing my new shades, I looked like Tom Cruise from *Risky Business*. At that moment, I became a different Ron, more robust and proud, a guy who knew what he wanted and how to get it.

Walking down to the beach, my eyes widened behind my lenses. I couldn't believe what I was seeing. Topless women were omnipresent. I saw boobs in every shape and size: saggy, pointy, teardrop, bell-shaped, upright—you name it, they were all there. What a glorious day this turned into. The blazing sun was illuminating breast land. And to think, if I hadn't said **YES** to this trip, I would be home teaching tennis to some bratty pre-teens and fantasizing about Rachel's A-cup breasts.

We found some space on the pebbly beach and plopped down on our cheap, paper-thin towels that we took from the hostel. I didn't even care that the rocks were pressing into my back. I was much too busy staring at the live show in front of me: men prancing around in their bikini bottoms with their bulges slightly protruding and women sunbathing and strutting around with their boobs jiggling. It was not like I hadn't seen my fair share of boobs in the pages of my dad's *Playboy* magazines that he kept hidden in his bathroom, but to see so many in the flesh was like a dream come true.

"Check out that hottie," Skeeter said.

A pruned woman with deflated boobs almost hitting her knees walked past us. "What? Dude, that's so gross. That lady looks older than my grandmother. I guess topless isn't always great."

"No, shithead, that one." Skeeter pointed to a sun-kissed brunette, her hair held back with a yellow silk scarf that matched her bikini bottom. She stood at the shoreline, letting the waves crash against her ankles. Her round, full breasts looked like a perfect C-cup.

I stood up and started to walk toward her.

"Ron, what are you doing? You're not going to talk to her, are you?"

"**YES**, I sure am." Up close, she was even more beautiful. She had high cheekbones and full lips. I greeted her in a sing-song voice, "Bonjour."

"Bonjour," she said.

"Do you speak English?" I asked.

"A little. You are American?"

"I am. I've been watching you and came here to tell you that you're the most attractive woman I've ever seen."

Her cheeks flushed. "Merci."

The next few minutes were like an out-of-body experience. First, I asked her to tell me about herself. Her name was Brittanie. She was twenty-four and worked at a women's clothing boutique in Cannes. She pushed her sunglasses on top of her head.

"Your eyes sparkle like the ocean," I told her, aware that my pickup line was super cheesy, but she totally fell for it as she must have been used to French guys pulling that stuff all the time. After the compliment rolled off my tongue, I leaned toward her face, inhaling the coconut scent from her glowing skin, opened my mouth slightly, and kissed her, soft at first, then deeper. My first true French kiss.

She stopped me and whispered in my ear, "Would you like to come back to my apartment?"

"**YES**! **YES**, I would," I responded, sounding a bit too excited.

Jack and Skeeter's mouths fell slack when we walked past them. Brittanie held my hand as she led me off the beach and toward the sidewalk to her apartment. On the way, I silently gave thanks for everything: my magical sunglasses, Rodin's *Thinker* and, last but not least, Rachel, for stomping on my heart. After all, hitting my lowest point enabled me to rise to the highest version of myself.

The following morning, Skeeter, Jack, and I sat outside a café, drinking espressos and eating chocolate croissants.

Skeeter looked at me, a smear of chocolate stuck to his upper lip. "Okay, Ron, spill it. We want all the details."

"C'mon," Jack interrupted. "I'm proud of you, bro, but I'm not interested in hearing a play-by-play of your sex life."

Skeeter shook his head. "Jack, why do you always have to kill the fun?" He took another bite of the croissant and made smacking noises while he chewed. "What the hell happened to you in Paris, Ron-Bo? You're definitely not the same guy who started this trip with us. But, buddy, you got game, and I'm impressed."

A couple of tables over, Skeeter turned to look at three attractive women. They had different shades of blonde hair and porcelain-white skin. "Zowee, you guys see those ladies over there? There are three of them and three of us. It's kind of perfect, don't you think?"

"Skeeter, let me handle this," I said, getting up from my chair and grabbing my small plate with my uneaten chocolate croissant.

"Do you believe this shit? Your cousin thinks he's some kind of Tom Cruise ladies' man," I overheard Skeeter tell Jack.

Standing before the women, I placed my croissant in the center of their table. "Have you ladies tried these chocolate croissants? You need to. They're hands down the best in Cannes."

"Thank you. That is so sweet of you," the woman with honey-colored hair said in a melodic accent that didn't sound French.

"You're not from here, are you?" I asked.

"No, we are from Sweden," Honey Hair announced. "We are here on holiday. And let me guess, you are from the States?"

"Is it that obvious?" I smiled. "My name is Ron. What are your names?"

Honey Hair pushed her shoulder-length locks behind her ears and said, "I am Astrid. This is Greta, and this is Kerstin." Greta's butter-yellow hair was pulled back in a ponytail. Kerstin had dirty blonde hair and bangs.

"It's a pleasure to meet you all. We were thinking about heading to Sweden after this, but we have yet to figure out where we want to go. Do you have any travel tips you can share?"

"Why don't you and your friends sit with us at our table? We will tell you everything you need to know about our beautiful country," Astrid said in her sweet voice.

I waved to Skeeter and Jack, signaling they should come to the table. The women spread their chairs apart, allowing us to sit with them. I took a seat on the other side of Astrid. For the next hour, we got to know each other. They were from Gothenburg and worked together in a bank. If I had to guess their age, I would bet they were in their early thirties. The way Astrid threw her head back, laughing at my dumb jokes, I could tell she was into me. After the previous night with Brittanie, I sensed I was on a roll with the ladies. Astrid and I were about an inch apart, and I could feel the sexual energy running between us. I wondered if she had any idea how old I was. When Skeeter and Jack mentioned that they had just graduated from college, I didn't say anything about how I had just graduated from high school. However, if she discovered how old I was and didn't want me because of my age, then so be it.

"We have to catch our train in a bit," Astrid announced. Then she turned to me and said, "Why don't I give you my home number and address in Gothenburg, and if you change your trip itinerary and go to Sweden, I can show you around, and you can stay at my place for a few days."

"That would be great."

We all stood up at the same time and hugged each other goodbye. Then, when the women walked away, we gave each other a high five.

"How about that?" Skeeter said. "Ron, you're getting laid on this trip and helping us get laid too. Who would have thunk it? Kerstin invited me to stay with her too."

"And I'm going to Greta's," Jack chimed in.

Skeeter pulled out the *Fodor's* book from his backpack. "Before going north, we should plan where we're going from here and what to cut from the trip to make this Swedish smorgasbord happen."

And that was when the bickering began. When people spend every minute with one another, conflict is inevitable. I wanted to travel to Italy next. Skeeter wanted to hike in Switzerland, and Jack wanted to go to Germany. We went back and forth, arguing with each other. We were three stubborn guys, and none of us would give in.

The only solution was to return to the Old Testament and King Solomon's wisdom of "split the baby." I suggested we split up, travel solo, and then meet in Zurich at the train station at noon in two weeks. From there, we would take the long trek together to Sweden.

I didn't even wait for an answer. I said **YES** for us all. Without realizing it, giving an automatic **YES** was becoming more natural. Then, tearing the pages for each country chapter from our trusty *Fodor's* book, I handed them their respective pages, stood up, and said, "We have our marching orders, boys."

We returned to the hostel to gather the rest of our belongings.

On the way out, I yelled, "See you in Zurich."

All Roads Lead to Rome (And Zurich to Sweden, Of Course)

After checking out of the hostel, I was on my own for the first time in my life. Unlike many of my wealthy peers from Long Island, I had never been to overnight camps or over-priced teen tours. Traveling alone was a big deal and allowed me to practice my thinking skills. While in Rome, a city filled with old ruins rich in history adjacent to modern structures, I spent a great deal of time pondering and realizing the value of learning from our past and using that knowledge to create a better future. I tried to hit as many historical sites as possible, touring the Colosseum and the Sistine Chapel and throwing coins into the Trevi Fountain.

I could've spent more time there, but instead, I headed to Florence, where I took my picture with Michelangelo's *David* and treated myself to a new leather jacket. Next, I went to Venice, where I hopped on a water taxi through the Grand Canal. I overate gelato, carbonara, pizza, fresh pasta, and gnocchi.

Everywhere I went, I chatted with locals. I met a photographer, Luca, who grew up by Ponte Vecchio and always wore a fedora. I got rejected by a stunning Venetian woman, Bianca, who had green eyes and silky black hair. But, of course, that didn't stop me from hitting on Francesca, a petite brunette who smeared red lipstick across my face when we made out at a bar in Florence. I didn't notice my clown face until I returned to my hostel.

It is interesting how certain places become tied to you. For me, London, Paris, the South of France, and Rome are cities I would return to repeatedly for different reasons, each playing an important part throughout my life.

Two weeks later, I reconnected with Jack and Skeeter in Zurich. Spending time away from each other was good for us. Reunited again, we embraced and traded stories about our solo adventures. Before heading to Sweden, we decided to continue our European adventures. We took overnight trains and hit as many cities as possible in various countries.

When we finally arrived in Sweden, we contacted our lady friends, separating again while we crashed at their different apartments. Astrid took a few days off from work and showed me around the city. We split giant cinnamon buns from a café, ate shrimp sandwiches, spent an entire day at the Liseberg amusement park enjoying the rides, and best of all, we had sex all over her apartment—in her galley kitchen, on her gray loveseat, in the bedroom, and in the shower.

Our flights back home were scheduled for mid-August from London, but none of us were ready to leave, so I called my father with my calling card to let him know I would be staying longer.

"What do you mean you're extending your trip?" my dad yelled through the phone, making my ears pound. "You need to be in school for freshman orientation next week."

"Don't worry about that, Dad. I'll make it back in time for my first class."

"You're making a big mistake, son. College starts the rest of your life, and you don't want to be late. Do what you want, but you'll need to get to school on your own if you're not back in time."

After hanging up with my dad, I contacted Jack at his Swedish lover's house. "Hey, bro. How's it going?"

"Great. I've been eating many Swedish meatballs and having fun with my beautiful lady friend."

"That's funny. Astrid and I have been eating lots of meatballs too." We both laughed. "I just got off the phone with Dad. He was pissed when I told him I wanted to extend the trip."

"I get it, but forget about Dad. Sometimes, you've got to do what's in your best interest. Skeeter and I want to check out Norway for a few days. You in?"

"Nah. I'm not ready to leave Astrid yet. And I want to keep eating meatballs."

"All right. I'll call you there when we get back."

That night, after I told Astrid I wanted to stay, she said, "I think you need to start looking for a job. Can you get a work visa?"

A work visa? Was she nuts?

Suddenly, I realized the meatballs were getting cold, and the sex was getting old. Astrid was almost double my age, and considering I was a week away from starting college, she needed to find someone much older and established. When Jack and Skeeter returned to Sweden, I told them it was time to go. Astrid understood when I broke the news to her. After hugging her goodbye, we pretended we would see each other again, but deep down, we knew that would never happen.

Cruising to College

Jack, Skeeter, and I took an overnight cruise from Sweden to London. To celebrate the last of our European excursion, we drank too much liquor and sang the theme songs from *Gilligan's Island* and *The Love Boat* at the top of our lungs until we passed out.

The day I landed back at JFK airport, I had to pack the Uhaul for school and get myself to Delaware before the start of classes—no big deal. I threw my clothes in Jack's old college duffel bags and drove the two-and-a-half hours from Long Island to Newark, Delaware.

Arriving on campus, I made my way toward the student center. College students, wearing blue-and-yellow logo apparel, ripped and bleached jeans, Bermuda shorts, and tank tops swarmed around The Green (the central grassy area on campus). I watched a disc fly over my head, almost hitting some girl with stiff, hair-sprayed hair.

Meanwhile, I was feeling good in my Vuarnet sunglasses, golden-copper complexion, and with a little more meat on my too-skinny high school body. I walked up the steps of the student center, and once inside the air-conditioned building, I asked a man wearing thick bifocals and a bow-tie where I was supposed to go.

"Are you a freshman?" he asked.

"I am," I responded.

"Young man, you missed orientation. It was yesterday."

"I know, but I'm here now," I said with a certain flair, as though they should count themselves lucky to have me grace them with my presence. "Where do I go to check in? And let's get this party started!"

He shook his head in annoyance, and I followed him into an office, where I was given my dorm assignment and key. After thanking him, I left the building, ready to begin the next chapter of my life as a **YES**-man with *Confidence*.

Lessons Learned Chapter 2: Building CONFIDENCE

Confidence Comes from Action, Not Perfection

True **Confidence** doesn't come from a pair of *Risky Business* sunglasses (though they help) or pretending to have it all together. It comes from facing fears, stepping into new situations, and trusting in your ability to figure things out as you go. **Confidence** is not about eliminating doubts or insecurities but acknowledging them and about taking bold steps forward despite them.

Let's recap:

Finding Strength in Vulnerability

When Rachel broke up with me, my self-esteem hit rock bottom. I doubted my worth and carried that insecurity across the Atlantic. But my solo visit to the Rodin Museum in Paris, and the quiet contemplation of *The Thinker,* gave me the space to reflect. Why was I letting Rachel dictate my view of myself? In that moment, I realized I had the power to change my perspective and to create the life I wanted by instead focusing on my strengths.

    Key Takeaway: *Confidence* doesn't come from external validation. It comes from reframing your perspective and believing in your ability to grow.

Taking Bold Action

With my newfound mindset, I approached Brittanie on the beach in Cannes—a decision my former self would have hesitated over. Even when my friends doubted me, I leaned into boldness, striking up a conversation, landing a kiss, and ultimately spending an unforgettable night with her.

Key Takeaway: *Confidence* grows when you act on your instincts. Say **YES** to opportunities that feel exciting, even if they scare you.

Becoming the YES-Man

From negotiating with my friends to split up and explore solo adventures to sitting down with three Swedish women at a café, I embraced **The Power of YES**. These decisions brought me closer to new experiences, like exploring Rome alone and staying with Astrid in Sweden.

Key Takeaway: *Confidence* builds as you prove to yourself that you can navigate new and uncertain situations. Every **YES** is a step forward.

Overcoming Imposter Syndrome

On my first day at college, I missed orientation and walked into the student center wearing my Vuarnet sunglasses and newfound swagger. Despite not having everything figured out, I still carried myself like someone who belonged, and that made all the difference.

Key Takeaway: You don't need to have it all figured out to show up confidently. Trust your ability to learn and figure it out as you go.

CHAPTER 3

TIME MANAGEMENT

HOW TO GAME THE SYSTEM

Officially liberated from the insecure eighteen-year-old I was before Europe, I strutted around campus with my new persona: an outgoing, self-confident ladies man, ready to conquer the next four years of college with self-assurance. And conquer I did.

How did I do that? Simple. I began formulating a process that has guided me in making decisions and planning in different aspects of my life ever since. This process eventually evolved into **Ronnie's Steps to Success** (as seen in the workbook).

Classes Begin at the University of Delaware

1985

When classes started, I had one goal: to earn straight As from the honors college and graduate with a kick-ass, high-paying job on Wall Street.

I knew I had to learn how to play the system to achieve my goals. I got to know my professors on a personal level. Here's an important tip to remember: Most people, when given a chance, love talking about themselves. I used that point to my advantage and grilled my professors to get to know them better. I inquired about their background, their interest in the subject matter they were teaching, and their journey to becoming professors. I asked them everything from where they grew up to why they chose this career. Whatever questions I could think of, I spewed out. Most of the time, once I got my professors chatting, they would spill their life stories. And bam!, we connected. I was no longer a random student. They knew Ron Stein, the tall, friendly, interested student who took his academics seriously.

Once I established a good rapport at the beginning of the semester, I would ask each professor to review the syllabus and rubric. This ensured that I knew what they were looking for from their students to earn an A in their class. I'd also meet with each of my professors before a test, and inevitably, they'd give me some insights about what I should study.

TIME MANAGEMENT was a mandatory component to my success. I would allocate blocks of time for studying, resting, and recreational activities by working smart. As a result, I never had to do the extra readings. I mean, after all, why bother? I didn't need to fill my brain with extraneous information, so instead, I showed up for class and listened, participated, sometimes took notes, and sometimes not. But no matter what, I made sure I was seen and heard. Thanks to clues from my professors, I never wasted my time studying unnecessary material because I knew ahead of time what I should concentrate on.

And guess what? It worked. While my friends were knee-deep in their big fat textbooks, stressed out, I was partying and playing—and they couldn't understand how I managed to do well when I didn't appear to be working as hard as them. Mastering the art of studying efficiently and fostering relationships with my professors was the key to acing the educational game.

How a D3 (at Best) Athlete Made the D1 Tennis Team

My next challenge was making the tennis team after the coaches told me I wasn't good enough. I had played tennis most of my life, and even though I was definitely not close to D1 material, I had a strong desire to try out and a fearless determination to make the team.

I begged and pleaded with Coach Doc, the head of the tennis program, to let me play against one of his top recruits. To shut me up, Coach Doc finally acquiesced and told me I could go up against David, a blond-haired, blue-eyed freshman from Florida attending on a tennis scholarship. We were scheduled to play the following afternoon.

"Ron, I hope you know you're going to lose," Coach Doc told me, his tone condescending.

I wanted to thank him for having no faith in me, but I kept my mouth shut. It was apparent he didn't want me on the team. From his perspective, I was a cocky kid who didn't stand a chance against one of his hand-picked recruits.

The day before our match, I studied David's every move on the court and couldn't understand why he and many other top recruits were playing tight, not hitting through, and missing so many easy shots. I watched David swing his racket, hitting the ball over the net and grazing over his opponent's head, landing outside the line.

"I thought these guys were supposed to be amazing," I whispered to the cute girl wearing a blue-and-yellow Delaware hat, sitting next to me on the bleachers.

"I think they're really nervous. Most of them are on tennis scholarships, and if they don't win their matches, they could lose their scholarships too," she said, then blew a small pink bubble with her chewing gum. Bingo. This girl had just revealed to me the ticket to a winning strategy. All I had to do was mess with David's head—in other words, I needed to outsmart him psychologically.

Before our match the next day, I approached David and said, "Wow, man, this is going to be hard for you."

"What the hell is that supposed to mean?" David asked, clenching his jaw.

"Well, you know I'm just playing for fun, but you, on the other hand, have a lot at stake. You could potentially lose your scholarship if you don't play well."

I heard David say, "Fuck you" under his breath as he stormed to his side of the court.

We were on serve for the first eight games, scoring 4-4. David was about to serve this must-hold game. He walked up to the line, served the ball, and it went long. He served again, and I took advantage of the second serve, ripping a forehand down the line. David announced the score, "Love-15." Standing at the line for his next serve, he smashed the ball into the net. Frustrated, David slammed his overpriced Prince Pro racket on the ground, completely cracking it.

Shame on you, I thought. Bad sportsmanship was not a good look for him, but it sure as hell made me look good.

David reset for his second serve with his spare racket while I hovered over the service line, in position and ready to pounce. Serving the ball, he double faulted and continued to crumble under pressure, allowing me to win the game. The score was 5-4, and the set was mine. I held my serve and took the set 6-4. David kept deteriorating as the second set began, and this time, I crushed him, winning the set 6-1.

Yay for me—beating David got me on the tennis team. The moral of the story is that you need ***Doubt Management*** because you can't go through life with fear. You must have faith in yourself and stay calm when things aren't going your way. My opponent was exponentially better than me, but I preyed on his vulnerabilities by letting him know he had everything to lose, adding to his insecurities.

Keep in mind that at eighteen years old, my brain was not fully developed, and I wasn't giving much thought to how my actions would affect David in the long run. Looking back on this experience, I realize that I came across as insensitive, and my behavior seemed selfish. Since then, I've consciously tried never to intentionally harm others for my benefit.

Going Greek: Doing It My Way

Similar to the movie *Animal House*, I wanted to join a social group like a fraternity. But something about being told what to do by a bunch of wise-ass college guys wasn't sitting well with me. I also don't like following orders that make no sense or being forced to do something dangerous or stupid. Rushing a fraternity generally encompasses all that, and since the new, improved Ron was a creator, a doer, and not a follower, I had to discover another approach to joining Greek life. One afternoon, I was hanging out with Fitz, a friend from the Honors program. He is easygoing, and I have always enjoyed chatting with him.

When I asked Fitz if he was interested in joining a fraternity, he said, "Nah. I'm not really the type."

"Yeah, me neither," I agreed.

"Really? You get along with so many of those guys. I would've thought for sure you'd be in a frat."

"I wouldn't mind being part of a social group, but I don't want to be forced into doing things I don't want to do."

"I heard a group of guys on my floor from the Honors College talking about how they are starting their own frat," Fitz said with a wry smile.

"Dude, that's brilliant. We should totally get in on that and help them make it happen."

"We totally should. Plus, I know those guys, and they can definitely use our help."

I thought about Frank Sinatra's song, "My Way," and then I said **YES** to doing it our way and fixing the issues with the old establishment, enabling me to avoid rush. It also gave me an opportunity to create a new set of fraternity guidelines that would work better for me and my fellow brothers.

I quickly learned that working with a *Strong Team* is a crucial step toward achieving success.

And, just like that, we got the ball rolling. Garrett, an anal-retentive overachiever, had already gotten the rules down and did all the paperwork. He contacted the Office of Fraternity and Sorority Life to learn how to start a fraternity. From there, he researched different national fraternities interested in expanding to the Delaware campus, which would fit us.

We met with representatives from three different national frats. During our interview with Kappa Delta Rho (KDR), we discussed our vision for the fraternity. Following a warm exchange, one of the representatives shared how their community service projects always stem from a collective effort among all the brothers. Ultimately, we chose them because of their *Positive* attitude and members' involvement in decision-making. Next, we had to find a faculty advisor to sponsor us. Someone suggested asking the dean of students, who had never been in a fraternity and wanted to be part of one. Fifteen minutes after meeting with him, he was so excited I thought he would pop out of his pants.

Our next task was to rush at least fifty guys, which we did quickly. We were also expected to maintain a certain GPA. That wasn't a problem—many of the recruits were members from the Honors College, so our grades were already embarrassingly high compared to the average frat guys, adding to our geek status.

Once our fifty members, sponsors, and applications were filled out, we had to participate in the Greek games as the new KDR chapter at the University of Delaware. Did you see the movie *Revenge of the Nerds*? Well, that was us—a bunch of nerds trying to compete against big, muscular jocks. Not an easy feat at all. A first look at us didn't leave the best impression: a group of frail dorks whose only weight-bearing exercise was lifting their textbooks and tennis rackets. Then again, we were geeks, and geeks knew how to put their brains to good use.

Our fiercest competition was Tug-of-War, and we were going up against the football and lacrosse teams. Our motley crew—many wore over-sized spectacles and had Mr. Spock haircuts and middle parts—gave everyone a good laugh. We had to win two out of three matches to beat the other team by pulling our opposition over the center line. Considering we weighed significantly less than the football players, and the weight distribution had to be even on both sides, we had fourteen people on our team versus nine on theirs. Spending hours in the library weeks before the competition, we researched Tug-of-War strategies and pored over microfilm articles and photographs of competitions to learn from the techniques used by other teams. To gain an advantage, we had to concentrate on angles, foot placement, and leverage—everything depended on the initial pull—just like in life.

Moments before the competition, I used my tennis strategy and got in the football players' heads. "You guys are going to get destroyed by us wimps," I told them, grinning confidently.

"Yeah, right, dude. You don't stand a chance," the six-foot-two, two-hundred-twenty-pound defensive lineman with a missing front tooth said with a grunt-like laugh.

Lined up on our side, we waited for the announcer to begin. We pulled when he called out, "Three, two," before he yelled, "One." Pulling first gave us the edge we needed. I knew the referee wasn't going to call the whistle on us. After all, one look at them and one look at us, and nothing about this game seemed fair. But guess what? We shocked the world and beat them, a feat comparable to the US Olympic Hockey team's victory over Russia a few years earlier—ha!

At the official Greek school induction ceremony, there was an alcohol shot competition. We picked the type of shot, and then four of us went against four of the best shot takers from the other fraternities. Again, we did our research and chose one of the hardest shots we could find: Prairie Fire, a mixture of tequila with Tabasco sauce. Let me tell you—it burned like hell. But the great thing about geeks was that we understood the value of practicing. We spent days mastering this newly acquired skill of repeatedly swallowing our shots in one gulp and keeping them down. The hours spent imbibing our alcohol worked wonders, as we nailed that event, impressing the cute sorority girls while the other guys puked.

We were officially established as a fraternity. I took on the role of the finance guy, and whenever it was time to collect dues, I'd call out, "Dues are due!" To this day, when I reunite with my frat brothers, they still joke about that. Over thirty-five years later, my son, Dylan, became the first legacy, following in my footsteps.

Do The Side Hustles

Since age thirteen, I have spent my summers working, taking on various jobs ranging from mowing lawns and landscaping to pool maintenance, cleaning toilets, teaching tennis, and even working on a lobster boat. My goal was simple: to **Work Hard** and earn as much money as possible from an early age. Now that I was a big-time college man, I wanted to make extra spending money—and, of course, use it to treat the ladies I took out. When I noticed a sign looking for referees posted on a bulletin board in the student center, I decided that would be the perfect side hustle.

After becoming a referee, I got another side hustle that made refereeing much better. The guy who hired me asked if I wanted to make the sports schedule for an extra twenty bucks. "I sure do," I replied. I got to work the games of my choice and cherry-picked the sororities I wanted to referee. That sure was fun.

I had another job with benefits: a flower delivery man, a minimum-wage job with bad tips that nobody wanted but me. I was hired in February, right before Valentine's Day. As the only floral shop in town, they were slammed. I worked eight-hour shifts, organizing the flowers by dorms and residential locations. Then, I used the shop's truck to deliver the bouquets, most of which were roses. Driving around in the truck, I played Motley Crew's "Girls, Girls, Girls" on repeat, and out of nowhere, I got a brilliant idea: I would take one rose out of each dozen and hand them to girls who weren't getting any deliveries. Whenever I walked by an attractive woman, I would say, "Here's a rose for your number." Saying **YES** to working in the flower shop made me turn a tedious job into a fun experience.

Although I never got in trouble for what I did, the guilt set in after the floral shop gig ended. Contacting the owner, I confessed and offered to pay for the flowers I stole from each bouquet. Appreciating my honesty, he told me not to worry about it. I thanked him, and he hired me for the next year. Honesty does pay off, and I made a promise to myself to never do something like that again.

Listen to Nancy Reagan and Just Say No

When my father landed a lucrative new job in Las Vegas, bringing in more income than he ever had, my parents relocated from our modest split-level home in Long Island, New York, to an upscale neighborhood near the bustling Las Vegas Strip.

Since this was the summer before my junior year, and I planned to live with my parents in Las Vegas, I needed to secure an internship with a good firm in the area in which I wanted to work full-time upon graduation. I landed a spot at Valley Bank in their equity trading department, where I specialized in statistical research. I hoped this position would serve as a steppingstone to becoming a trader after graduation. However, I soon discovered that staring at numbers all day was mind-numbing.

Desperate to let loose at night, I befriended a group of affluent, pampered guys my age who lived nearby. Unbeknownst to their parents, they were involved in a profitable side hustle, dealing cocaine for extra cash. My nights took a wild turn when I said **YES** to joining my new friends for some parties at the hottest nightclubs on the Strip. They often used a gram of cocaine as their ticket to access these exclusive venues. Hanging out with them, I witnessed firsthand the allure and perils of the drug trade.

One evening, I decided to play a practical joke. The guys had a substantial cocaine delivery scheduled, and we planned to celebrate afterward. While they were upstairs in one of their houses, taking an unusually long time primping, I got bored waiting for them. Deciding I needed a good laugh, I spilled flour all over the floor. Pretending to freak out, I shouted, "Shit, I dropped the coke everywhere."

Frantically rushing downstairs, one of the guys tripped and broke his leg. Though furious with me when they found out I was joking, they were relieved that their precious cargo remained intact.

Not long after the flour-capade, things took a turn for the worse. One of the guys found himself in a dire situation when he was pulled over by a cop for speeding. In a panic, my friend reached into his glove compartment to hide the drugs. When the officer spotted this, he thought my friend was going for a gun and fired his weapon, injuring my buddy. Despite my friend's recovery, he landed himself in jail for several years. These events served as a wake-up call for me, and I realized that not every **YES** is successful. Saying **YES** to hanging with drug dealers was not a wise decision and that I should just say NO to drugs (even selling them).

Meeting the Big Guy (and It Didn't Even Cost Me Ten Percent)

While at the University of Delaware, I discovered another important aspect of saying **YES**: don't worry about why you agreed to do something or how you will get there. Instead, it's about staying open and *Positive* to a **YES**'s possibilities.

To clarify, as a member of the Honors College, we were offered many enrichment opportunities, such as panel discussions, dinners with faculty and alums, and invitations to hear renowned speakers. In my freshman year, I came across a flyer on a bulletin asking for volunteers in the Honors College to clean up after all the events, and if we stayed on the cleaning committee for two years, we would receive a reward at the end. I had no idea what kind of reward I would receive, but I decided to take my chances and said **YES**. After every event where food was served, I got down and dirty, folding chairs, cleaning dishes, throwing away dirty napkins, moving tables, and picking up garbage. It wasn't the most glamorous job, but *Working Hard* is necessary for success and always pays off in the end. I never asked what kind of prize I would receive because I assumed it would be worth my while.

When I completed my two-year stint, I received my reward. At the next keynote speaker dinner, I sat next to one of the special presenters, the Democratic senator of Delaware—Joe Biden. Forty-five-year-old Biden looked old to me back then. I was a twenty-year-old college kid having a one-on-one political discussion with a senator. I brought up topics to debate with him from economics to large government.

When I told him I thought his strict, anti-drug stance was fueled with racism because it targeted black people more than whites, our talk got heated, and our voices grew loud. At one point, a member of his security team approached us and asked Senator Biden if he wanted me removed from the table. Biden responded, "Absolutely not. Ronnie and I are friends. We're discussing and sharing our opinions. Healthy debate is the cornerstone of our democracy."

I appreciated that. When the guard left, Senator Biden asked, "You're okay if I call you Ronnie?"

"Sure." No one had ever called me that before. But from that day forward, I credit Biden with giving me a new nickname. I never would've imagined that saying **YES** without knowing the outcome would turn into such an enlightening experience.

Job Search: The One That Got Away

1989

In the last part of college, I began to think about planning my **Life Volume II: Post-College Careers** by developing a process to increase the likelihood of achieving my goals, **Ronnie's *Steps to Success*** (as seen in the Workbook). In the first step of this process, I had to determine what I wanted. No big deal—I knew exactly what I wanted to do post-grad—secure a job on Wall Street. Despite facing a significant hurdle getting there, it never stopped me from keeping my legs moving like a running back, even when I appeared to have gotten stuck.

Goals are like destinations on a map with countless routes to arrive there. Some roads are direct, and others are windy, but despite the direction you take, if you keep your eyes *Focused* on the end game, saying **YES**, when possible, you will eventually manifest your desires.

Even though I was graduating from Delaware with a double major in finance and economics, I would soon find out that meant nothing when competing against the crème de la crème—the Ivy League graduates. Additionally, Wall Street was steeped in nepotism, and since I had no connections, I was at a disadvantage. But I had no intention of letting my lack of pedigree stop me, nor would I allow the unfair system to get me down. I went on a crusade and put myself out there: sending résumés, writing cover letters, **Networking** with professors, and making cold calls.

Somehow, I managed to get twenty-one job interviews, and believe it or not, I got nineteen offers right away. Unfortunately, most of the offers were with mid-level banks in Baltimore and Philadelphia that didn't interest me, and the pay was pretty low.

The one job I didn't get was with an options trading company out of Philadelphia. During the last round of interviews, the head trader said, "I only have one question for you, and if you get it right, you'll become an options trader at our firm." He waited a moment before asking, "Are you ready?"

"Sure."

"What's the square mileage of Mexico?"

I raised my eyebrows in confusion, wondering if this was some kind of joke.

"That's it," he said. "You have one minute to answer it."

I drew a blank, completely clueless on how I should answer this question. Beads of sweat began to trickle down my forehead. *Was this guy nuts? How the heck was I supposed to figure this out?* The wheels started turning in my head, but not in the right direction.

"I can tell by how you're doing it that you won't get the answer."

Finally, a random number spilled out of my mouth.

"Nope," he replied, his expression smug. "I knew you wouldn't get the correct answer."

Obviously, I didn't get the job, but I needed to understand the meaning behind the question. "How should I have answered that? I mean, after all, how many people memorize the square mileage of foreign countries?" I asked.

"That's what you should've been thinking about, trying to figure out a sensible, logical approach to determine the answer. Mexico is shaped like a triangle, and if you know how to get the area of a triangle and you know the size of Mexico against the United States, you can tell they're close in length. From there, you can take an educated guess. I asked you that because I'm looking for thinkers, problem solvers, and people who remain cool under pressure."

I learned a few valuable lessons from that experience. My first mistake was not remaining calm and failing to use *Doubt Management*. Instead, I let my fear get in the way of my thinking. My next mistake was not taking the time to process how to find the answer. From that day forward, I try to set aside time each day just for thinking, allowing my thoughts to flow and interpret information. Doing this lets me clear my head meditatively, enabling me to fine-tune my problem-solving skills.

The Big Apple and Broadway, Here I Come

The last firm that made me an offer was Arthur Andersen, who was looking to start a management consulting company. The only problem was that they wanted me to work in their Philadelphia office. I asked if I could work in their New York office instead, but they gave me a firm no and said I could transfer there after two years. When I told them that wouldn't work for me, human resources suggested I re-interview in the final round in Manhattan. However, if I didn't get the role, I would have to give up my slot in Philly. Willing to take the risk, I said **YES** to interviewing in NYC, the location I had chosen to reside in while planning **Life Volume II**.

The NYC office contacted me and set me up with flights, a midtown hotel, and an interview schedule. The morning interviews went well, and after that, I had a lunch meeting at the upscale landmark restaurant The Russian Tea Room with Bill, one of the partners, who would ultimately decide my fate.

I took a few deep breaths before entering the opulent restaurant decorated with rich gold accents, lush velvet curtains, and elaborate chandeliers. Once inside, the maître d' escorted me to the table where a middle-aged man was seated. He was wearing an expensive suit with a blue silk tie.

Bill shook hands and said, "I already ordered the tasting menu with caviar and a bottle of Château Lafite Rothschild." I knew little about wine at twenty-two, but it sounded expensive. "I have one question to ask before the food arrives, and your answer will determine my decision. Either way, we'll enjoy the food and wine."

Oh boy, here we go again—another stumper question. But, this time, I was ready to nail it.

"Where do you want to be six months after you start this job, and how will you make that happen? And please don't give me a stupid generic answer. Speak from your heart."

Sitting up straight and looking him in the eye, I told him I wanted to work in the NYC office, starting as a management consultant, and I planned to rise quickly to the top and work as a trader on Wall Street. I waited for the sommelier to pour our wine, and then I added, "I am willing to do whatever it takes to succeed and plan to have crazy wild fun getting there."

Bill didn't utter a word as he took a sip of the wine. Then, placing his wineglass on the table, a huge shit-eating grin spread across his face, "Welcome to Andersen, New York City. I will be your mentor, so you'll only work for me. I have a good feeling about you, Ron. The only difference in your plan is that you will accomplish your goals as a rising partner with me." He picked his glass back up again. "Now, let's toast to your bright future and enjoy this fine meal."

Graduating and Heading into the Real World

Ed Bradley, a CBS News reporter, gave the commencement speech at my graduation, and I'll never forget one line he said: "Life is filled with tests, and you just need to keep passing them." I could not agree more, but to do this, I would have to dig deep and use the life skills I had developed over the past four years—concentrate on my goal, say **YES** whenever possible, and work the system to my advantage. Last but not least, I had to keep moving toward my goal even if it meant going over the door, under the door, busting through it, or building a ladder.

My job at Arthur Andersen was set to begin in September, which meant I had time to play. Since I'd already had my European adventure, I wanted to see the great US of A. When my roommate, Fitz, asked me to take my old, beat-up car, which I had purchased from my parents, to travel with him across the country, I said **YES.** I love America, the Land of Opportunity, and couldn't wait for more fresh, exciting experiences.

Lessons Learned Chapter 3: Mastering TIME MANAGEMENT

Time Is Your Most Valuable Asset. Spend It Intentionally (can make money but can't make time).

In Chapter 3, I discovered the power of working the system by being *Focused* and intentional with my time, efforts, and connections. My ability to manage time effectively was a key driver behind my success in academics, sports, Greek life, side hustles, and career-building. Managing time isn't just about fitting tasks into your day—it's about strategically allocating your time to what truly matters.

Let's Recap:

Efficiency Is Key

I aced the academic game by leveraging my professors as allies, focusing only on the most important material, and strategically cutting out unnecessary work. I maximized results while minimizing effort by working smart, not hard.

   Key Takeaway: *Prioritize* tasks that provide the highest impact. Don't waste time on busywork when targeted effort can deliver better results.

Preparation Can Beat Talent

By studying my opponent's weaknesses and leveraging psychological tactics, I made the Division 1 tennis team despite not being the best player. Preparation, combined with *Confidence*, gave me the edge to overcome stronger competitors.

Key Takeaway: Being well-prepared is often more important than innate talent. Outwork and outsmart your competition.

Leveraging Opportunities

My side hustles, like being a referee and delivering flowers, weren't just about earning money—they were opportunities to connect with people, have fun, and think creatively. Even a tedious task like delivering flowers became a memorable experience through my innovative approach.

Key Takeaway: Look for ways to maximize every opportunity, even in small jobs or everyday tasks.

Strong Teams Create Strong Results

When helping to found a fraternity, We built and relied on a team of complementary talents: the planner, the researcher, and the visionary. Together, they turned an ambitious idea into reality.

Key Takeaway: Surround yourself with a *Strong Team* to amplify your strengths and offset your weaknesses. Collaboration drives success.

Saying NO Is as Important as Saying YES

I learned to balance when to embrace opportunities and when to walk away—like distancing myself from dangerous friendships in Las Vegas. Knowing when to say NO is as critical as knowing when to say **YES**.

Key Takeaway: Be discerning about your commitments. Say NO to anything misaligned with your goals or values.

CHAPTER 4

NETWORKING

I'LL SHOW YOU, MR. IVY LEAGUE

1989

Fitz and I had taken a road trip the prior September and things had gone well. After graduation, we hopped into my blue 1977 Chevrolet Impala and drove from Delaware to Provincetown, Massachusetts, located on the tip of Cape Cod. Arriving in the vicinity late at night with no place to stay, we slept in the car at a rest stop and woke up early in the morning to a loud banging on the window.

"What are you boys doing?" a police officer asked. "You can't sleep in your car, and it's illegal to have sex in there."

"No, don't worry, officer," I said through the open window. "We're just taking a little nap, and, by the way, we're not gay."

"Well, then, move along, not-gay, gay boys."

Laughing, Fitz and I watched the officer drive off, and we went into a rest stop bathroom to brush our teeth and wash our faces. Cleaned and refreshed, we drove into Provincetown proper and parked the car. Strolling down Commercial Street, we got coffee, wandered into some shops and galleries, ate pizza and ice cream, and watched everyone meandering around in neon-colored beach clothing.

"Fitz, do you notice anything weird here?" I asked. "Everywhere I look, I see two girls holding hands and two guys holding hands, but there are no male and female couples."

"Yeah. You're right. That is kind of strange."

We'd had no idea Provincetown was known as one of the friendliest gay (now LGBTQ+) towns in the US, but now that we did, we realized we had a lot to learn about America. After Cape Cod, we officially embarked on our cross-country road trip. We spread the maps on the dashboard and took turns driving and co-piloting. Reading and tearing pages out of our *Fodor's* guide (just like on the Europe trip) helped us determine where to go next and gave us some background about each place we visited. Listening to Bryan Adams's "The Summer of '69" on the drive, we belted out the tunes, replacing '69 with '89.

Anytime Fitz suggested a new city to check out, I said, "YES," embracing the idea of exploring everything. (Having many diverse experiences enables you to discern your likes and dislikes.) We drove eight to thirteen hours a day, amazed that my old clunker got us anywhere safely. Since the car was leaking oil, we had to add another quart every time we filled up with gas. We saw some amazing places along the way. Heading south, we visited Virginia Beach, Myrtle Beach, Charleston, and then headed over to Atlanta. But while driving through Mississippi on our way to New Orleans, we had a run-in with a cop who pulled us over.

"Show me both your licenses," the officer demanded in a Southern drawl.

Fitz was driving the car, so I thought it was strange he asked for mine too, but I handed it over, not wanting to get in any more trouble.

"What's a Christian and a Jew doing together in Mississippi, of all places? You boys must be crazy." He shook his head in disbelief. "You better hustle out of here. I'm tired," he said, yawning. "My shift is almost over, and I don't want to deal with you two and the paperwork."

High-fiving each other, we drove away, relieved. From there, we explored the French Quarter in New Orleans and then headed west, visiting Houston, San Antonio, and Carlsbad Caverns in New Mexico, sleeping in tents there until a windstorm blew them away. After that, we headed to Santa Fe, the Grand Canyon (and some hiking), stopped in Las Vegas and gambled a little, and cruised up to San Francisco, where we walked across the Golden Gate Bridge, ate chocolate at Ghirardelli Square, and checked out Fisherman's Wharf.

Everywhere we stopped, we bought bumper stickers and plastered them all over my car, which was on its last leg of our drive to Los Angeles, our final destination. Unfortunately, by then my brakes had worn out, making stopping on the Pacific Coast Highway difficult. I bit my nails down to the quick on the entire journey, praying we would arrive safely. Fortunately, we did. Fitz's girlfriend had invited us to stay in Los Angeles at her parents' house. We arrived tired, dirty, and hungry, and slept on and off in her living room for nearly thirty hours.

After a few days of recovery, it was time to ditch the car. Not to mention, we were desperate for cash. Given the condition of the vehicle, we drove to a South Central LA car lot. A short, heavyset Mexican man with a thick mustache greeted us when we pulled up.

"Can I help you two amigos, and you are not policía?" he asked in broken Spanglish.

"We're looking to sell this car," I responded, opening the door and stepping out.

"I see, señor," he said, inspecting the vehicle, wide-eyed. Then, un-latching the hood, he looked inside, smiled, heard a clicking sound, and nodded in disapproval. "Bad leefters. I'll only give you $600."

"I'll take it," I replied and reached out my hand to shake on it, shocked we even got that much, considering the broken car and stickers plastered all over it.

We used that money to buy ourselves the cheapest possible round-trip package deal to Hawaii and finished off our epic cross-country road (and now air) trip on Waikiki Beach.

The party ended when I landed back in New York, and I was ready to experience the real world. But little did I know I was in for a rude awakening. While at the University of Delaware, I was a big fish in a small pond, living in a controlled environment. Everything I planned and worked at came to fruition, making the tennis team, a piece of cake;

earning all As, easy; helping to start a frat, no big deal; and getting a post-college job, a success. But looking back on my four years of college made me realize I had been living in a bubble. As I moved into my new reality, I had come to realize from the trip and meeting so many different people that it was not all about me. I had to have the right amount of humility, enabling me to be open to *Listening and Learning* to grow.

Life Volume II Begins: First Day of Full-Time Work

On the first day of my job, I woke up early and dressed in my brand-new blue pin-striped suit from Brooks Brothers, where I had recently purchased a new wardrobe. The clothes were simple, good quality, and didn't totally break the bank. They also made me feel good and looked professional, but in the end, it wasn't about that. My clothing wouldn't make a statement—I would.

I walked uptown from my studio apartment, on the corner of 16th Street and 7th Avenue. It was a two-mile trek to the office, but since most New Yorkers walked, I did too. Not to mention, it saved the cost of a subway token and became the start of my healthy habit of walking whenever possible.

Arriving at the office, I entered the small conference room. Twenty men and women, wearing high-end designer suits (not from Brooks Brothers), most of whom graduated from prestigious schools, sat around the mahogany table, waiting for the manager to enter the room and begin the training session. I sat next to a guy with a friendly smile and introduced myself.

"Nice to meet you, Ron. Call me Popper." We shook hands, and then he rambled on about himself, letting me know he graduated from Vassar College and how excited he was to start this job, which took him months to land. Although he did most of the talking, I liked his good energy, and even though I didn't know it at the time, Popper would become one of several lifelong friends.

After work, a bunch of us went to Rosie O'Grady's for happy hour. Happy hours were popular back then because they were fun and social and gave out free food and cheap beers. Since I was on a tight budget, and most of my colleagues were frugal (often the case for wealthy people), the nuts, pretzels, trail mix, rubber meatballs, dried-out chicken wings, and alcohol became our dinner almost every night for the next few weeks.

That evening, the packed bar was bustling with young professionals, men wearing suits, their ties loosening around their necks, and women wearing knee-length skirts and buttoned-up blouses. Unfortunately, Popper couldn't join us, but I was looking forward to getting to know my other colleagues. We sat around a high-top table and talked.

"Ron, what university did you graduate from?" Jordan, one of my coworkers with a military-style crew cut, asked me.

"Delaware," I responded, taking a sip of my beer. "What about you?"

He laughed out loud, his beer spewing out of his mouth. I had a feeling he was mocking me. Then, wiping his mouth with his napkin, he said, "Wharton. And Joe was one of my fraternity brothers at Penn."

Jordan gave Joe, who had a pointy, pinched nose, a fist pump. Then he turned to Billy, a guy with short, gelled hair, and said, "Jessica graduated from Stanford. And John is finishing up his MBA from Harvard." John had red hair and freckles that reminded me of Howdy Doody. "How the hell did you get this job? You must've had a crazy connection."

"I didn't know anyone. They begged me to come here." I grabbed the pitcher of beer, refilled my glass, and then topped off Howdy Doody's cup.

Jordan shook his head. "No, they didn't."

"I'm telling you the truth," I insisted.

"Well then, you must be making less than everyone else," Jordan said, smug.

I grabbed a mozzarella stick off the appetizer plate. "Why don't we go around the table and find out," I suggested. "Everyone put a twenty-dollar bill in the middle of the table, and the one getting paid the most keeps the pot. Kind of like the rich get richer."

"All right." Jordan took a bite of a saucy buffalo wing. "I'm making 32K."

Joe was next. "32K too."

"35K," Harvard John called out.

And finally, Jessica said, with tear-filled eyes, "28K."

When it was my turn, they all looked at me, their mouths dropping in disbelief when I said, "I got 42K plus 3k for moving expenses."

"How the hell did you get that?" Jordan asked, his eyebrows furrowed.

"I negotiated," I announced in a matter-of-fact tone. But, of course, I didn't tell these guys that I didn't just negotiate—I asked Bill to assist me by telling his boss I was unattainable and that I had other offers for more money. Bill had taught me to always negotiate with leverage, and that playing hard-to-get works wonders sometimes, so he loved the plan.

"I didn't know you could do that," Howdy Doody said.

I jumped up, grabbed a shot of tequila from the round I ordered, slammed it down, and grabbed the pile of twenty-dollar bills. Then I proudly declared, "That's because you all went to Ivy League schools, but unfortunately, they don't teach you what you need to know in the real world." I had a smirk on my face for the rest of the evening.

Getting the job at Arthur Andersen taught me another valuable lesson: never underestimate your self-worth. Obviously, these guys had better credentials than I did, which helped them get in the door. As for me, I didn't grow up with a silver spoon. I didn't attend a fancy private school or boarding school, and a degree from Delaware didn't have the prestige compared to the schools where my colleagues graduated.

But I **_Listened and Learned_** at Delaware and in the world around me. Of course, life will always pit you against people who, on paper, have better credentials, but those are just labels, and you can crush paper. I am anything but a label. If I wanted to make it in the world, I couldn't let my seemingly inferior degree hold me back. I had to prove that I was just as worthy, had more grit and determination, and would stop at nothing to be the best version of myself at whatever job I landed.

If we allow every setback or put-down, every person who is more intelligent and prosperous, to make us feel bad about ourselves, ultimately, we will lose the most important game of all—the game of life.

Winners never stop trying. And they never stop moving forward, like the running back.

Maybe my coworkers had the privilege of learning from distinguished professors. But guess what? I had some great professors too. Real learning had more to do with my perception of myself and belief in my inner strength. I am not better than anyone else. But every human on planet Earth can tap into their power. It begins with the right mindset, embracing an I-think-I-can-I-know-I-can attitude, and it was that mentality that got me more money than my Ivy League colleagues and would propel my career forward from here in a completely insane, nontraditional, and ultimately successful way.

The Old Bait and Switch

A few weeks into the job at Arthur Andersen (now Andersen Consulting), I was given a coding book, which I was instructed to read and study. Unfortunately, I had no coding experience, and when I was hired, I was told I would be working on Wall Street. Since my white whale was to become a trader, I hoped this position would eventually lead me there. I did not want anything to do with technology consulting, but if I wanted the job, I didn't have a choice.

Everyone had to attend a three-week training program in St. Charles, a distant suburb outside of Chicago, in the middle of nowhere, to learn how to code. It was brutal. We were locked in a windowless office seven days a week with no breaks, coding all day for nineteen consecutive days. I passed out in bed at night, dreaming of algorithms. If I wanted to keep the job, I had to complete the training and pass a test. I had to **Work Hard**—nineteen consecutive days of grueling twelve-hour coding sessions was not my idea of fun. Ugh!

Many employees in today's workforce view their jobs as a four-letter word (starting with an f or s). Of course, work can be challenging, tedious, nonsensical, irritating, humiliating, etc., but when the going gets tough, it doesn't mean it's time to quit or give up. Instead, remain **Positive** and try turning an unpleasant job into a game by setting goals, using resources around you, and making assignments into a fun experience.

I hated programming, and it wasn't what I signed up for, but rather than complaining about what I viewed as a bait and switch, I made imaginary games to help me get through assignments. I also relied on my good buddy Popper, a savant who never took a computer science class in college, to help me whenever needed. All I had to do was stay the course, and as a result, I would enjoy the fruits of my labor following my programming prison sentence.

The Chicago Blues

Our team leaders finally decided to give us a much-needed break. Before the twenty-one-day training ended, they organized a celebratory trip to downtown Chicago on a Saturday morning. Providing us with a bus stocked with alcohol for the ride, they dropped us off on the corner of Division and Rush Street, a bustling neighborhood where we would spend the day and evening barhopping. It all seemed perfect, so what could go wrong?

Having spent nearly three weeks studying code with little to no downtime, I felt like a caged animal who was finally set free. Upon our arrival, we were given strict instructions to be back on the bus at 1:00 a.m., and if we failed to make it back on time, we would be fired, mainly because our final exam was scheduled two days after our outing.

On the bus, we passed around a bottle of Jack Daniels. At the first bar, we drank endless pitchers of beer. At the second bar, we ate deep-dish pizza and downed pints of mind erasers. At the third bar, I drank more beer, but at that point, my mind was almost erased. Finally, at the fourth bar, I met a hot woman with light brown hair and golden highlights who looked like Heidi Klum. I mean, I think she did. At least, that was what my drunk goggles made me believe. Inebriated, I had no clue what her name was or anything about her except that we were both into each other. For the sake of storytelling, I'll refer to her as Heidi II.

"Ron, I think this is the last call," Popper informed me. "The bus is going to be here in about fifteen minutes."

Heidi II whispered in my ear, "Don't go, Ron. You can spend the night at my place." She started kissing my neck.

"The bus is outside," someone yelled.

"I've got to go," I stuttered.

"If you stay the night, I'll take you to Da Bears' game. My uncle works for the stadium, and I've got great seats on the field." Heidi II rubbed her breasts against my chest.

How could I pass up that offer? A night of sex with Heidi II, and then a football game?

"YES!" I screamed. "I'm in." I realized I would probably get in trouble for this, but in my sloppy state, I assumed I'd figure out a way to get out of it.

"You won't regret it," Heidi II promised. "This is going to be the best night ever."

In that moment, my YES seemed like a no-brainer, but let's be honest: I had no control over myself and could barely stand or see straight. Stumbling to the bar to pay my tab, I noticed the other guys had left. When Heidi II and I got outside, the bus was pulling away. I gave everyone a bouncy wave, and then I heard someone yell out the window, "Ron, you're definitely getting fired!"

There Has Got to Be a Morning After

The following morning, the blinding sun woke me up. My head felt like someone was whacking it with a hammer, spinning the room. When I turned to my left, the bed was sloshing around, and I flailed my arms in a feeble attempt to get up. What was going on? I had no idea where I was. A pink floral blanket covered my naked body. I tried to remember the details of the night. Where was I? And how did I get here? I felt seasick every time I shifted in the bed, and it dawned on me that I was in a waterbed. Finally, I forced myself to stand up. At the same time, a woman, her hair in a loose bun and wearing a robe, walked out of the bathroom.

"Ron, do you want to shower?" she asked. "We have to get moving. Otherwise, the traffic will be brutal."

Traffic? What was she talking about? Where were we going?

I heard a beeping sound from my jeans pocket, draped over the wicker night table. I pulled out my beeper, and my heart stopped for a second when I read the message from my boss: *I'll give you a second chance if you're back in the office in one hour.* Oh shit. The memories started flooding back to me: laughing when the bus drove past me and laughing even harder when I lost my job. Mind-blowing, drunken sex in the elevator with Heidi II. The invitation to the football game. I had to get out of there ASAP.

"Thank you so much for a fun night, but I have to get back to my office."

"What do you mean?" Heidi II asked. "You can't leave. You said you wanted to go to the game with me."

"I know. I'm so sorry." I kissed her on the cheek. "Actually, can you give me a ride to my office?"

"No fucking way."

"Okay then." On the way out the door, I said, "Hey, if you're ever in New York City, call me. I'd love to take you to dinner and make it up to you."

She gave me the finger.

Mistakes Are Okay if You Own It—Apology Accepted

Dashing down the steps of her apartment building, I screamed in my head—YES—to getting my job back. Outside her apartment building, I asked a mother pushing her baby in a stroller to point me toward the train station. I caught the next train back to the training facility, but unfortunately, the entire journey took well over an hour. When I walked into the auditorium with my wrinkled clothes reeking of stale alcohol, my team stood up and gave me a standing ovation.

The lead manager, his eyebrow raised and arms crossed, stood up and announced, "Ron, you're fired!"

As he was escorting me out of the auditorium, I begged him for forgiveness and another chance.

"It's too late," he said, pointing at his watch. "You knew the rules and chose to ignore them."

I spent the next five minutes giving him the same heartfelt speech I had given to Bill during the interview lunch. Afterward, he said, "All right, I'll tell you what, if you're willing to be an example and admit your wrongdoing in front of the trainees, then I'll rehire you."

Standing before the entire training group on the final day of the program, I apologized humbly, admitted that what I did was immature and disrespectful, and that it reflected poorly on myself and Andersen Consulting. I also added that I learned from my inappropriate behavior and would never let it happen again.

When I finished, the lead manager said, "Thank you, Ron. It sounds like you learned your lesson, and you all should take note. You can have your job back."

Even though it all worked out, I realized that a drunken YES is not always the best kind of YES. However, I also understood the value of owning up to your mistakes. Acknowledging and taking responsibility for our errors is a crucial step in personal growth and development.

This Ain't the Real Wall Street

After coding training hell, my first consulting assignment was at Goldman Sachs, where I had to report to a woman named Carla. She had a permanent scowl and wore shapeless dresses that accentuated her hefty rolls. For some reason, Carla, whom I nicknamed Crayla ('the dragon') behind her back, had it out for me and put me on photocopy duty. She would give me three-hundred-page binders daily, ensuring that I sat day and night making copies. Although I earned lots of extra cash working overtime, taking advantage of the heyday of consulting in the early 1990s, I had to pass the trading floor each time I walked into the copy room, which only fueled my hunger to get a job there.

Feeling bad about that assignment, my boss, Bill, invited me on an all-expense-paid trip to London to teach me how to sell to clients. I said "YES" immediately. Although I had to give up a few social commitments in New York and my weekend role as a volunteer coach for the Special Olympics, these were minor sacrifices I was willing to make for the sake of my job. Despite that, I was excited to *Listen and Learn* from Bill and experience the upscale side of London. We were booked in suites at The Dorchester, a five-star hotel, ate at Michelin-star restaurants, and drank fine wine.

One evening, a messenger knocked on my door, handed me a large file of papers, and said, "Good evening, sir. Your boss would like you to print this file and have it ready for breakfast."

"Are you kidding me? It is almost midnight," I responded.

"Don't worry, sir. I will get you some assistance straightaway." Ten minutes later, the messenger returned with four men: one holding a printer, another with the paper, a third to work my computer and print the file, and the fourth making and pouring me tea.

Smiling, I sat back and watched, enjoying this assignment. And then Bill stopped by, wearing a dressing gown underneath his hotel robe, grinning from ear to ear. "Making copies in London at The Dorchester, quite different than the office in NYC, huh, Ron?"

"Good one," I said, laughing and sipping my hot tea. Bill had a great sense of humor and knew how to enjoy and appreciate life, a valuable quality every workplace should incorporate. As my mentor, he took me under his wing. Bill taught me how to be a professional consultant, guiding me through everything from selecting the right wine to order, dressing appropriately, *NETWORKING* effectively, and distinguishing between a sales call and a business meeting.

Michelle Pfeiffer, Or So I Thought

One evening after work, I walked into a card shop on the bottom floor of my apartment building in NYC, looking for a birthday card for my mother. I did a double take when I noticed the cashier. She looked like Michelle Pfeiffer with shoulder-length blonde hair, blue eyes, and high cheekbones. When I brought the card to the counter to pay, I smiled and said, "I know you're closing soon, so do you want to grab a drink with me?"

"Sure," she responded, batting her eyelashes flirtatiously.

We had a few drinks at a bar nearby, and then she asked, "Should we go back to your place for a nightcap?" You better believe I said YES—maybe even a little too enthusiastically. For the next few weeks, we spent a lot of time together, getting to know each other on every level. She was an avid reader and shared fascinating facts about her favorite history books and exotic places she'd seen in her travels. The more I hung out with her, the more I liked her.

About a month into our relationship, the Beatle's song "I Want to Hold Your Hand" came on the radio while we were having dinner at a restaurant. "I want to hold your hand and much more, Ron," she said in a low, sexy voice while touching me.

"Of course." I took her hand in mine.

"I remember hearing this song on the *Ed Sullivan Show* years ago."

"Oh, yeah. My parents used to love watching that show on TV."

"Well, I saw it live."

"What do you mean you saw it live? How is that possible? The show ended in 1971."

"I know. I saw it right after I graduated from college." I did the math in my head, and my eyes almost popped out of their sockets when I realized she was forty-eight, three years older than my mother. How did I not know she was that old? Noticing my ashen face, she asked, "What's wrong?"

"How old do you think I am?"

"I don't know," she said, caressing me with her long, red-lacquered nails. "You have some grey hair and always look professional and put together in your suits, so I guess you must be in your mid to late thirties."

I didn't have the heart to tell her I was only twenty-two. After that night, I tried to take her out again but couldn't get past the age differ-ence. Looking back, saying YES to dating Michelle Pfeiffer's doppel-ganger made for a memorable Mrs. Robinson experience.

Not long after my fling with "Michelle Pfeiffer," I reconnected with my college flame at my university's homecoming reunion. Dating her exclusively, I popped the question less than a year later, and she ac-cepted my proposal.

Exit Stage Left

"Bill, I've got some exciting news to share. I just got engaged," I an-nounced, grinning.

"Oh, wow. You're too young, but whatever. Good for you."

The next week, Bill handed me an envelope. "Here, take this. It's your next assignment."

"What's this?" I asked, pulling a key out of the envelope.

"It's your key to life."

"What's the key to life?"

Laughing, he said, "Your new apartment in Harrisburg, Pennsylvania. I'm putting you on the Pennsylvania Department of Transportation tech project. They're one of the first states moving to a non-paper card, and they're already behind schedule, so you'll have your work cut out."

"But I'm not in the government sector, and as you're well aware, I really want to work on Wall Street."

"Sorry, but the guys here want to see if you can handle the challenge. They think I baby you too much. We'll deal with the Wall Street situation when you get back."

"Okay," I said in a sour tone.

"You sound like a whiny baby. Man up, go home, and tell your fiancée you can't help her plan the wedding." He released a loud, evil-sounding cackle.

Since this project was not in line with me and what I wanted to be doing, while I went as instructed, I then started planning my exit strategy.

Living and working in the burbs of Pennsylvania was worse than I had imagined. I spent six months there, putting in twelve-hour days, six days a week, calculating driver's license fees based on a person's birth date and code. I would do the four-hour drive back every Saturday night and early Monday morning. While in the office, the team and I watched *The Simpsons* and binged on cheese steaks, buttered pretzels, and Pennsylvania Dutch potato salad. The pounds piled on, but it was nothing compared to the real issue I faced—getting out of there. Tirelessly ***Networking*** by calling everyone I had ever met and established a relationship related to business asking for their help, advice, and access to their network; within a few weeks I got an interview with Morgan Stanley in New York City in the accounting group and landed myself a new job. It wasn't the trading floor on Wall Street yet, but it was definitely one step closer.

Lessons Learned Chapter 4: The Power of NETWORKING

"Your network is your net worth."

This often-quoted maxim couldn't ring truer, as ***Networking*** is one of the most effective ways to unlock opportunities, broaden your horizons, and build lasting relationships. My experiences—from cross-country road trips to corporate consulting—highlight the immense value of building authentic connections and how they can propel you forward in unexpected ways.

Let's Recap:

Genuine Engagement Over Transactional Interactions

Whether it was joining Fitz on a road trip or leveraging mentorship from Bill, my success came from engaging with people authentically. *Networking* isn't about asking for favors, it's about creating mutually beneficial relationships.

Key Takeaway: Approach ***Networking*** with the mindset of building friendships, not just making contacts.

Be Open to Listening and Learning from Everyone

From police officers in Mississippi to coworkers at Andersen, every encounter gave me insights and perspectives. Some connections, like the one with my boss, Bill, become longtime mentors.

Key Takeaway: Treat every interaction as an opportunity to learn, even if it's with someone who seems very different from you.

Leverage Mentorship and Guidance

Bill didn't just guide me professionally; he taught me how to navigate life—whether it was negotiating salaries, handling career setbacks, or *Networking* over fine wine in London.

Key Takeaway: Find mentors who will invest in your growth. Don't be afraid to ask questions, listen, and apply their advice.

Adaptability and Resilience Are Critical

My career path wasn't linear. Coding wasn't my *Passion*, and Pennsylvania wasn't my dream destination, but I made the most of every experience while planning my next move.

Key Takeaway: When faced with less-than-ideal situations, maintain a *Positive* attitude and use the time to strategize your next steps.

Networking Opens Doors

My proactive *Networking* got me an interview with Morgan Stanley, which became a stepping stone closer to Wall Street.

Key Takeaway: Your next big opportunity will most likely come through someone in your network (and you don't know which one). Cultivate relationships that align with your aspirations (people you want to be like and/or respect).

CHAPTER 5

PRIORITIZING

SUSHI, SUSHI, AND MORE SUSHI

After putting in my two years at Andersen Consulting and realizing that the job was not leading me to my ultimate goal of getting to the Wall Street trading floor, it was time to reset and move in another direction. I reached out to my contacts, and almost immediately, found a headhunter who placed me in an accounting job supporting the trading department at Morgan Stanley, promising that the position would eventually lead me to my goal of being a trader.

In the meantime, after starting at Morgan, I kept my *Listen and Learn* acumen sharp, continued to *Network* with other professionals, and stayed busy learning new skills outside of the job. In the evenings, I took classes at New York University to get my MBA while studying for my CPA exam. In addition to school and work, I helped plan a wedding and got married.

My hectic schedule was a challenge, to say the least. I woke up at 4:30 a.m. to commute via train from my house in Westchester to Manhattan. Most nights, I didn't get home until after 10:00 p.m. The key to my success was *PRIORITIZING* and then employing my *Time Management* skills by allocating specific periods or chunks of time to each activity. This allowed me to *Focus* and get more done in an efficient manner.

Classes vs. The Slaughtered Lamb

I enrolled in two night classes per semester at New York University Stern School of Business, beginning with accounting, a course that would help me with my job and prepare me for the CPA exam. On the first day of class, I sat next to Julian, a brilliant all-American Wasp who graduated from Harvard in three years and was already a big-time trading success on Wall Street. His firm required an MBA before they could promote him to management at age twenty-five. Julian and I hit it off (just like when I sat next to Popper on the first day of Andersen Consulting). We ended up taking every class together and became good friends. It seems more than a coincidence when like-minded individuals unwittingly embark on comparable journeys that lead to connections at similar times.

Initially, it was hard to keep up with my schoolwork. I managed to get through by using the same method that worked at Delaware: figuring out the essential material needed for the exam and studying. Hard. Getting a handle on the workload appeared difficult early in the semester until my genius friend, Julian, pointed out that grad school should not be that difficult because professors typically taught to the lowest-level students in the class. He was right. To my shock and chagrin, most of the students did not know much at all.

Each night, after checking into our first class, Julian and I would quietly sneak out and head over to The Slaughtered Lamb, a pub in Greenwich Village near the NYU campus. There, we would devour supersized cheeseburgers and French fries (Julian, of course, put mayonnaise on everything) and drink a few yards of beer. We would discuss our future plans and how to achieve them. Then, we would secretly head back to the end of our second class, apologizing to our professor with a made-up excuse that our bosses needed us to stay late at work. Soon enough, we mastered the attendance portion of our grade and excelled in testing and assignments, as they were way too easy, just as Julian had said.

Pre-AI and Pre-Zoom

While at Morgan Stanley, I developed a new accounting system to allocate the firm's expenses back to the money-producing trading floor. Since I didn't have an accounting background, I put forth tremendous effort studying for my CPA, which was the quickest way to learn everything I could about accounting, while simultaneously fulfilling the work requirement needed to earn a CPA. It took ten months, working eighteen-hour days, reviewing and learning the material during breaks and meals. The unyielding effort I put forth branded me with an even harder work ethic, like a hot iron.

One major obstacle I faced on a work project was allocating expenses to units that rolled into other units first, sometimes involving several roll-ups. Then I had to reallocate those costs, making each concept clear and easy to process. We actually hired a NASA rocket scientist to develop a repeating iterative algorithm, which ran on a supercomputer that we rented overnight for thirteen iterations back-to-back. Each learned from the previous, adjusted the algorithms accordingly, and used the newly revised data. FYI, we were using self-correcting algorithms (what is better known today as Artificial Intelligence (AI), laying the foundation for some of my current work). Back then, the technology took overnight to compute, but now it is done in seconds.

Upon finishing this arduous task, my boss asked me to teach the other offices worldwide how to use the program. I said **YES** to doing it, but there was a significant issue—I did not have the time to fly to thirty-plus offices worldwide. In addition, it was the early 1990s, so video conferencing solutions didn't exist yet.

The only option was to create a videotape explaining the process that could be copied and then be sent to all of the offices. I got to work writing a script, hiring a crew, and filming the training sessions on a large Betamax tape (**YES** Betamax – Ha!). Little did I know that this would become a precursor to my future in the film industry, demonstrating that skills learned can potentially be utilized at any point in life. I had also insisted that we use two cameras to split screen time between my talking and pointing out the relevant information on a computer screen. This method (now called "screen sharing" on Zoom) showed our foresight in adopting technology ahead of its time. After the staff watched the recording, I reviewed the steps on a conference call.

The success of this project marked a significant milestone in my career, my first-ever six-week international business trip to Tokyo, the home of Morgan Stanley's biggest accounting office that handled all of Asia. Obviously, I said **YES** to an all-expense assignment in Japan and gave a double **YES** to the credit card I was given to use for all my sightseeing trips and restaurant excursions. Despite the incredible opportunity, being a newlywed added a layer of complexity. The extended time away from my wife, who chose not to join me, as she decided she did not like to travel anymore, undeniably strained our relationship. But otherwise, it was a great gig for a guy in his early twenties.

Turning Japanese, I'm Turning Japanese, I Really Think So

Flying first class on Japan Air was quite a treat. Throughout the lengthy direct flight, I traded off working, watching movies, eating gourmet food, back rubs, and listening to music on a cassette tape on my Sony™ Walkman with The Vapors' "Turning Japanese," which I played dozens of times.

Upon my arrival, I was struck by the homogeneity of the population. It was anything but a melting pot back then, with only three percent of the country, including tourists, not Japanese. Morgan Stanley put me up in a small one-bedroom apartment with a tiny kitchenette on the top of a fancy hotel in Tokyo. I never used the kitchenette because someone from the office was designated to take me out every night. Each morning, I went down to the lobby for the complimentary extravagant Japanese wild raw salmon breakfast, where greeters waited to say "Hello" and "Have a nice day" in English.

I drank a lot of sake and ate a lot of sushi. Nowadays, sushi is ubiquitous in the United States. It's almost as popular as pizza and hamburgers.

But, back then, since nobody I knew frequented Japanese restaurants, I had never been exposed to sushi nor did I know much about it. But that was about to change. In Japan, I tried every piece of sushi offered to me and became a connoisseur of sorts.

The first time I tried sushi, a dainty Japanese woman from my office, Ayaka, took me out. Ayaka had shiny, shoulder-length black hair, short bangs, and pearly-white skin. When she asked me if I wanted to try her favorite sushi restaurant, I gave her a firm **YES**.

The brightly lit restaurant was narrow, with only counter seating. Glossy poster images of the various sushi options hung on the walls with the names of each piece written in Japanese. A conveyor belt ran along the length of the restaurant and into the back kitchen, with different colored small plates of sushi pieces moving on the belt.

"Just take whatever plate you want, and we will pay at the end of the meal," Ayaka instructed me in her soft-spoken voice.

I took a red plate, then a blue plate, then a yellow plate, and continued trying every colored plate in the rainbow. Whenever I ate something I liked, I grabbed that same color. I had no idea what I was eating. Some fish melted in my mouth, sliding down my throat like butter; some tasted sweet, and some had a tough and chewy texture. Busy trying everything, Akaya and I didn't speak much while eating. One of the pieces of sushi made me gag, and I had to spit it up twice before I could get it down on the third try. Ayaka almost tossed her cookies while watching me. Finally, when I couldn't fit another piece of fish in my belly, we stood up and brought our plates to the register. Ayaka handed her plates to the cashier first. I wasn't sure how I ate twenty-two sushi plates while she only ate three. We were charged per colored plate. Needless to say, it was a pricey meal, but I didn't care. Thank you, Mr. Morgan Stanley.

At another memorable sushi restaurant, I tried to put my life at risk. Talk about fresh, the fish swam around in large tanks. It was a good thing I had excessive sake running through my veins before eating there with Hiroto, another Japanese colleague whose perpetual smile offset the frown-like shape of his oval eyes. Chefs pulled out the fish right in front of us and sliced it while it wiggled around. And then, with the heads off, the fish continued to jerk, and I was instructed to pick it up with my chopsticks and eat it. I tried not to gag, convinced the dead fish wasn't dead as it danced down my esophagus and into my stomach.

"Are you ready to try a Japanese delicacy?" Hiroto asked, his smile widening.

"Sure, of course," I responded, wondering when and if the fish I ate would swim down my sphincter and out my asshole.

"It is called fuku, which means blow."

"Wait a minute, do you mean blowfish?"

"Hai," Hiroto said (Hai is a Japanese term for showing agreement). "You've had it before?"

"Um, no. Aren't blowfish poisonous?" I remember learning about the toxicity found in blowfish in a marine biology class I took in college, and from what I recalled, which may not be entirely accurate, there's no antidote for the poison. The toxic fish causes paralysis in the muscles and a painful death within twenty-four hours. So I followed my **YES** response with a prayer to the man upstairs.

"Don't worry. These chefs are highly trained and will try not to kill you."

"Try not to? That doesn't sound too convincing. But I guess I'm in."

Hiroto nodded to the chef, indicating that we would eat the blowfish. The chef pulled the blowfish out of the tank and placed it on the wooden counter. He cut the head, the tail, and the fins using his sharp knife. Next, he removed the guts and skin. Finally, he sliced the fish into paper-thin pieces and arranged them on a plate. I waited for Hiroto to eat his first before trying it. Once he swallowed, I grabbed a piece, chewing the slimy, mild fish slowly.

"Do you like it, Ron?" Hiroto asked as soon as I swallowed.

"Considering I'm not dead yet, **YES**, I liked it. It tastes pure and clean."

After the meal, I bowed to the chef in gratitude for his skillful preparation of the blowfish—and for not killing me.

A Head Above

For the entire duration of my Tokyo stay, I only interacted with two Americans. One was a friend from New York, Gary, who was also spending time in Japan on business. One day, Gary and I planned to meet during peak hour at the Shinjuku Train Station, the busiest Tokyo station in the business district. From there, he wanted to take me to one of his favorite sushi restaurants.

"Gary, are you crazy? How will I find you in the middle of the train station?" as I had flashbacks to the European backpacking trip.

"Trust me, Ron. Just look up when you get to the main JR East platform. You'll find me," he said in a matter-of-fact tone.

I thought I would never find him, and since cellphones weren't mainstream, I had no idea what would happen if I didn't see him there. As it turned out, he was right, and I was wrong. Stepping onto the platform, I found myself in a sea of people, filled with men and women dressed in business attire, holding briefcases, and swarming everywhere. Commuters wore straight-faced expressions, their eyes fixed on their destination. Keeping my head high, I looked up, and in a few moments, I spotted Gary at the same time he spotted me. Standing in the crowd at six feet, six inches, Gary looked like Andre the Giant, surrounded by shorter people who appeared to be under five feet, six inches tall. As for me, I was probably the second tallest guy there at over six-one.

"I told you you'd find me," Gary said, hugging me.

Outside the train station, we walked a few blocks, catching up on business and discussing our favorite sites in Tokyo. Upon entering the restaurant, which reminded me of a New York diner filled with booth seating and a long sushi bar along the side, we were handed a clipboard with the number thirty-two on it. I followed behind Gary as he approached booth thirty-two, and we sat across from each other. There was a small touch screen that reminded me of a jukebox at the end of the table.

"Look at the screen and hit the red button under the piece of sushi you want, and the server will bring it out," Gary told me.

Everything was written in Japanese, so I randomly hit buttons with pictures of sushi that looked like things I had tried in the past. After trying each piece, I reordered the sushi I liked when a server brought them out. No such restaurant existed like this in the United States, and I felt like I was playing a video game. By now, I had become an expert at eating exotic-tasting raw fish and enjoying the unique ordering experience. My palate became much more refined during my stay in Japan.

The Insider

The other American I spent time with was Jerry, a guy who worked in the Tokyo office with me, and his Japanese wife, Yoko. Originally from a Midwest farming family, Jerry had white hair and a jolly-looking, pasty face, reminding me of Santa Claus or Jerry from the *Parks and Recreation* TV show. Jerry's father had been in the Air Force and was transferred to Japan when Jerry was in grade school, so he grew up on a base there and became fluent in Japanese.

One weekend, Jerry and Yoko invited me to their country house, a two-hour train ride from Tokyo. Their home was a traditional, small Japanese three-bedroom house made of wood beams and panels with walls of thin materials called shoji screens. Unlike many American homes with oversized, heavy furniture, their house had a sparse décor. Instead of beds, we slept on rice-straw tatami mats. Getting comfortable while sitting in the low wooden chairs in the living room was somewhat challenging, but we spent most of the weekend drinking sake, making sushi rolls, and taking turns belting out songs on the karaoke machine. Yoko worked for Japan Airlines and spoke eight languages. She also had an incredible singing voice, reminding me of a tiny, pale-faced, Japanese Whitney Houston.

Jerry and I went to a hole-in-the-wall restaurant, resembling an abandoned brick shack, in a desolate alley. Inside there were about seven tables, four of which were occupied by diners. The ceilings were so low I had to crouch my head. Jerry and I stood out as the only two Americans in there (maybe ever). I felt everyone's eyes glaring at us.

Jerry sometimes hid his flawless Japanese dialect for fun. Speaking in English, he told the man with deep-set facial lines and gray hair, who I assumed owned the restaurant, that we were a party of two. We followed the owner to our table, and then, after we were seated, I heard the owner say something to one of the servers, a younger guy with messy black hair and narrow lips. Laughing and looking at us, it was apparent we were the butt of their joke. Jerry, of course, knew what they said. I later discovered they were mocking Jerry's round belly and my height and referring to us as dumb Americans. Jerry stood from the table and asked for a piece of paper and a pen. Then he wrote them a note in perfect Kanji telling them they should be embarrassed by their behavior and how dare they make fun of us. When the owner read the note, his face fell. He apologized profusely and gave us free food the entire night. Go, Jerry—he showed them.

Saying **YES** to working in Japan allowed me to immerse myself in Japanese culture, subsequently opening doors for me to engage with and learn about the ways of life in other countries and around the world. I also learned the basics of the Japanese language and left with a lingering taste of melt-in-my-mouth sushi.

The Revolving CPA Door

Fun fact: It took me over three-and-a-half years to graduate and earn my MBA while switching jobs halfway through school. Unfortunately, the graduation ceremony was held on May 12, the same day my wife gave birth to my eldest daughter Casey. Of course, I bailed on graduation to be with my wife in the delivery room and hold a leg. Despite my busy schedule, this reinforced my belief in *Prioritizing* the essential things and continuing to try to master the art of *Time Management*.

After earning my MBA, it was time to schedule my CPA test. But I had realized that working as an accountant felt monotonous and unfulfilling.

I mainly did number crunching and back-end work that lacked the creativity and energy I craved. Walking to the exam that day, I had an uneasy feeling rumbling in my belly that had nothing to do with how prepared I was. I asked myself: *Should I bail on the test and switch careers again?*

YES!, the voice in my head screamed. I took this as a sign that I should not pursue an accounting career. Not to mention, I didn't want to turn into a guy who fixed books or was expected to know all the tax codes and risk ending up in jail. Strolling into the exam center, I froze and pushed the revolving door back and forth, going through it multiple times. Meanwhile, everyone stared at me like a circus freak who didn't know how to enter. Finally, I turned around and darted home.

The Two-Year Rule and Off Again

My mentor, Bill, from Andersen Consulting, had always told me that I needed to stay at any job for at least two years to gain the right amount of experience. This would give the job enough time to see if it was right, look for an upward path, get the maximum bonuses, and show commitment on a résumé. Also, when quitting a job, I would do it in August after accruing all my vacation days, giving me much-needed quality time with my family. After a well-rested break, I would start my next job after Labor Day when the kids returned to school.

Every job and every experience I've had, including Morgan Stanley, proved valuable and allowed me to grow and learn. I tried to make the most of everything I did there. Traveling and gaining extensive accounting knowledge became an invaluable skill set that I utilized in all my future careers. Even though it ended up not being the right job for me in the long term, and I did not accomplish my goal of getting to the trading floor, it was not a mistake, nor was it a waste of time. Regrets only happen when you make decisions for the wrong reasons or against your better judgment because you listen to the bad advice of others instead of your gut.

Fortunately, after leaving Morgan Stanley at the two-year mark, the same recruiter with whom I had made sure to keep a close, personal relationship with (***Networking***) had put me to the top of his list and lined up another supporting role for me. This time, however, I was promised a direct timeline to become a trader. (Here I go again, feeling like Charlie Brown with Lucy, the recruiter.)

Inspired by one of my favorite books, *Moby Dick,* I knew I would fulfill my dream of stepping onto the trading floor—my white whale.

Lessons Learned Chapter 5 – PRIORITIZING (with Precision)

"Priorities define your purpose."

In Chapter 5, managing an intense workload such as juggling an accounting job, MBA classes, CPA studies, and personal life taught me the importance of aligning my time with what truly matters. *Prioritizing* is more than just organizing tasks; it's a strategic way to balance ambition, productivity, and personal milestones without sacrificing what's essential.

Let's Recap:

Genuine Focus Over Multitasking Chaos

From studying for my CPA to building an innovative accounting system, I realized success didn't come from trying to do everything at once but from *Focusing* on what truly mattered. Breaking my day into specific designated blocks with achievable timelines allowed me to tackle one task at a time, reducing stress and maximizing productivity.

Key Takeaway: *Prioritize* tasks that move you closer to your long-term goals or personal happiness and *Focus* on them with intention.

Strategic YES, Purposeful NO

Opportunities often come disguised as distractions. Saying **YES** strategically allowed me to embrace career-expanding experiences—like working in Japan and creating a global training program. But saying NO to misaligned paths, like the CPA test, helped me avoid long-term dissatisfaction.

Key Takeaway: Accept opportunities that align with your goals, but don't hesitate to say NO to distractions or obligations that don't serve your purpose.

Adaptability Fuels Growth

My time in Japan forced me to step outside my comfort zone, immersing myself in a new culture while building professional relationships. It taught me that being open to unfamiliar experiences can yield invaluable personal and career growth.

Key Takeaway: Be willing to adapt, *Listen and Learn*, and embrace change—it's often where the greatest growth happens.

Balance Ambition with Personal Life

Skipping my MBA graduation to be in the delivery room for my daughter's birth reminded me that no career milestone can replace life's irreplaceable moments. Even during my busiest years, I learned to *Prioritize* what matters most.

Key Takeaway: Personal milestones (can include family, working on one's health, religion, friends, etc.) deserve just as much—if not more—attention as career goals. Balance is key.

Listen and Learn from Every Experience

Although accounting wasn't my ultimate career path, the skills I gained at Morgan Stanley became invaluable for future roles. Every step, even the less glamorous ones, contributed to my overall growth.

Key Takeaway: No experience is wasted if you *Focus* on the lessons and skills it teaches you.

Chapter 6

Listening and Learning

The Wild West on Wall Street

September 1993

On to my next opportunity: Lehman Brothers. This time, I scored a desk, working in technology support on their fixed-income trading floor, the setting for Michael Lewis's book *Liar's Poker*. I was close enough to the action but still considered a second-class citizen. The traders and salespeople had no problem reminding me of that. And let me tell you, back then, Lehman Brothers resembled the Wild West. Guys were raking in the dough, and I wanted to swim in the green waters too. To get there, I applied the philosophy I learned in college: know the end game and figure out how to work the system.

Getting Warmer and Making Cash Along the Way

My goal was still to become a trader, so I managed to position myself as a much-needed commodity to gain maximum leverage. While at Lehman Brothers, I became good friends with my young boss, Tim Remember him from chapter one? He was the guy I had tea with in London before heading to Cannes (another lifelong friendship).

One morning, Tim asked if I'd be willing to take charge of the technology help desk. This was a significant responsibility for management, as it meant overseeing hundreds of people, most of whom were much older than me. By now, I'm sure you know my answer, a loud **YES**.

The help desk was not the most glamorous position. My job entailed providing my colleagues and customers with technical support and fixing computer issues. If my coworkers couldn't work because they were having IT-related problems, they would come to me screaming and begging for help. After all, if their computer didn't work, they couldn't trade. And if they couldn't trade, they couldn't make money.

Once a trader starts earning boat loads of cash, it becomes like a drug addiction. They are never satisfied until they have more. Money was like cocaine to the traders, and their computers were the dealers. If the dealer couldn't supply the drug, the traders, like people with an addiction, became desperate. That's where I came in, preying on my coworkers' addiction.

One day, a trader, whom I'll refer to as Cocky Money Bags, came running up to me, his hair in disarray and voice shrill. "Ron, dude, you've got to help me. I spilled coffee on my keyboard, and now my computer won't turn on."

"Wow. That's a bummer," I replied. "I can get you a new one, but it may take a week."

My response made Cocky Money Bags jittery, his face turning pale. "No, man, I can't wait that long. Look, how about I give you a thousand bucks if you get me a new one today?"

Dollar signs flashed in my head. "All right, I'll see what I can do."

"Thanks, Geek," Cocky Money Bags said.

"For calling me a geek, that'll be five thousand dollars," I replied, channeling my inner Bob Barker from *The Price Is Right*.

Grumbling, he agreed.

Thanks to this encounter with Cocky Money Bags, I created a side hustle for myself. Every day, it seemed like someone else's computer coincidentally broke down. Hmm . . . I wonder how that happened?

Whenever a trader's computer needed to be repaired, I offered my rush service for a fee and rummaged through our storage room filled with computer parts and fixed whatever was broken. Brilliant, I know, considering these guys were earning so much money. They spent it lavishly on expensive porterhouse steaks from Delmonico's a few nights a week and washed them down with Macallan's single malt whisky. They gifted their lady friends fur coats and diamond tennis bracelets, drove to the Hamptons in flashy sports cars, and took private jets to Paris for dinner over a weekend. Giving me a few thousand bucks meant nothing to guys like Cocky Money Bags.

Sitting at the help desk daily meant I was in the middle of all the trading action. When I wasn't busy with tech issues, I soaked up knowledge like a sponge, ***LISTENING and LEARNING*** from the traders. I gained an understanding of the challenges they faced on the trading floor, mainly focusing on how to make trading more efficient.

During my downtime, I collaborated with my nerdy computer friends at the firm and with a new startup company called Bloomberg. I even had the opportunity to work directly with Michael Bloomberg himself to design and write a new government bond trading system. Lo and behold, it was a huge success, and my program enabled me to get closer to becoming a trader.

The only problem was I hadn't taken my Series 7 exam, without which I couldn't trade. A few days before my scheduled appearance on the trading floor, my friend Felix—who had trained me when I first arrived and with whom I bonded over our shared love of sushi—kindly offered to let me use his Series 7 certificate.

"Really? Are you sure? I don't want either of us to get in trouble," I said, voicing my concerns.

"Don't worry. They'll never know. Just hand in the certificate face down to HR. They won't even read it. They'll just put it in your file," Felix assured me.

I followed Felix's advice, and luckily, it worked. (This could never happen today in the digital age, and looking back, I never should've done something so unethical.) I traded for a few months, but there were signs indicating that the Lehman Brothers trading dynasty was nearing its end.

I reached out to that same headhunter and informed him that my two years were up and that I had become a trader. I asked if he had a fantastic trading opportunity available. While transitioning to my new position, I also began studying for my Series 7 to become a legitimate trader.

Finally Arrived, Harpooning the White Whale

September 1995

I left Lehman Brothers and took a job at Merrill Lynch on their sprawling trading floor, bigger than an actual football field, at the prestigious options desk as a real trader. Sometimes, when you get to where you strive to be, it is not all it's cracked up to be.

I finally caught my white whale. However, success isn't always sweet, and this whale did not taste good (too much blubber, I guess). I reached nirvana and realized it was not the top of the mountain but rather the base, and I still had much more to climb.

I figured out that trading, my dream, was no longer what I wanted to do. The countless hours I spent staring at numbers on the computer screen, playing a high-stakes game—earning money, losing money, making more money—gave me an unsettling feeling that all I had to contribute to the world was excessive cash. And there was nothing creative or altruistic about being a trader. Not to mention, I didn't enjoy working with a bunch of dumbass Neanderthals in an industry fueled by greed.

Don't get me wrong, I wanted to make lots and lots of money, but it didn't seem like the path that would make me feel fulfilled. I looked around the room to see who I wanted to be like, and there was no one. Julian, my graduate school buddy, was there, but he operated on a different echelon, and it was clear I wasn't meant to be on that level at this time. Not everything is within reach. For instance, lacking the height or basketball talent meant I could never go pro. (No matter how much I wanted to *be* like Mike, I couldn't be Michael Jordan.) But despite these limitations, there are still possibilities.

Recognizing this, I threw in the towel on getting my Series 7. I decided it was time to reset and go back to technology in the short term. My new goal was to use my MBA and work experience to become a successful businessman within high-level management.

This experience gave me a better understanding of myself as I recognized my preferences, strengths, and areas for growth in my career. Knowing I excelled in learning quickly, problem-solving, and project management enabled me to gain insight into my capabilities and aspirations.

Only through this self-awareness can you determine how to elevate your skills to the next level. By identifying what you're good at, you can pursue work that aligns with your ***Passions*** and provides ample opportunities for growth.

Back to The Future

September 1996

Now what was I going to do? Faced with the prospect of waiting two more years, I knew I couldn't stay. I was not ***Passionate*** about trading anymore, nor did I want to deal with that headhunter again. From that day forward, I decided to fully reset, take complete control of the plane, and pilot my career.

I called Bill, seeking advice. The key to managing your mentor is to avoid asking trivial questions and instead present real problems for discussion. You don't have to stay in touch daily, weekly, or monthly—just enough to let them know you're around and to update them on positive developments and successes.

Bill insisted we meet in person for drinks that night, and to my surprise, he seemed overly enthusiastic to talk to me. We met at the rooftop of the Peninsula Hotel, a hot spot for high-end business people and high-end call girls, go figure.

"Welcome home," Bill said with a giddy smile when I sat beside him at the bar.

Before I could ask him what he was talking about, he continued. "Things have changed since you left, and we are now Accenture. We just started a new program at the firm, which I'm spearheading. Instead of recruiting recent college and MBA graduates, we're looking for well-rounded employees with industry experience. And I want you to come on board as one of the twenty hires to be the poster boy of the program."

Bill took a sip of his drink. "Since your last three jobs were on Wall Street, and now that you have experience in accounting, back office, and leading-edge technology and money-making trading, you can be the subject matter expert and client front-man for all financial services in New York City and London. We will close so much business together, and I'll make you the youngest partner at Accenture. You in?"

Shaking Bill's hand instantly, I yelled "**YES**" at the top of my lungs. I left Merrill Lynch and returned to technology and financial consulting at Accenture, reporting directly to Bill.

"Great," he said. "Remember, you're with me now, and I am not letting you go. You'll be my clients' emergency kit. Breaking the glass only for the biggest and toughest clients."

Around The Globe Faster Than the Speed of Sound

On my first day on the job, I went to Bill's office, and without a word and still wearing that goofy smile, he handed me an envelope. "This is your first assignment, if you choose to take it."

Inside the envelope were tickets on the Concorde (the fastest commercial plane in the world) to London, scheduled to leave three hours later. When I first met Bill, he told me to always carry my passport. To this day, I don't leave home without it.

"Upon arrival in London, buy yourself some fancy suits at my favorite tailor at the company's expense. I'll let him know you're coming."

You bet I said **YES** to that. Now I was the giddy one, traveling to London at supersonic speeds. The trip would be a mere fraction of the time it would normally take. Amazing.

Dressed in my dapper new clothes, Bill and I headed to meet with Marc, the CIO of Deutsche Bank, in their new London offices. Bill warned me ahead of time to agree to go wherever Marc instructed, adding, "I don't care about the travel cost—keep going, no matter what. I have faith in you. Just continue to be uber-*Positive*."

Marc looked like a giant-sized version of Homer Simpson, and when I reached out to greet him, he grunted, "Why are you here? I need you in Frankfurt this afternoon to be my spy in the German-led technology meetings at their data center in Eschborn. Report every important detail back to me right afterward in a voicemail. Can you do it?"

"**YES**," I responded.

Marc shook Bill's hand, awarded us the major account, and then the two of them sat down to go over the details and the contract. I pulled up my chair to watch, and Marc looked at me and said, "Why are you still here? Get your ass to Germany *now*!"

Paranoid the bank was trying to overthrow him since he was American, Marc sent me on a wild goose chase around the world to attend every meeting he thought might be important since he could not be there himself.

I flew first class from London on Lufthansa, partly owned by Deutsche Bank, to Frankfort, Germany. Outside the airport, a huge Mercedes Benz limo took me to Eschborn. The high-security data center had six-inch-thick bulletproof glass and was guarded by German soldiers with machine guns and massive German Shepherds.

When the meeting ended, I called Marc and left him a voicemail detailing the meeting, which, to be honest, was boring and not important.

Soon after, I got a message from Marc's pager telling me to call him ASAP.

"Ron, the meeting has been moved to London. Get on the next flight, and don't miss it!"

"Okay. Will do," I said and grabbed a car to the airport, where I ran to the ticketing agent and bought a one-way first-class ticket to Heathrow, scheduled to leave in an hour.

When I arrived in London, I went over to the phone bank to check my voicemails and received another message from Marc informing me that the meeting had been changed again and that I needed to go directly to Singapore. I made my way to the Singapore Air counter and bought another first-class seat. With some time to kill before my flight, I went to the best lounge in the world, showered, got a massage, and boarded the plane for the long flight. Just because you have to work like a dog doesn't mean you can't enjoy the good stuff too.

Upon arrival, I checked into a huge suite at the Shangri-La Hotel. When I found out the meeting was pushed to the next morning, after three days of nonstop travel around the world, I crashed hard in the softest, most comfortable bed I had ever slept in (luxury has its perks), praying this would be my last stop.

I remained in Singapore for the next seven days with my two seasoned gray-haired colleagues from London, Andrew and John. Little did I know, these connections would prove invaluable in the future, as both reported to me, emphasizing the importance of nurturing solid professional relationships. You never know when paths will cross again. Despite the scorching summer heat and humidity, the London guys wore formal attire, dressing in thick, three-piece wool suits throughout our stay. We scheduled breakfast meetings at 7:30 every morning.

Every day, I woke up to an early phone call from Marc, notifying me that the meeting was moved to the following day. For shits and giggles, I didn't tell my colleagues and watched them walk in and out of the hotel, hot, sticky, and with sweat dripping from every pore of their bodies to the outdoor restaurant, where I waited for them in a bathing suit, short-sleeved shirt, and sunglasses. They didn't appreciate my joke as much as I did.

With no work responsibilities, I explored the many tourist attractions. One of the highlights was visiting the Gardens by the Bay, walking around the expansive gardens, and admiring the diverse range of plants and trees. Escaping the sweltering heat, I cooled off in the air-conditioned National Museum and toured the Buddha Tooth Relic Temple. I also indulged in traditional food, like spicy laksa, savory satay, and flavorful chicken rice. The chili-spiced food was music to my taste buds, and the extra heat made me perspire that much more.

During this period, coinciding with one of the High Holy days, as a Jew, I sought out a Sephardic temple to attend services. It marked my inaugural experience, during which I was instructed to remove my belt and shoes, which were not permitted attire. Though I managed to follow the services, I found myself constantly readjusting my suit pants and catching a whiff of my sweaty feet.

Not having any meetings for a week worked well for me, allowing me to immerse myself in Singaporean culture. On the seventh day, I received a call at 6:30 a.m. letting me know the meeting had been moved to New York City. To the airport, yet again, but this time, I was finally heading home to see my family—or so I thought.

Lessons Learned Chapter 6: Mastering the Art of LISTENING and LEARN-ING

Active listening and the ability to Listen and Learn from your environment are indispensable skills, particularly in high-pressure and fast-paced settings like Wall Street.

In chapter 6, I leveraged these abilities to transform a tech support role into a stepping stone toward my dream of trading. By immersing myself in the culture, dynamics, and needs of the trading floor, I not only gained valuable insights but also created opportunities that led to substantial career growth.

Let's Recap:

Be Present

Success starts with paying full attention to the environment around you. Avoid distractions and *Focus* entirely on the task or conversation at hand. Take notes to retain critical information and revisit it when needed.

Key Takeaway: Active engagement is the foundation for meaningful learning.

Ask Open-Ended Questions

Asking thoughtful questions like "how" and "why" encourages deeper understanding of processes, strategies, and goals. This not only demonstrates curiosity but also helps uncover nuances others might miss.

Key Takeaway: Never hesitate to ask questions that enhance your understanding and show your commitment to growth.

Observe Dynamics

Pay close attention to interpersonal interactions and organizational structures. On Wall Street, this meant learning the unwritten rules, observing how traders solved problems, and understanding their motivations.

Key Takeaway: Observation is just as important as action. It reveals the power structures and workflows that can guide your decisions.

Adapt and Apply Knowledge

Listening and Learning are only as valuable as their application. Use what you observe to identify inefficiencies and contribute solutions. For example, I worked with Bloomberg to design an innovative bond trading system by translating what I learned on the floor into a practical tool.

Key Takeaway: Take what you learn and apply it in ways that create value for your organization and personal growth.

Build Relationships

Strong relationships amplify learning. By collaborating with mentors like Tim and teaming up with technology experts, I gained critical insights and support that accelerated my career.

Key Takeaway: Surround yourself with people who challenge and inspire you.

Reflect and Refine

Schedule regular reflection to assess your learning and identify areas for improvement. This helped me understand how my contributions shaped the trading floor and how I could build on those successes.

Key Takeaway: Continuous improvement is key to long-term success.

Leverage Challenges as Opportunities

Every task, no matter how mundane, holds a lesson. My help desk role was not glamorous, but it became my vantage point to observe trading inefficiencies and build impactful solutions.

Key Takeaway: Embrace every role and responsibility as a *Listen and Learn* opportunity.

CHAPTER 7

WORKING HARD

TO BE OR NOT TO BE PARTNER? THAT IS THE QUESTION

I managed to pass my travel test with flying colors and earned my wings. Not long after, when I was back in NYC, Bill asked, "You still want to make partner, correct?"

"I sure do," I replied, over zealously.

"How badly?"

"I'll do whatever it takes, but you already know that."

"Good, Ron. That's exactly what I want to hear. For your next assignment, Marc specifically asked for you to lead the Accenture team at Deutsche Bank. The bank is considering moving its IT headquarters back to Frankfurt, Germany. If that happens, Marc is out because Frankfurt already has a CIO there. To determine how to do this fairly, Deutsche Bank agreed to have two consulting firms conduct the study jointly: a German firm, McKinsey & Co Consulting, and us. If we win, Marc promised to give us the entire revamp of the IT group, which would be a billion-dollar-plus budget. It's all or nothing, Ron, baby. I need you to fly to Amsterdam to battle it out with them. This is your chance. If you succeed, I'll make sure you become a partner. Remember what I told you. *Positivity* and **WORKING HARD** always wins. There is no such thing as failure. You'll have plenty of time to sleep when you're dead. And, finally, if you're not living on the edge, you're too close to the middle."

"I'm on it, Bill," I told him, unsure how I would get this done, considering Frankfurt had better technology than the Americans and McKinsey was the top consulting company in the world, with their best and brightest assigned to this project. But, somehow, I knew I would find a way.

My Secret Weapon: The Red Light District

Days later, I sat in a conference room at the Grand Hotel in Amsterdam with two colleagues, along with McKinsey's two top German employees, Karl and Hermann, and Anil, a younger British guy who moved to Germany after college. The meetings started on a Wednesday. We planned to work through the weekend and return to Germany on Monday for the final documents and presentation to the *Vorstand*, the board of Deutsche Bank, on Tuesday.

Working nonstop day and night, we went over sheets of data. I knew the Frankfurt McKinsey team had more experience and had been doing it longer. Not to mention, Karl, the German lead, was a partner and absolutely brilliant. I was way out of my league regarding knowledge and experience for this project. Karl even spoke English much better than I did.

Knowing I had to win, I made sure to paint the data in a way that cast us in a favorable position. Keep in mind, all is fair and unfair in love and war. We were prepared to stop at nothing to beat the Germans (sound familiar? Ha!). By Thursday night, despite my underhanded work, it still wasn't looking good for our team. The odds were in their favor, and with the report nearly eighty percent complete, it looked like I was about to get defeated. But as usual, I refused to give up until it was over, working even harder.

Besides showering and sleeping late at night, we remained in the conference room for nearly forty-eight hours. Finally, yearning for some downtime, we decided to take a break and finalize the last twenty percent on Friday. The junior guys on each team still had to present their data, but with our heads spinning, we ended the meeting early, and the six of us went out for dinner and drinks.

We drank Amstel beer from the tap and filled our bellies with stamp-pot with smoked sausage on the side, gawked at the prostitutes in the windows of the Red Light District, danced with blonde-haired Dutch women under the neon strobe lights at Escape Club, and finally crashed in our hotel rooms sometime in the middle of the night.

We agreed to meet at 8:00 a.m. in the conference room the following day. However, that was when everything went awry. In life, it's always good to expect the unexpected. Five of us were sitting around the table, ready to hear the last data collected. My junior Accenture manager, Kevin, was prepared to present. Anil would go next, but he never showed up.

"I think we need to begin without Anil," I told Karl, smugly.

"We can't. Call Anil's room immediately. We need him. He has all our information," Karl barked out in his thick German accent.

Sipping coffee, we watched Karl pick up the phone and ask the front desk to connect him to Anil's room. "He is not answering."

"Well, maybe he's in the shower or something. Let's just get started," I suggested. "Hopefully, he'll show up soon."

"*Nein*!" screamed Karl. Panicking, he began to sweat for the first time.

I knew I had the advantage now. Super composed and measured from the onset, I hadn't seen Karl this frazzled before.

"I will go to his room and bring him back myself," he said in his heavy German accent.

I grabbed a Danish off the plate of pastries and took a bite. "Okey dokey. Don't take too long. We really, really need to finish the report right away. You know how important it is to stick to schedules," I said. Then to rub it in further, acting like a wise ass, I pointed to the big clock on the wall. "The proverbial clock is ticking—tick tock, tick tock."

By the time Karl stormed into the conference room with a concerned look, we had polished off the entire plate of pastries. "Anil is not in his room. I don't think he came back last night."

"What do you mean he never came back? How do you know?" the other German guy asked.

"I asked security to open his door. His bed was still made, and house-keeping wasn't there today. We need to call the police."

"That's quite odd. I thought we all returned together last night. Did anyone notice if he wasn't with us?" Kevin asked.

"No, I assumed he was with us when we returned," I replied. "Al-though I did consume a lot of beer, so I guess it's possible I just didn't notice him missing."

Karl called the police and hung up a few minutes later, frustrated. "We cannot file a missing persons report until he's been gone for twenty-four hours."

"Well, I don't mean to seem callous, but we need to complete our work," I stated. "We don't have much time left."

Karl's cheeks reddened, and he spoke English in his heavy German accent. "Mr. Shtein, we cannot finish without Anil presenting our data. You know how it will turn out."

"Sorry, man, but this is due on Tuesday, and we're flying back in two days. We need to compile the two-hundred-page report, print twenty copies in German and English, and we do not have the luxury of waiting for your colleague."

"*Fick dich*, which means F-you, Ron," Karl yelled. I thought I saw steam coming out of his ears. "We cannot complete it without him. No, I refuse. No, no, no!"

"Relax, buddy, and stop acting like a baby," I said. "It's not our re-sponsibility that you lost track of one of your team members. We have a significant amount of work to do. My team does not have time to orga-nize a search party. Your team can do it. This needs to get done before Monday, utilizing our collective data. No other solution is logical."

Kevin distributed the stack of papers to everyone, ensuring that all the positive data was directed toward our team. He meticulously included it line by line in the report and later in the conclusion. Meanwhile, Karl crossed his arms over his chest, sulking for the rest of the day while we continued working.

The following morning, we still hadn't heard from Anil, so Karl contacted the police once again, demanding action. With Anil still missing on Sunday, they called his parents in London. Through the phone, we could hear his mother yelling, questioning how Karl and McKinsey could lose their son. Anil, who hailed from an upper-class family in Kensington and had attended prestigious boarding schools. After graduating from graduate school at Wharton in the States, he had been working for McKinsey Consulting in their Frankfurt office. He was always punctual, sometimes working late and on weekends, and completed his reports ahead of his colleagues. His sudden disappearance made no sense. Was he kidnapped? Was he dead? We had no idea what had transpired.

In my mind, and not to be a total ass, of course, I cared and prayed that he was safe. However, since Anil could not present his report, the ball was now in our court. We finalized our work, printed it, and placed it in binders. Then, we jointly submitted our report, and fortunately, we emerged as the winners. Lucky for me, I was on my way to becoming a partner at the firm.

We later found out what happened to Anil, and thank goodness no harm had come to him. Returning to the hotel after our night out, Anil waited for us to go to our rooms and then doubled back to the Red Light District. Earlier that evening, he'd spotted a girl in one of the windows, and the sparks flew between them. It was love at first sight for him. Yep, that's right, Anil hired the young woman for the night and fell head over heels for her. He convinced her to leave her profession and marry him. She agreed, and Anil returned to Frankfurt, terminated his apartment lease, and opened a souvenir shop in London with his new bride. Way to go, Anil.

Don't worry. I'm not heartless and felt relieved and grateful once Anil was found. But winning the deal was even sweeter, knowing he was safe and embarking on his life journey. Although Karl swears to this day that I orchestrated the entire situation and hired that prostitute—even though I am not that skilled or ruthless—sometimes all it takes is a stroke of luck, impeccable timing, and the strength and *Confidence* to power through.

The Genie Grants Me Three Wishes

As a reward for my success, Bill had three surprises in store for me on my journey to becoming a partner.

The first reward was a three-month executive program at INSEAD (European Institute of Business Administration), located outside of Paris, focused on international business. This immersive experience involved being placed in groups of four with students from France, Spain, Japan, and the U.S. Each class was taught in a different language, and we had to collaborate to complete projects. We were also provided apartments in Luxembourg Gardens in Paris, allowing us to enjoy three-day weekends. While living there, I spent time revisiting *The Thinker* statue at the Rodin Museum, indulging in morning walks in the gardens, and playing American-style pick-up basketball with some Parisians. There was also an amusing incident when our driver on the way to Paris smelled so bad, we asked him to pull over and call us another car. As soon as we stepped out of the vehicle, we puked on the side of the road.

The second reward was a three-day Covey Methods training course in Colorado Springs, taught by Stephen Covey. During the course, I acquired and refined various skill sets, including Blocks of Time and Sharpening the Saw (scheduling blocks of time for *Focused* tasks), which I subsequently incorporated into my life lessons and decision-making processes.

For the third award, Bill invited me to the partners' global conference held at Disney World™, exclusively for a select group of senior managers and their families. Among the various entertaining events, we had the opportunity to enjoy Epcot Center, which was closed to the public. At one of the afternoon sessions, all the partners gathered in the conference room, and to our surprise, Mickey Mouse made a special guest appearance and introduced the group to Henry Kissinger. Mr. Kissinger delivered an hour-long speech, a memorable highlight of the event. Unfortunately, throughout the event, I was asked to complete duties for work, pulling me away from quality time I could have spent with my family.

Prepare to Turn on a Dime

September 1998

For my next assignment at Accenture, I ran the account at Bankers Trust (who had just acquired Alex. Brown & Sons, the first investment bank in the U.S.) and helped do some of their integration work. While there, I met and became good friends with Valerie, the senior executive. Valerie seemed to value my advice on just about everything (Accenture-related or not). We spent a lot of quality time together, developing an easygoing rapport, and she trusted me, the key to any good relationship.

In her early forties, Valerie was one of the most intelligent, ambitious women I had ever met. She worked her way up through the ranks of corporate America, commanding respect in every room she entered. With a sophisticated demeanor, she was not formally business educated but rather trained as a classical pianist. But despite her prim-and-proper appearance and soft-spoken nature, Valerie had a secret weapon: her lipstick. Valerie always made a point of reapplying her lipstick whenever she was in meetings with men. It was a subtle power play, reminding those around her that she was a female boss who should not be underestimated.

Valerie never let her gender hold her back, making her mark in a male-dominated industry. She was a straight-shooter known for her strategic thinking and ability to close deals. Unafraid to speak her mind, Valerie had a reputation for mastering the art of direct communication and an ability to cut through the noise to get to the heart of the matter. I respected and looked up to her.

One afternoon, Valerie and I sat in a red corner booth in Gallagher's Steakhouse, eating a late lunch in the dimly lit, classic, and smoky restaurant with dark wood paneling. A hodgepodge of black-and-white photos of celebrities and sports figures covered the walls.

Out of nowhere, Valerie announced that she had something important to ask me. "Ron, you're a solid worker, and you're smart. I see a lot of potential in you. I know you're about to make partner."

How the heck did she know that? I never told anyone, and I didn't think Bill had either.

"That is such a major and impressive accomplishment. I could not be happier for you or prouder." Reaching her glass in my direction, she toasted me.

Wow, I thought. Gaining accolades from one of the top executives on Wall Street was so important to me and made me feel amazing.

We took big sips, and then she said, "I want you to quit!"

Hearing this, I spit wine out of my mouth over the tablecloth, and we both chuckled.

"You should work for me now. You'd be a great asset at the bank and a trusted lieutenant in my army," she continued as she finished the last sip of her red wine. "I'll pay you three times your partner's salary, give you a huge signing bonus, and an out clause in your contract in case things don't go as planned."

This really threw me for a loop. The wheels in my head began turning at the speed of light, and I started to weigh the pros and cons of leaving my current job. *How could I leave, especially when Bill went out of his way to groom me?*

I flashed back to a meeting I had recently with the top thirty partners in the firm, secretly informing me that I was on track to achieving my goals by age thirty and becoming the youngest partner in Accenture history. They all told their life stories, one by one. How they fought to make partner, and how much they gave up personally. We indulged in expensive caviar and champagne from Petrossian, a gourmet restaurant, and they convinced themselves that the trade-offs were worth it.

It wasn't until this moment that I realized I had kept my head down so much I failed to lift it up to assess whether the end goal genuinely aligned with my desires. The truth was, I didn't aspire to be like any of them, and they did not value family and personal time. Despite their mega-success, their personal lives were in disarray—marked by divorce, estranged children, and missed family milestones. They never appeared happy. The Beatles were right, "Can't Buy Me Love." The partners' work lacked creativity and adventure. It was a routine, working-for-the-man grind. Again, in life, it is essential that you not only have the goal but can see people you want to emulate when you get there. This conversation made me realize I wanted to be more like Valerie than any of those Accenture partners and remain on my own path.

I took it as a sign when I noticed a photograph of Babe Ruth hanging on the wall above Valerie's head. Reflecting on how the Yankees' acquisition of him from the Red Sox propelled his baseball career, I decided that leaving Accenture was the right choice.

"**YES**!" I announced, throwing my napkin on the table. "I'm in."

"I knew you'd make the right decision. I'll fax you an official offer from HR when you return to the office," she assured me.

Her *Confidence* rubbed off on me.

Something Happened on the Way to the Promotion

Later that afternoon, when the fax came in, my eyes grew wide in excitement when I looked at the salary offer. Just as she had promised, I would earn significantly more with an equally larger signing bonus than I was currently making. I called Valerie to let her know I received the fax.

"Okay, now go into Bill's office and tell him to call me on speakerphone," Valerie said. "And then break the news to him that you're quitting. I want to hear his reaction and help you if things get tough. Oh, and Ron, consider me your mentor now."

Cue the *Star Wars* moment where Darth Vader drops the bombshell to Luke, "I am your father."

The door to Bill's office was open. He was standing in front of his desk, his back facing me, gathering a stack of papers.

"Got a minute?" I asked, walking in.

He turned around. "Oh, hey, Ron. Of course, for you, our youngest and brightest new partner. C'mon in." Bill came over and put his arms around me in a partial hug, and then he leaned his back against his desk, pointed to two Cuban cigars, and said, "These bad boys are for us to smoke tonight to celebrate. Can't believe this day is here."

I'd never felt such a high level of apprehension. A knot, a burn, and an unfamiliar pain churned in my stomach, signaling this wouldn't end well. This must be what it was like being caught in bed with the neighbor's wife for the first time. I had no idea how to start, and my planned speech was irrelevant and out of my head. *Do it quickly, like pulling off a band-aid*, I told myself.

"I just came back from having lunch with Valerie. She wants you to call her on speakerphone," I blurted out. My entire body became a pool of sweat.

Nodding his head sideways, he gave me a questioning look. "You don't look great. Don't be nervous. As of this morning, you are already officially a partner."

He dialed Valerie's phone. When she picked up, he said, "Valerie, it's Bill. I'm with Ron. We are so proud of him. What can I do for you?"

"Ron has something he would like to tell you." Her voice sounded louder than usual coming through the speaker.

Bill looked at me. I couldn't talk. I opened my mouth, and nothing came out. This was much harder than my marriage proposal.

Bill and Valerie simultaneously said, "Come on, Ron, out with it."

"Valerie offered me a job at her firm, and I'm taking it," I exclaimed quickly to him.

Valerie called out, "This is not a joke or a fire drill. It is real."

There was a deafening silence. My head was ringing so loudly I was afraid it would burst. Bill's face turned beet red. He stood up without saying a word, picked his paperweight up off his desk, and threw it through his office glass wall. "You can't be serious, Ron. What the hell?"

Venom spewed from his mouth. "After everything I've done for you, you're leaving me the day you made partner here!"

In all the years I had known Bill, I had never heard him raise his voice. All I could do was stare in horror as he continued to rage on.

"I can't believe you're doing this. Do you know how embarrassing this will be for me? I'm going to ruin your career, you stupid piece of shit," he fumed.

"Calm down, Billy," Valerie interjected through the phone. "Ron's got me now. Stop acting like a child. This is business."

My mind began to spiral, wondering if I had made the right decision. Then, as if Valerie had read my mind, she said, "Ron, leave Bill's office. I need to talk to him in private."

Moments later, Bill got off the phone, no longer scowling but staring up at the ceiling and wearing a forced relaxed expression on his face. "Sorry about that, Ron. I guess I overreacted. Congratulations, and best of luck on your new, exciting career change. It will be great. I will let everyone know."

I later discovered that Valerie issued a bold ultimatum to Bill. She made it clear that unless he improved how he treated me immediately, she would cease all business with Accenture—a potential loss of one-hundred-fifty million dollars annually. Furthermore, she revealed that my initial role would involve overseeing all the consultants for the bank, and I held the authority to reduce Bill's income to zero. With her leverage and formidable negotiation skills, Bill had no option but to grin and bear it. Two weeks later, I started my new job, working for Valerie.

I admired and truly appreciated Bill, and I felt terrible about leaving. Unfortunately, I never managed to repair our relationship, and given what I did, I understand.

Mentor Switcheroo

As the head of all consulting assignments at the bank, I was also tasked with reducing expenses. Valerie made it clear to everyone that they were accountable to me and advised them constantly to maintain a cooperative attitude. My primary responsibility involved devising various initiatives to trim unnecessary costs. I had inside knowledge of the projects and consulting. Whenever, for instance, we had a team of six individuals proposed or currently working on a project, I would streamline the workforce by making the consulting company eliminate two members, confident that the job could be done with just four. I trimmed one-third of the massive IT consulting budget, and Valerie took care of me at bonus time (the savings more than justified my huge pay). As a result, my reputation within the organization took on a tough demeanor, often likened to the hitman. Nevertheless, Valerie staunchly supported and defended me against criticisms of my age and questions about my ability to deliver results.

Occasionally, Valerie would employ me as a pawn to achieve desired outcomes. She told me to let others do my dirty work while maintaining my composure. Additionally, she emphasized that success comes at a price, and although it wasn't easy, it could be enjoyable. For example, if I managed to slash over twenty million dollars from the budget, resulting in discontent among the consulting team, Valerie would acknowledge their concerns and advise them how to retain five million back. This enabled her to be hailed as a hero for maintaining a balanced approach and salvaging the company's finances in the long run.

Cigar Bar

When I worked at Accenture in 1999, Valerie suggested I start doing small consulting jobs on the side (to keep sampling) and told me to keep it on the down-low because doing so was against company policy. She offered this advice to keep my mind active and explore potential opportunities or my next direction.

My first gig was for a guy named Arnold, who I later found out was a complete sham. He was taking money from people to start a business and skimming off the top. I didn't know this when he hired me, and I told him I would do the job for twenty-five thousand. Arnold gave me five thousand dollars to get started. When I finished the job, and it was time for him to pay the balance, Arnold told me I had done amazing work, but he didn't have any money because he had put it in his new startup concierge business. This taught me an important lesson: never start a job without a checkpoint. Payments should be broken into thirds: one-third up front, one-third in the middle, and the final one-third at the end.

"How the hell are you planning to pay me?" I asked, about to tear him apart limb from limb.

"Oh, I was going to pay you with free concierge services."

"But I don't need concierge services. I need my money."

"I'll tell you what, I'll give you a year's membership at the Grand Havana Room, a high-end cigar bar in NYC."

"Why the hell would I want that? I don't even smoke cigars anymore." The truth was, I used to smoke them regularly but stopped when my five-year-old daughter begged me to give them up after she caught me smoking on the porch one day. She had heard at school it would kill me. And when you make a promise to your kid, you keep it.

"Trust me," he said. "You'll meet a lot of really cool people."

Knowing I probably wouldn't see a dime from him no matter how much I protested, I said **YES** to the membership. I mean, why not? At least it was something in return for my work. And while I was there, I could actively utilize my *Listening and Learning* skills for any new opportunities that came my way.

Cigar smoking tends to be a bonding experience. Guys will insist you try their favorites and want you to smoke them together. But since I was no longer an avid smoker, I wasn't sure how to avoid cigar camaraderie without offending someone. Rather than making anyone uncomfortable, I decided to say **YES** to accepting a cigar when offered for the sake of *Networking*, assuring them I would smoke it later.

The first time I went there was midweek, after work. Upon entering the club, I walked through a stunning marble foyer to the main lounge area. It had plush leather armchairs, paneled walls, and silver ashtrays on top of mahogany wood tables. Ambient lighting gave the space an intimate feel. When the host, a white-haired man wearing a suit and tie, approached me, I introduced myself and asked if there was a place where I could watch the Yankees game.

"Of course. Come with me, and I'll take you there," he said. I was close behind him when he stopped in front of a man with a receding hairline and light brown eyes, who was sitting in a tufted chair, smoking a cigar. "Hello, Mayor Giuliani. This is Ron Stein, one of our new members."

"Ron, how do you do?" Giuliani reached his hand out to shake mine.

"I was going to take him into the other room to watch the Yankees game."

"Don't be silly. Ron, have a seat here. We'll watch the game together. They'll pull a TV out for us." I sat down in the chair across from him, and moments later, a server wheeled out a TV on a stand for us to watch. "You don't mind if another friend joins us?"

"Not at all," I said.

"Good. We'll have plenty of food and drinks. It'll be great watching the game together." We were glued to the TV when a heavyset black man with long, slick-backed hair and a mustache sat in the seat next to me. "Oh, hey, Al," Giuliani said to him.

I reached over to shake his hand and introduce myself, even though I knew who he was.

"Al Sharpton. Nice to meet you," he said, giving me a firm handshake.

I felt good about myself then, relishing this quintessential New York experience. Of course, had Arnold paid me the money he owed, none of this would have happened. But in hindsight, it worked out in my favor, and I got to hang with two high-profile characters, The Reverend Al Sharpton and Mayor Giuliani, on a random evening, watching the Yankees.

During a commercial break, I decided to initiate a conversation, so I asked Giuliani a political question. "I recently read that you favor education vouchers for underprivileged kids to attend private schools. Is this true?"

"Ron, we don't talk politics here," Giuliani said. "We only smoke cigars and talk baseball."

"That's not true. We also talk women," Al added, chuckling. They were correct, baseball and women were much better topics to discuss than politics.

Another evening at the club, Arnold sat me next to Alec Baldwin at the bar and asked me to try to convince Mr. Baldwin to join. Seated at the end of the bar, I ordered a tequila on the rocks. While waiting for the bartender to hand it to me, I turned to Alec and said, "Hey, I'm Ron."

Nodding, he took a swig of his drink and kept quiet. Maybe he was bothered that I refused to acknowledge his celebrity status.

Whatever. *His loss*, I thought.

The bartender handed me my drink, and I thanked him before I took a sip. Alec and I didn't exchange one word for the next ten minutes.

Then, finally, he said, "You're not going to say anything to me?"

"No, why? I tried to introduce myself, but you made it clear you didn't want to make conversation, which I understand. I'm guessing you probably had a hard day at work in the office." I was still playing it cool, pretending I didn't know who he was.

"Oh, okay. Well, I'm Alec Baldwin."

"Ron Stein," I said, shaking his hand.

"You seriously don't know who I am?"

"No, I do. I just don't care."

"Cool," he responded. "Can I get you a drink?"

"Sure."

He waved to the bartender and ordered another round. "You've got to smoke one of my cigars," he insisted, handing me one from the interior of his jacket pocket.

When Arnold noticed I was talking to Alec, he came over and butted into our conversation. "Ron, tell Alec how great this place is and that he should get a membership in the club."

"Yeah, all right, Arnold." When Arnold walked away, I told Alec, "Place is great, and you should probably join if you like it, but that Arnold guy is a douchebag."

"Really? Wow, I agree and appreciate your honesty."

Alec and I chatted for the rest of the evening. When we said goodbye, I assumed I wouldn't see him there after that. I brought a few work clients to the club a few weeks later. We were seated at a table in the back corner. When I looked over at the bar, I spotted Alec sitting in the same spot where we hung out. Noticing me, he got up and came over to our table.

"Ronnie, how are you?" he asked. I stood up, and we hugged it out. Then he leaned into my ear and whispered, "Hope that impressed your friends."

Ron, the Hitman

Valerie called me into her office one morning to inform me that Deutsche Bank (DB) was buying Bankers Trust. She was working on the transition team and wanted me to do the same job for all of DB. This was a huge promotion, and she assured me that the buyout clause in my contract, similar to a baseball player's contract, was valid if I decided to leave. Valerie then asked me if I would be interested in taking on an additional short-term assignment in London.

"There's a guy in the office named Hank, and quite frankly, I can't stand him because he's treating everyone in the office disrespectfully. I need you to give him a taste of his own medicine and make his life so miserable that he'll quit. Do you think you can do that?" she asked.

"**YES**, absolutely," I confidently replied. Poor Hank had no idea what was about to happen to him.

Assuming the role of Valerie's hitman, I flew to London, ready to embark on my first terminator assignment. Hank had a classic case of the Napoleonic complex, reminding me of an evil version of Austin Powers with crooked teeth and a terrible comb-over. According to Hank's staff, he frequently made women cry by spewing derogatory comments about their work and then calling them out for it in front of everyone in the office. Hearing first-hand accounts about Hank's lousy reputation ignited my excitement about giving him a taste of his medicine.

Upon my arrival at the London office, I immediately bombarded Hank with an overwhelming amount of work. I assigned him two-hundred-page reports, all diligently expected to be completed by the close of the day. Whenever he finished working on a project, I would inform him that his efforts were incorrect, forcing him to redo them. In a desperate attempt to deflect blame, Hank would often accuse one of his subordinates of the mistakes I pointed out. However, I would publicly admonish him, reminding him that it was solely his responsibility to ensure accuracy. Crafting assignments out of thin air, I mercilessly tore apart every task he attempted until he finally broke. Hank resorted to whining, crying, and even hurling curses in my direction. By the end of the second week, Hank had reached his breaking point and resigned. I promptly contacted Valerie to deliver the news. "Assignment complete. Hank is gone."

"Fantastic work, Ron," Valerie said with a smile in her voice.

Aruba Tradition Begins

Upon Valerie's insistence that I take some vacation time, emphasizing the importance of breaks from work to clear my mind, I embarked on a ten-day trip to Aruba with my family during the winter break from school. That initial getaway marked the beginning of an annual tradition spanning over twenty years. We made the most of every moment, engaging in various activities, such as water sports, relaxing at the beach and pool, snorkeling adventures, Jolly Pirate sailboat, and off-road explorations in the desert. We also befriended several families who, like us, returned year after year. Together, we watched our children grow up and forged lasting friendships. I have maintained relationships with a number of them including: Paul (good buddy), Mark, Brian and Haley, Lance and Elise, James and Cindy, Michael and Marina, Bill and Jen, and Ken and Lisa, and Magic Mitch.

Additionally, I became friendly with local Dutch residents, including a renowned chef, Denis, and a sommelier named Glen, who would later visit me in NYC. The annual trip taught me the immense value of vacations, especially when spent with family. The Aruba tradition will always hold a special place in the hearts of me and my kids who all grew up there as well.

The Payout: No More W2s and Working for the Man

I managed to advance my career in a short period—thanks to giving a confident **YES** whenever necessary. Upon my return home, I assumed control of the London office, operating it remotely from New York.

In February 2000, I turned thirty-three when the Y2K scare was finally over, and Valerie informed me that it was time to move on. She was leaving IT to run the Deutsche Bank Venture Capital group and encouraged me to start my own company using the money I had accumulated from the bank. We embraced each other, and she assured me she would offer advice whenever needed, although she cautioned against excessive reliance. So, I went ahead and hit the button on my buyout package from Deutsche Bank. About a month later, I received a substantial payout. Having secured the funds, I achieved my goal of amassing one million dollars and having at least two kids by the age of thirty, only three years behind schedule (not bad).

I was ready to embark on my next venture. Although I hadn't decided on the nature of this venture yet, one thing was certain: I was going to seize this opportunity to become an entrepreneur and vowed never to be a W2 employee again, choosing instead to be my own boss.

Lessons Learned Chapter 7: WORKING HARD with Purpose and Persistence

Hard work goes beyond sheer effort; it requires strategic Focus, creativity, and resilience to achieve meaningful and impactful results.

This chapter illustrates how purposeful dedication and adaptability helped me overcome challenges and seize opportunities—even when faced with unexpected obstacles or emotionally charged decisions. And always go the extra step/mile.

Let's Recap:

Set Clear Goals

Clarity about your objectives provides the foundation for impactful work. Define what you want to achieve and outline smaller, actionable steps to track your progress.

    Key Takeaway: Break down your aspirations into manageable milestones to stay *Focused* and motivated.

Think Creatively Under Pressure

High-pressure situations demand innovative solutions. In the Deutsche Bank project, I reshaped the data to present our team in the best possible light, giving us an edge over our competitors.

    Key Takeaway: Challenges are opportunities to think outside the box and create unconventional pathways to success.

Stay Positive and Confident

Confidence fuels resilience. By embracing a "Be, Do, Have" mindset, I maintained a calm, self-assured demeanor during critical moments—like taking control when Anil disappeared—allowing me to steer the project toward success.

Key Takeaway: Positivity and self-assurance can turn adversity into opportunity.

Work Smarter, Not Just Harder

Strategic *Prioritization* amplifies the impact of your efforts. Delegate tasks effectively, *Focus* on what matters most, and leverage collective strengths, as I did with my team during the Deutsche Bank assignment.

Key Takeaway: Quality of effort often matters more than quantity. *Prioritize* high-impact tasks.

Expect the Unexpected

The unexpected is inevitable but being prepared enables swift adaptation. Our ability to continue working efficiently despite Karl's team's disruption ensured we stayed on track and delivered results.

Key Takeaway: Always have contingency plans in place to adapt to shifting circumstances.

Listening and Learning from Mentors and Leaders

Mentorship accelerates growth. Bill and Valerie each influenced my path in different ways, showing me the value of leadership styles and pushing me to define my unique trajectory.

Key Takeaway: Absorb wisdom from leaders you admire but use their lessons to forge your own path.

Balance Persistence with Self-Awareness

While persistence is critical, it's equally important to reevaluate whether your goals align with your values. My realization that I didn't aspire to be like the Accenture partners prompted me to choose a path that resonated with my personal goals.

Key Takeaway: Periodically reassess your goals to ensure they align with your values and long-term aspirations.

CHAPTER 8

ACT DECISIVELY

CRASH AND BURN

Unsure of my new direction, I called Valerie and asked her for guidance. She suggested we meet at a teahouse near her home in Greenwich, Connecticut. I sat across from Valerie at a table by the window in the quaint restaurant she had selected. The walls of the teahouse were lined with bookshelves, and the heat from the fireplace added to the warm and cozy feel. Valerie spoke to me in her usual calm, cool, and collected tone and told me about all the investments she had made in dot-com companies, many of which were founded by young people who weren't that bright.

"We're in the middle of a dot-com bubble, and you need to come up with a dot-com idea while the opportunities are hot," Valerie said. "I'll help you raise money with my connections. And in the meantime, a few of my portfolio companies could use a smart and experienced person like you to manage them. The money you earn from that job will give you cash to live on with a potentially large upside. It's time for you to have a financial advisor. I recommend seeing Lisa, a woman I mentored, who is on her way to becoming a top advisor at Alliance Bernstein. Call my office tomorrow and ask for my secretary; she'll provide you with Lisa's contact information."

We continued talking for another thirty minutes about the dot-com expansion (a period when internet-related stocks soared during the late 1990s). Valerie was a wealth of knowledge and gave me excellent advice. I left the teahouse feeling inspired and motivated. I knew I had to come up with a great idea, and in the interim, she would get back to me with a job managing one of her companies. I was confident this would all play out somehow.

Joining the Dot-Com Craze

While working at Accenture, I became good friends with Mitchell, a young junior consultant. We often discussed innovative dot-com ideas but never came up with anything solid we wanted to pursue. After meeting with Valerie, I contacted Mitchell and suggested we get together for a brainstorming session. He agreed, and we had a breakthrough after a few breakfast meetings. We came up with a dot-com business idea targeting university students called U-Connections, a platform offering various online and offline marketing services to college students. We believed that U-Connections would provide a much-needed, valuable service by connecting students with businesses.

As we explored the concept, I realized there was a massive demand for this platform. The student marketplace was enormous and businesses needed to figure out how to reach that audience effectively. Taking a chance on the idea, I said **YES** to investing money to get the business started.

I leaned on friends and family and, with the help of Valerie, secured additional funding from other prominent investors, including a wealthy individual, Sam, from Long Island, who gave us twelve million dollars. Though we didn't know it then, Sam had been in jail for a Ponzi scheme but managed to hide most of his wealth in overseas bank accounts while serving time.

With our funding, we rented a trendy loft space in SoHo. A decorator helped us design the space, creating a hip, energetic vibe with green textured fur wallpaper and a pool table in the center of the room, surrounded by sleek, modern office furniture.

While building our dot-com business, I also worked for a newly formed global consulting firm based in NYC and London called M&A Partners. I had previously collaborated with several of the partners, including Andrew, Bharat, and John, from the Accenture Singapore trip. Leveraging my client base from large banks, I contributed to developing our sales strategy. We also organized two remarkable offsite events. One occurred in Dublin, where we enjoyed freshly brewed Guinness at the brewery and joined in singing sessions at local pubs with strangers who became like family. The other event was held in Southern England, at a castle estate near the River Dart.

The flexibility of both jobs allowed me to incorporate my *Time Management* skills. Whether during late nights, early mornings to accommodate London's time zone ahead of us, or a few hours spent in the SoHo office, I managed to balance technology delivery effectively.

Stories about young adults getting rich from dot-com startups were all over the news, and everyone wanted to get in on it, making it easy to hire a *Strong Team* of employees. Naturally, I turned to my inner circle of trusted friends. Fitz, my college buddy, was head of AT&T call centers, handling customer interactions, and he joined our team. Popper, the guy I sat next to on my first job, was the head of *Star Wars*™ toys at Hasbro and came on board to do marketing. We also recruited student representatives from the University of Delaware and the University of Michigan. Jay, an eighteen-year-old freshman at Rutgers, helped us get U-Connections off the ground. He became the head of human resources, managing a team of two-hundred-fifty people while he was a student at school, hiring and firing student reps and adults as he saw fit.

As we worked to get U-Connections up and running, we faced numerous challenges, including the need for high-tech equipment to support the expected influx of online users. Instead of spending on luxury trips and Ferraris like other dot-com executives, we invested millions of dollars in the latest technology and even had to lift servers into our office via crane. Despite the obstacles, we remained determined to make U-Connections successful, adding other ingenious services to the platform. Using existing technology, cellphones, pagers, and fax machines, we created an online food ordering system called U-Eats, similar to what Grubhub™ and Uber Eats™ are today. We also developed a social group and dating service called U-Date before the emergence of Tinder™ and Bumble™.

We spent hundreds of thousands of dollars purchasing custom U-Connection gear, like T-shirts, water bottles, pens, etc., and gave them away to help spread the word. I traveled to different universities to get people to join our online community and slept on floors in sleeping bags with the college students who worked for us. We were going strong for a while, expanding and getting closer to making our business profitable. Soon we were only a few weeks away from closing on a new funding round of forty-eight million dollars, which would catapult us to the next level.

Dot-Com Bubble Pops With a Flush

One April morning, while taking a crap on the toilet in the U-Connections office, I heard all six fax machines going off nonstop. Then, my cordless phone rang, which I had brought into the bathroom with me.

"Dude, you sitting down?" Sam, our most prominent investor, asked.

"Actually, I am. What's up?" I tried to suppress the musical noises coming out of my ass.

"It's over. The dot-com is over. We're losing everything!"

"What are you talking about?"

"The dot-com bubble has burst. The market is over-saturated and overvalued, and stock prices are rapidly declining. Businesses are going down left and right. Take whatever money you can from the accounts and go."

I hung up the phone, got off the toilet, ran over to Mitchell, who was typing on his computer, and told him, "I just took the worst shit of my life."

Mitchell's face turned snow-white when I explained what was happening in the industry and that we would have to walk away from it all. During the dot-com boom, tech companies invested in each other's businesses. We were owed about four million dollars from various dot-com companies, one of which was eBooks. This partnership was forged following a significant collaboration, initiated after a trip to Kentucky where we had the privilege of meeting the former governor on his private plane.

Scrambling, we tried to figure out what to do with our employees, the office space, and the large computers and high-tech equipment. With so many businesses going under, we couldn't sell anything we had. And since I co-signed for everything, I had to negotiate to get our bills closed as fast as possible. When it was all said and done, we left and abandoned the office.

After the chaos died, the pain of losing my entire life savings—about a million dollars—hit me hard. With two young kids at home and the breadwinner of the family, I couldn't bring myself to tell my wife. Instead, I decided I needed time to gather my thoughts and determine my next move. In my gut, I knew I'd be okay. I was young, healthy, and had earning potential.

Unfortunately, timing is everything in business, and the crash of our dot-com company made it evident that, despite how close we were to a breakthrough, the world was not ready for this technology. Maintaining a ***Positive*** outlook, I knew I would overcome this challenge by plowing ahead and finding another route to success.

Sam called me again a week later and asked if I wanted to meet him for a drink. Sitting across from him at a table in a small, dark restaurant in SoHo, we each ordered a scotch. I took a long sip of my drink, letting the amber liquid move through my veins, easing the tension in my body, and said to Sam, "I'm really sorry I lost your money."

"I don't care about the money. Most of it was other people's money I had raised anyway."

Hearing him say that felt like a weight lifted off me.

Sam continued, "You need to learn from this experience. You went all-in, and that's okay. I made a lot of mistakes in my life too. Real winners know how to bounce back from something like this. Find your core strength and *Focus* on rebuilding your wealth. But do it as you go along—like when you're at a casino. When gambling, you don't bet it all on one hand. Instead, you put in a little, take some out, and eventually play with house money. This was a great lesson for you. You need to wear the loss and bankruptcy like a badge of honor and learn from it."

B to C

In chapter five, when planning **Life Volume II**, I mentioned that I had been developing **Ronnie's Steps to Success**, a guideline I follow, enabling me to achieve objectives that stem from a **YES** response. As I continued to refine the steps, I first had to reset and decide what I wanted and what I would have a *Passion* for. Although I wasn't clear on my direction, I knew the endgame and developed my goal: pursue a career in New York (location was important) that gave me the financial security to support my family with the flexibility to remain present and involved in my children's lives. To achieve this, I had to start with research and *Networking*, another critical step in my process. I called Valerie yet again for advice, and she told me I could work temporarily as CIO of one of her portfolio companies, Adeptra, a startup SMS firm, with offices in Stamford, Connecticut, and London. This would give me income for the next six months.

"That's great, but what do I do after?" I asked.

"Go back to what you know best, your core. Consulting." She paused for a moment and then continued. "*Focus* is going to be the key here. Put all your energy into starting a mini-Accenture with an experienced project management team. As you know, these companies never have the right people or the clients they crave. And then, I want you to build the shit out of it. Got it?"

"**YES**." My *Focus* would be the driving force to success, an approach I was prepared to undergo in consulting.

"Good. I'll sit on your board and help with oversight and client intros. Make sure you get a significant and recurring revenue stream, and then, when the time is right, we'll sell it."

I knew Valerie was correct. Everyone should attempt to get a mentor like her to guide and catapult their career, and I was grateful to have her support and encouragement at every turn.

Going back to consulting reminded me of playing tennis in college. I never loved tennis, but I was good at it, so I continued to play on the team. At times, it's necessary to engage in work that aligns with your strengths, even if they aren't your preferred choice, and strive to infuse them with creativity and fun. Sometimes, you need to **Focus** on the mundane tasks to reach the more rewarding aspects. Doing that enabled me to discover a new **Passion** for entrepreneurial growth.

The next day, I started my consulting firm, Management and Planning Implementation, MPI (what a creative name – ha!). Mitchell, willing to take no pay for the first six months, joined me in my new venture as a junior partner while everyone from U-Connections ran back to where they came from, begging for their old, conventional jobs like everyone else in the dot-com world was forced to do. They were done with entrepreneurial adventures.

Opening a new consulting startup with no money proved challenging. I didn't even have enough cash to rent a one-room office space. Initially, we met with prospective clients at a Starbucks near Grand Central Station. Our first gig, which Valerie helped us get, was a two-person assignment consulting for the Bank of Bermuda. Instead of getting paid by the hour, I devised a better system to get paid by the job. I learned it was much more lucrative to bill this way and not let the client know how many people we had working on the job and how many hours it took to complete. As a result, Mitchell and I did the work of five people, putting in countless hours to ensure that we got the job done with minimal overhead, producing large profits immediately.

Before securing our next assignment, I had to hire a few consultants. To **Network** effectively, I reached out to my contacts at Accenture, inquiring if anyone was interested in joining our startup consulting firm.

We offered more competitive compensation than traditional consulting firms, along with better assignments and clients. Only three people jumped at the opportunity and joined our team. Kristy (one of the greatest people on earth) would consult, hire, and help me run the entire firm. Harry was ready to tackle assignments with his IT wheelhouse once we had a client signed on, and Kelvin, older and a bit more senior, came on board as a junior partner. Cheers to me. I now had three consultants, but the problem was I didn't have any work for them.

Even though I still hadn't found another gig, I continued to have unbridled *Confidence* and *Positivity*. I said, "**YES**, I've got this. **YES**, I can make this happen," and "**YES**, I will be successful," just like the *Saturday Night Live* skit, "Daily Affirmations with Stuart Smalley," where Smalley would look in the mirror and say, "I'm good enough, I'm smart enough, and doggone it, people like me." Those affirmations became my fuel, giving me assurance to keep moving forward. But I also heard Valerie in my head, telling me I didn't need a business plan—I just needed to get the eff out there and do it.

"Stop being a baby, Ron, and close the next deal," she told me ad nauseam.

And then, just like that, it happened. I got a call from someone I knew at UBS Bank who was interested in hiring my firm to help them manage a massive consulting project.

Kelvin and I drove to their headquarters in Weehawken, New Jersey, in the pouring rain to meet with the head of the bank. We sorted our paperwork and prepared our presentation on the way out of the city.

"Kelvin, listen up," I advised. "You're a partner now, and you need to act like it. We have to land this job, or else we won't get this company off the ground, and if that happens, this partnership will be meaningless."

The bank was looking to hire a firm to manage their project teams and coordinate changing their interior and exterior logo signs from the old Paine Webber to the new UBS three-keys logo. And they wanted it to happen on the same day, worldwide.

"Do you really think we can do this, Ron? You and I have never managed a facilities project before," Kelvin said as we pulled out of the Lincoln Tunnel.

"**YES**, partner, have faith, exude *Confidence*, and act like we have been there before, presenting ourselves as a big firm. We've got this," I reassured him.

As I entered the conference room, my heart raced with nerves, yet I displayed no signs of it outwardly. Taking a deep breath, I introduced myself and Kelvin. Scanning the room, I noticed half a dozen men and women seated at the conference table, all dressed in suits and looking expectantly at me. We were the last of three firms to present.

Clearing my throat, I began my presentation, my voice steady and robust. I had done my research and outlined my qualifications and experience, highlighting our goals and projections. As I spoke, I could see the interest and skepticism on the faces of my audience. These were intelligent, successful people who wouldn't be easily swayed. But I was determined to convince them we were the right group for the job. I ended my presentation with a strong closing argument, stressing the value I could bring to their company and the positive impact I could have on the bank.

There was a tense silence when I finished, and then I added, "We understand the importance and urgency of your situation here. We can put twelve people on the job with Kelvin leading the project full-time, and if you choose us now, he'll start this afternoon."

Then, one of the men stood up and approached me. "Thank you for your presentation," he said. "Give us ten minutes to discuss."

When they left the room, Kelvin turned to me and said with his eyes bulging, "Are you crazy? We can't start now. You're out of your fucking mind. First, I have a dentist's appointment this afternoon, and second, we don't even have twelve people." A vein pulsated in his forehead as he spoke. "I take that back. We don't even have anyone hired for this project. How the hell do you plan to find a dozen people to come on board this fast?"

"That's the least of our concerns. Let's get this deal, and then I'll find the consultants."

A few minutes later, the tall guy with glasses and gray hair walked back into the room, followed by his minions. He reached his hand out and said, "Okay, you've got the job. Ron, please, please don't fuck this up. Kelvin, you can use the conference room in the back as your office and command center."

"Great. Kelvin will begin now." ***ACTING DECISIVELY***, I smiled and shook the boss's hand, my heart overflowing with gratitude and relief. I had done it. I had convinced these important men and women that I was the right person for the job, and it would be a twenty-three-million-dollar project, of which MPI was making twenty-five percent, amounting to over five million dollars in six months.

Kelvin was in complete and utter shock. Much to his disbelief, I left him to begin the project. Not only was he missing his dentist's appointment, but he also didn't have a ride home. Of course, I knew he would probably give me hell for that, but so be it, at least we closed the deal. On the drive back to the city, I called Kristy. "We just landed a huge assignment for UBS Bank. I need you to find me twelve more consultants immediately."

"Ron, I would ask if you're serious, but knowing how you operate, I'm sure you are. This task is arduous, and you're not giving me much time to find the right people. And we don't even have an office to meet potential candidates and interview them. But I'll get it done because I am that good. However, I want to remind you that you're insane and an idiot," she said, then cackled.

"You'll find them. Offer them fifty percent more money. If you manage to get them for less than that, you keep the difference on top of the bonus you'll earn for each hire."

Starbucks: Our HR Office

We were all-hands-on-deck within no time, running this massive project for the bank. When I formed the company, I offered all senior employees small partnership buy-ins. However, besides Mitchell and Kelvin, nobody else was willing or able to take a lesser salary for the partnership. And given the recent dot-com crash, most people lacked faith in startups and were risk averse. I offered profit sharing to the rest of my employees instead. They were paid a salary plus a bonus for every day they worked, based on the amount the client paid us. I paid my employees immediately, so they didn't have to worry about me taking away their year-end bonuses. This was a much better deal than they previously had.

Post 9/11—Lest We Forget

Not long after we scored big with UBS, I landed us another whopper of an assignment. A woman named Linda, the head of Keefe, Bruyette, and Woods (KBW) called me and said a close friend had recommended MPI for an important and unique project. She asked me to come to her office, which happened to be in the same building as UBS, to discuss it.

Linda's door was wide open, and when I stepped inside, she looked up from her computer and stood up to shake my hand with a firm grip. She had dark boy-short hair and wore a blazer, pants, and a button-down shirt underneath. Behind her chair was a substantial over-sized painting of the Twin Towers and, in bright yellow letters, "Lest We Forget."

"I heard from a friend that you're really good," Linda said as she gestured for me to sit across from her desk in a leather chair while she shut her office door. "Here's the thing, Ron, I am not sure you know our history, but we lost over a third of our people at KBW on 9/11, including our CEO's son. We recently moved into these offices, and everyone, including me, is still distraught. It's hard to think straight, and I can barely keep everything afloat with so much to do. I need a consigliere, someone I can trust to have my back but not be in the spotlight and overshadow me. I want to create a three-year IT and operations program to rebuild and get us back on track with some immediate wins."

I was blown away. "Wow, Linda, I got this. **YES**, I will be your con-sigliere, acting like an in-the-closet partner for you. I can start now and place Harry, my top IT senior manager, to lead the effort, reporting directly to you," I told her, determined to do my best.

"Really? You're serious?" She smiled. "Okay. Let me know your price. Money is no object."

I hesitated, not wanting to seem greedy. "My fee is 60K a month, and that's for my time and two-and-a-half days in the office a week. And, of course, I will work offsite as well. I'll also give you a fair and reasonable price for my team, which is slightly below market rates."

"You got it, and you can use our office at the end of the hall to work out of when you're here. Do you really think you can do this, Ron? You might make a lot of people angry. We've got a bunch of old-timers here that aren't open to change."

I gave Linda (who has been a friend and someone whom I learned so much from) an assuring look with *Confidence*. "You and KBW need me. I'll act as your in-the-closet consulting partner and make you look good. Trust me, my team and I will be successful."

"Great. And one more thing I want you to know." She paused for a moment, grinning. "Please don't ever use that term 'in-the-closet consulting' again. I'm a lesbian, so it's not kosher to say that."

"I had no idea," I responded sarcastically, and we both laughed so hard we couldn't breathe. It was the beginning of a fantastic friendship.

My 9/11 Memory

On September 11, 2001, I was supposed to be at the top of the World Trade Center restaurant for a breakfast meeting about options tech-nology. I had already purchased my ticket to head up there but was called away for an urgent meeting at the Adeptra office in Stamford, Connecticut. I was one of the lucky ones, and I am beyond grateful. I lost several friends and work associates that day. Watching the towers burn on TV, I felt helpless and hopeless and couldn't believe my life had been spared while so many perished on that fateful day. Working with the people at KBW allowed me to make a slight difference, helping those directly affected by this horrific tragedy.

Lessons Learned Chapter 8: The Power of ACTING DECISIVELY:

Success often hinges on the ability to make bold decisions swiftly, even when faced with uncertainty or incomplete information.

In this chapter, I navigated the collapse of a dot-com business, leveraged mentorship, and pivoted back to consulting—all while acting with *Confidence* and resolve.

Let's Recap:

Trust Your Instincts

After the dot-com bubble burst, my gut told me to pivot quickly and *Focus* on a field I knew well: consulting. It was this instinct that kept me moving forward despite the setback.

   Key Takeaway: Trust your inner voice, as I did when transitioning from U-Connections to founding MPI.

Gather Key Information Quickly

When the dot-com collapse hit, I acted immediately, leveraging Valerie's advice and guidance to reset and plan my next move. I didn't wait for perfect clarity.

   Key Takeaway: Don't delay decisions waiting for complete certainty; act on the most critical data at hand.

Weigh Risks but Commit Fully

Securing the UBS project meant taking a bold risk by committing to deliver a solution with a team I hadn't fully built yet. Despite the uncertainties, I presented with *Confidence* and made it happen.

Key Takeaway: Even when risks exist, fully commit to your decision and figure out the details as you go.

Leverage Relationships and Resources

Valerie's mentorship and my professional *Network* were invaluable in securing new opportunities, from consulting roles to funding and introductions.

Key Takeaway: Relationships, like my connection with Valerie, can provide the resources and support needed to rebuild and thrive.

Act Decisively with Confidence

When pitching MPI to UBS, I exuded *Confidence*, presenting us as a large, capable firm even though we were just starting out. This assurance inspired trust and landed the deal.

Key Takeaway: *Confidence* in your decisions and presentation is crucial for gaining buy-in, even when the odds seem stacked against you.

Adapt to Changing Circumstances

The dot-com collapse was a stark reminder of how quickly things can change. My quick pivot to consulting helped me regain stability and momentum.

Key Takeaway: Stay flexible and ready to pivot when circumstances evolve, as I did when transitioning back to consulting after the crash.

Reflect and Learn

The failure of U-Connections became a valuable learning experience, teaching me to diversify risks and adopt a more measured approach to future ventures.

Key Takeaway: Transform setbacks into stepping stones for growth and future success.

CHAPTER 9

FOCUS

A HOME RUN: MPI GROWTH, SALE, AND PARTY

At MPI I went out of my way to build a *Positive* company culture by encouraging a space where everyone's voice mattered. Facing challenges together sparked innovation and research, and staying ahead of the competition became a group effort. It was never about me pushing my ideas around but rather encouraging everyone to get creative, explore new solutions, and utilize the latest technology.

Success didn't happen overnight, but as our reputation grew we started to attract new clients. Within a year, MPI had grown exponentially. I had dozens of consultants working for me and an influx of projects daily. The dot-com failure strengthened me, reinforcing the importance of *Working Hard* and having *Confidence*.

Kristy, My Number One Employee

I have been fortunate to have had great mentors throughout my life, and I have *Prioritized* paying it forward by doing the same for others. Kristy, my first consultant and lifelong friend, has always valued the life lessons and business philosophies I have shared with her—even if she does sometimes think I am crazy.

I remember a pivotal moment a few years into our working relationship when MPI was taking off and she said, "Ron, I don't know what it is about your advice, but I followed it and just wowed them with my *Confidence* and personality. They gave me the new assignment right then and there."

I felt a sense of pride and accomplishment hearing her words.

"I've learned a lot from you, Ron," Kristy continued. "Your guidance really helped me develop my self-assurance and understand the value of being myself in the workplace."

I first talked to Kristy about the importance of self-assurance in business early in her career when she struggled with insecurity and uncertainty. I explained that by believing in herself and her abilities, she could tackle any challenge that came her way.

Kristy's words that day touched me deeply, and I felt grateful that I had been able to have a *Positive* impact on her career, and I appreciated her influence on mine, constantly reminding me of who I am.

Going Out on the Way to the Top

In 2006, three years after starting MPI, I had more than two hundred consultants working for me. I was generating nearly forty million dollars in revenue annually, and we projected that revenue would double within the next two years. Despite being exhausted from running the company and consulting, I was eager to give my board meeting report.

After my presentation, Valerie, who naturally sat on my board, spoke in a composed tone. "Amazing work, Ron, but now you must sell the company. The timing is ripe, and pigs get slaughtered. You've got to do it on the way up because you don't know how long it will last. Also, I've heard chatter that the financial markets may not be as strong as everyone thinks."

Remarkably, she always had a pulse on everything.

Moving forward with Valerie's advice, I hired an investment bank she recommended out of Washington, DC, to help me find the right company to buy us. Many people criticized me for selling when I did because they assumed I'd make more money if I waited, but I was ready and, quite frankly, exhausted from working so much.

As always, Valerie was right. Two years later, in 2008, the financial market crashed, and if I had waited until then, MPI would've been worth a small fraction of what I sold it for in 2006.

Montreal, Smoke on The Water

We got dozens of bids from companies that wanted to buy MPI, but in the end, it came down to three: one in the US, one in Canada, and one in India. The company in India offered the most money, but I didn't want to travel there every month. The US company, IBM, was huge, but the deal was complicated and had too many future goals to meet without our control. I ended up selling to CGI, the Canadian company, because they were looking for a US presence in New York in financial services consulting. In less than four years, I went from having no money in the bank to walking away with a multi-million-dollar check.

Before closing the deal, I flew to Montreal to meet with CGI's CEO, Jacque. A car service arrived at the airport and drove me to CGI's head-quarters. As I walked through the sleek glass doors, I was immediately struck by the opulence of the space with its marble floors and expensive artwork. I took the elevator up to the top floor. The receptionist greeted me warmly and said Jacque was waiting for me in his office.

My eyes were drawn to the sweeping city views once I was inside Jacque's office. Seated behind a massive desk, Jacque had a full head of salt-and-pepper hair and wore an expensive Italian suit. When he stood up to shake my hand, I noticed the Panerai watch on his wrist, and then he offered me a seat on one of the plush chairs facing his desk.

"Welcome to Montréal," he said with a wide grin and a heavy French accent. "I'm glad you could make it."

We discussed numbers and projections and finalized operations for the next hour. We stood up simultaneously when we finished, and Jacque walked me out of his office.

"This is going to be a great deal," he said, slapping me on the back. "And I want you to work out of our office in Montreal one day a week. Don't worry about the expenses. We'll cover everything and anything you need. If you want any extras, like prostitutes or whatever, just let me know, and I'll have them waiting for you." He winked at me.

Who knew hookers would be part of this deal? Not that I would ever take him up on his offer, but it definitely made me see this was the right company, person, and deal.

After dining at a delicious, high-end French restaurant that evening and signing the paperwork the following morning, I flew home, ready to share the news with my employees and celebrate the windfall. A **YES** response doesn't always provide the results we anticipate. After all, I said **YES** to the dot-com business and that didn't pan out as expected. However, the failure of that venture led me on another path: saying **YES** to starting my consulting firm and staying one hundred percent *FOCUSED,* which resulted in a big, fat YES to selling.

Telling the Team

Initially, I hadn't told any of my employees about my plans to sell the company because I was concerned—more like paranoid—that the deal wouldn't go through if someone leaked the news ahead of time. It wasn't until two days before it was announced to the public that I called a company-wide emergency meeting at my friend's Greek restaurant in Tribecca, Thalassa, to share the news.

Everyone mingled in the open loft space on the restaurant's top floor that evening. Its brick-walled interior, high ceilings, sheer white curtains, and scattered round tables were a perfect ambiance and had been my preferred location for several of our company-wide meetings. I waited for all my employees to enjoy a few cocktails, hoping they would have a little buzz before I gave my talk. When the timing felt right, I whistled loudly to get their attention. As soon as the schmoozing stopped and all eyes were on me, I gave a short, direct speech about the sale of the company.

The group was stunned, and their jaws dropped open. An eerie silence filled the room. It was so profound you could have heard a pin drop, stretching for an eternity. Suddenly, as if on cue, the room erupted into chaos, and a chorus of loud, angry voices arose.

"How much did you sell it for? We deserve to know," someone called out.

"We all need a piece of the sale," another guy yelled.

I didn't want to disclose the amount I made because I knew it would only worsen the situation.

"Please, let's settle down. I promise you'll still have your jobs, plus you'll get an additional ten percent salary, and I plan to give you all bonuses paid upon the sale closing."

Many of my employees thought they were equal partners and assumed they deserved money from the sale because they were part of a startup. Unfortunately, they also conveniently forgot that after the dot-com crash, I offered the option of ownership if they were willing to take half their salary, but other than Kelvin and Mitchell, my junior partners, nobody wanted that risk. I was the only one who put myself on the line for the company.

After an hour, when things began to settle, I reiterated that the deal was done. Then I asked, "Did you make great money and enjoy yourselves here at MPI? Did I keep all my promises?" They nodded in agreement. "At this point, there's no going back, so we need to be *Positive* and move forward. I promise I won't abandon you. I'm here to help and advise you along the way. Please, just have faith. This will work out well for all of us today and in the future."

Time to Party

I did my best to put out the fires for the next week, and as soon as everyone received their bonus money and new contracts, they were much calmer. It was time to plan a fun party to reflect upon the company's achievements and celebrate the future. I went to the W Hotel in Union Square to see if I could host the party there.

"I know this is last-minute," I told the hotel manager, "but I need to rent the event space for Friday night. I want unlimited top-shelf alcohol, food, music, and the works. I'll pay you in cash if you give me a good price." A look of contemplation washed over his pimple-scarred face. So I added, "Dude, just say **YES**, and I'll make it worthwhile."

"Okay, 5K in cash, and it's yours."

"Done," I said, and then ran to the bank and pulled out the money. I was one hundred percent sure the scar-faced manager pocketed it after I gave it to him, but whatever, at least I secured a place.

Wanting to make a grand entrance before the party, I rented a horse and carriage for me and my junior partners, Kelvin and Mitchell. Riding down Broadway, the horse's hooves clacked against the pavement as we approached the crowd outside the hotel. A group of my employees waited by the entrance, waving and staring in awe at the sight of us. We likely looked ridiculous sitting in a flashy carriage with brass fittings and plush cushions, but I didn't care. It was part of the fun. When the carriage stopped, a few people gave a round of applause while others laughed. Finally, I stepped onto the pavement and greeted everyone with hugs and handshakes, and then we all walked through the hotel lobby and down to the party on the lower level.

Stepping into the event space, I was impressed by how well every-thing came together, considering I booked it at the last minute. A DJ played loud, upbeat music, and a few people were already dancing, their bodies swaying and jumping to the beat. Tables and chairs were set up around the room's edges, and buffet tables, loaded with carving stations and an assortment of pasta, lined the back wall. I ordered a tequila with a big ice cube from the bar, guzzled it down, and then hopped onto the dance floor, feeling the energy and excitement in the air.

Cube

At some point during the night, a group of about twenty imposing, loud black men dripping in flashy jewelry gathered by the room's entrance. Their hair was styled in various ways, ranging from buzz cuts to long braids to carefully sculpted fades, and many were covered in neck ink. I approached the group when I noticed a security guard talking to the man with the goatee, wearing a camo-print hoodie and matching pants, with plastic sunglasses perched on his head.

"What's going on?" I asked the hotel security guard.

"These men are trying to come in, and I keep telling them it's a private party."

"Who are you?" the goatee man asked.

"Ron Stein. And you are?" Up close, I realized who he was, the rapper Ice Cube.

"Look, man, I'm Ice Cube, and me and my boys are just looking for a place to party."

"You and your friends are welcome to join. It's on me."

"What do you mean it's on you? I don't need your money." He pulled out a wad of bills from his pocket to show me.

"It's no big deal, really. I'm hosting this shindig for my employees, but I'm sure everyone would be psyched to have you."

"You sure, man?"

"It'll be a lot of fun. And everyone in there will get a kick out of seeing you. Follow me to the bar. I want to get everyone drinks."

Ice Cube pulled me aside. "Man, people are always taking my money. They always want shit from me. You're a good guy, Ronnie. I like you. From now on, call me Cube."

I got Cube and his cronies a shot of whiskey and a beer. When we made our way over to the dance floor, Cube's eyes grew big and hungry when he noticed Gloria, our office admin, shaking her booty to the beat.

"Yo, man, who's that woman? She's hot. I got to meet her tonight," he whispered in my ear.

"Hate to break it to you, but she's engaged."

"Yeah, so what's your point?" he asked, deadpan.

Knowing Gloria could handle herself, I said, "All right then, I'll introduce you.

"Gloria," I yelled over the loud music. "Meet Cube—as in, Ice Cube."

"Nice to meet you," Gloria said, her white teeth glowing when she smiled. Cube moved closer to her, and they started gyrating on the dance floor. Their dancing got the crowd pumped up. The energy in the room was electrifying. Everyone was bopping up and down rhythmically to the music, laughing, and drinking way too much alcohol.

At one point during the night, when Cube was at the bar getting drinks for everyone, I noticed Gloria's face had a pale greenish tint. "You okay?" I asked her.

"No, I think I'm going to be sick," she said.

"Let me help you into a cab."

"No, thanks. I'll be fine. I just need to get out of here. Will you say goodbye to Cube for me?"

"Of course. Are you sure you'll be okay?"

"I think so," she said, bolting out of there.

Moments later, Cube handed me a beer. "Yo, where's Gloria?"

"She wasn't feeling well. She took off."

"She left?" An angry crease formed between his eyes. "Without saying nothin' to me?"

"She was about to puke. She told me to tell you goodbye."

"Yo, man, you got to give me her number," he demanded.

I assumed he would check on her to ensure she was okay, so I shared her contact info. I thanked him for the beer and then returned to the dance floor. The wild party raged on for another few hours.

There Has to Be Another Morning After

I woke up with a throbbing headache and a fuzzy recollection of how I got home. Groggily, I dragged myself into the bathroom, hoping a cold shower would clear my head, but it only made me dizzier and more disoriented. I chugged cold water from the refrigerator, which helped a bit. After getting dressed, I left my work apartment on Central Park South in Manhattan and wolfed down a greasy egg sandwich, diet soda, and a double espresso I bought from a nearby deli. Then, I went to the office to meet with Gloria and Mitchell. We had to finish the employee contracts before Monday.

Gloria and Mitchell looked worse than I felt. Gloria had dark circles under her eyes and messy hair, and she was nursing a large coffee, clutching the cup with both hands. Mitchell had bloodshot eyes and was leaning on the back of his desk, looking like he wanted to crawl into a hole. Despite our rough appearance, we did our best to push through our hangovers and work.

"Gloria, is that your cellphone ringing?" I asked, hearing a muffled tone coming from her brown handbag.

"Yeah, but I can't talk to anyone right now," she said, not bothering to check her phone. For the next ten minutes, the ringing didn't stop. Clearly, someone desperately wanted to get in touch with Gloria.

"Ugh, who keeps calling me?" She grabbed her bag and pulled out her phone. "Oh no," she said, her voice sounding freaked out. "It's Cube." She waited for the ringing to stop and looked at the screen on her phone. "He left me three voice messages."

She pressed play and held the phone to her ear. Her eyes grew wide as she listened to the recordings. "OMG. He said he wanted to take me away and buy me jewelry. This is crazy. Ron, what am I going to do? He's obsessed with me. I'm about to be married."

"Don't worry. Nothing happened. All you did was dance with him."

The color drained from her face. "I feel sick about this. I think I'm having a panic attack."

"Relax, Gloria. Take a deep breath." I watched her inhale and exhale a few times. "Call him back, tell him you had fun hanging with him, and then remind him that you're engaged and can't see him again."

I watched Gloria's finger tremble slightly when she dialed Cube's number. She repeated what I suggested she should say, her voice low and soft while she spoke. The call lasted about a minute, and when she hung up, she bit her lip.

"Well, how'd he take it?" I asked.

"He just kept saying, 'Yo, baby, you missin' out, and I'm really sad about that.'" His response made us chuckle. Saying **YES** to Cube joining my party may not have been the best for Gloria, but having him there was definitely a highlight of my evening.

Years later, I ran into Cube again while dining at a trendy restaurant in SoHo with some business associates. When he spotted me from a distance, he beelined to my table to say hello. When I saw his beaming face heading my way, I jumped up from my seat and hugged him, and then he turned to the other men and announced, "This guy, Ron, he is crazy, and he knows how to party."

After the sale of the company, I hit a major crossroad in my life. Retire? Find a new career? It was time to figure out what was next again.

Lessons Learned Chapter Ten: Cultivating FOCUS Through Meditation

The growth and ultimate success of MPI exemplifies how *Focus*, intention, and clarity can drive innovation, overcome obstacles, and achieve remarkable results. Chapter ten highlights the transformative journey of building MPI's *Positive* culture, fostering creativity, and navigating the company's sale—all of which were possible through intentional actions and the ability to remain grounded.

Let's Recap:

Start with a Clear Mind

When faced with challenges at MPI, like navigating cultural shifts or managing setbacks, I *Prioritized* creating an environment where every voice mattered. For instance, fostering open dialogue and encouraging innovative ideas during the company's restructuring required a calm, clear mind to lead effectively.

   Key Takeaway: Start with a clear mind through meditation or quiet reflection, like going for a long walk, giving yourself the time and space to think. This practice allows you to clear distractions and set meaningful intentions, just as I did to steer MPI toward a successful turnaround.

Practice Daily Mindfulness

Building MPI's collaborative culture required staying present in every interaction, from brainstorming sessions to team celebrations. This presence was especially critical when managing tense situations, like the emotions surrounding MPI's sale or navigating resistance to change.

   Key Takeaway: Incorporate mindfulness into your daily routine. Being fully engaged in conversations and decisions fosters trust, creativity, and intentional action.

Break Down Goals

MPI's journey from early struggles to ultimate success didn't happen overnight. Whether it was integrating new technologies, collaborating with employees, or refining processes, we grew step by step, tackling one challenge at a time.

Key Takeaway: Focused planning and small, actionable steps are crucial. Break large goals into milestones, as I did to both transform MPI and train for life's challenges.

Meditate to Sharpen Concentration

During high-pressure moments, like handling employee reactions to MPI's sale, staying calm and focused was essential. Walking meditations or breathing techniques helped me ground myself and make composed decisions, even when doubt loomed.

Key Takeaway: Dedicate time for meditation, long walks, or focused breathing to sharpen concentration, particularly in moments of stress or uncertainty.

Anchor Yourself in the Present

One of the most important lessons I've learned is the power of staying grounded during complex challenges. Addressing critical decisions at MPI and being present allowed me to lead with clarity and balance.

Key Takeaway: Use meditation and mindfulness as tools to anchor yourself in the present moment, especially when dealing with stress or overwhelming circumstances.

Reflect on Progress

Reflection has played a significant role in my success. Looking back on MPI's journey—from its early struggles to its celebratory sale—helped me refine my approach for future ventures and plan the next challenge.

Key Takeaway: Regular reflection, paired with meditation, helps you assess achievements, celebrate milestones, and identify areas for growth.

CHAPTER 10

DOUBT MANAGEMENT

CROSSROADS EXPECTED THE UNEXPECTED

Brief Retirement

June 2006

The sale of MPI marked a major turning point in my life, and the months leading up to the deal took a lot out of me. When I returned from Cannes, I was thoroughly exhausted, inside and out. (Reminder: At the beginning of the book in chapter one, I was in London to hand over the MPI office but bailed and went to Cannes for the film festival, where someone thought I was a producer and pitched a movie to me.) Heading into summer, I decided to rest and regroup before figuring out my next course of action in the movie business.

I was turning forty soon, too young to retire. Not to mention, I still had a lot of energy, an active mind, and four pre-college-aged kids at home. With a milestone birthday approaching, I had to answer the most important question: What do I want to be when I grow up? A firefighter? An astronaut? A movie producer? Or something else?

Mirror, Mirror on the Wall, Who's the Fairest of Them All?

As I began to ponder my life's direction, I discovered an ugly truth. While looking in the "magic mirror" one morning, the image reflected at me was anything but pretty. Instead of Snow White saying I was the "fairest of them all," I saw an obese, out-of-shape man. At six feet one inch, I weighed an astonishing two-hundred-eighty pounds. To put it in perspective, when I graduated from college, I weighed one-hundred-sixty-five pounds, and having played D1 tennis, I was in peak shape.

Over the years, as the weight piled on, I realized I must have been a jolly fat person because I felt fine and healthy and followed a simple eating plan: eat with no rules. In other words, I ate whatever I wanted whenever I felt like it. McDonald's for lunch? Absolutely. Two Big Macs, two large fries, and a supersized soda? Sure. Hungry for an afternoon snack? How about three or four slices of pizza? Yum. Doughnuts for breakfast? You bet. I indulged in everything from bottomless bowls of pasta, bread and butter, and ice cream sundaes with extra toppings, and washed it down with beer, beer, and more beer. My eating habits were a nonstop party, and my overweight physique paid the price.

The "magic mirror" implied it was time to set my goal to get healthy and improve my lifestyle. I said **YES** to losing weight and getting in shape. I recognized that achieving optimal health would require dedication and I would need to *Work Hard*, but I was determined to remain *Positive* throughout the process and not give up.

Richard Simmons to the Rescue

With my four kids away at overnight camp, I had a timeline of seven weeks to *Focus* on my health. I knew I had the *Discipline* and work ethic to get healthy, but the problem was, I had no idea how I would do it. The first thing I did was put on my mother-in-law's Richard Simmons VHS tape, *Dancing to the Oldies*. Donning my 1970s short shorts and tube socks, I tried his dancing workout. Not only did I look foolish, I felt foolish. I'm sure Richard Simmons has helped countless people, but unfortunately, I wouldn't be one of them. His workout didn't inspire me or give me the **Confidence** I needed. Conducting research, I determined what was possible and crafted a path with achievable checkpoints. I would train for a Sprint Triathlon. The next step was to **Act Decisively** and go for it.

Attaining the Initial Goal and Going for More

September 2006

By the end of summer, my weight dropped to two-hundred-thirty pounds, and I had a solid base, training in swimming, cycling, and running. But I still had a long way to go. With self-assurance, I continued to master my new diet and exercise regime, signed up for a sprint triathlon, and purchased a wet suit for the cold lake water.

On the day of the triathlon, I woke up at 4:00 a.m. and drove to Connecticut for the 7:00 a.m. start. Jittery with nerves, I set a simple goal: to complete the triathlon and not fall into the did not finish (DNF) category, which happens to over sixty percent of racers in triathlon events, especially their first one. Transitioning from one element to the next during the race is challenging for the body and the mind.

The weather did not cooperate that day. The sky was a thick gray blanket with heavy rain falling from the dark clouds, making everything damp and cold. But as soon as the gun went off and I jumped into the frigid lake, I immediately entered a zone, so **Focused** on my mission I barely remembered the swim itself. I also didn't recall scraping my knee against the rocks on the shoreline or puncturing a hole in my wet suit when I finished.

With no time to spare, I pulled off my wet suit. Since someone told me to spray my body with vegetable oil before the race, it came off easily. From there, I hopped on my bike and began a slow uphill trek, riding somewhat cautiously. The wet and slippery conditions caused a lot of accidents as the bikes were slipping on the road. Biking was my strongest of the three sports, and I completed it in my best time. Next up was the running portion, but by this point, my body had had enough. The first half of the 5K run was mainly downhill, while the second half was uphill, the real killer. This was the moment when my muscles began screaming, and my hamstring cramped. Powering through the pain, I maintained a steady pace and kept my eyes on the prize, the finish line. I heard Rocky's voice in my head: "You stop this fight, I'll kill ya!" With each step, I channeled that determination, knowing that victory awaited me at the end. When I completed the race, I was left with an incredible sense of achievement, the same feeling I got when I sold my company.

The Ultimate Dream: The NYC Marathon

I drove home, fueled by the adrenaline and proud of myself for accomplishing my goal. Sitting around the kitchen table with my kids the following morning, I told them about my experience competing in the race.

"That's great, Dad. What's next?" Casey, my eldest daughter, asked.

"What do you mean, what's next? It's done. It's over. And it's time to move on."

"That's it? You're about to celebrate a big birthday and haven't set a new goal. Lame, Dad. Lame," Casey said, shaking her head. "What about the New York City Marathon?"

It didn't take long for me to think about that. A moment later, I blurted out, "**YES**! Great idea. I'll do it."

After I said that, my inner dialogue took control. *Are you kidding yourself? You are only a decent runner at best, and the marathon is twenty-six miles, and you still weigh two-thirty.*

Shut up, doubting the nay-saying voice in my head, I commanded.

Using **Doubt Management**, I called Lisa, my runner friend (and my financial advisor), to ask for training help.

"Ron, that's a pretty lofty goal. Part of me wants to advise you not to do it, but I've known you too long to bet against you. Sure, I can help. See you at the finish line," she added before hanging up.

And just like that, I now had a new goal.

WTF Along the Way—The NYC Triathlon Too

I trained for the marathon by following a detailed, structured plan I had put together through much research. This plan included progressively longer weekly runs, as well as cross-training in swimming and biking. Nutrition, hydration, and ample rest were key priorities, and I tracked my progress in a training journal. In January, I ran the Disney™ half marathon with Kristy, who came down from Rochester. It was a magical experience sprinting through the castles.

One afternoon on a bright, sunny day in September, while running outside, an elderly woman sprinted toward me, pounding the pavement with a determined gaze, and caught up to me. Her silver-white hair was tied in a tight bun, and a sweatband hugged her creased forehead. She wore a sleek, moisture-wicking running outfit that clung to her fit frame. She greeted me with a smile and said, "Hi. What are you training for?"

"Is it that obvious?" I asked, wondering how she knew that.

"Lucky guess, I suppose."

"I am running in the NYC Marathon in November."

"That's nice. By the way, my grandson has an extra slot in his group for the NYC Triathlon in July next year. If you're interested, I can put you in touch with him."

"Thanks, but I don't know. A full triathlon is really difficult."

"C'mon," she replied sweetly. "Don't be a scaredy-cat."

This grandmother was badass. She would crush me in a race. "**YES**," I yelled as she blew past me.

"Thatta boy." She stopped momentarily and gave me her grandson's phone number.

I ran the NYC marathon with my buddy Popper in November, who was much faster than me. However, he was kind enough to wait for me at the finish line.

Then, after accepting the challenge from that grandmother to do the NYC Triathlon in the upcoming July 2007, I knew I had no time to waste. With just two months to prepare, I took my training to a new level, dedicating even more hours to honing my swimming, cycling, and running skills, pushing myself beyond my comfort zone. The pool became my second home as I tirelessly practiced my strokes, and my trusty road bike carried me through long, grueling rides to build endurance. As for running, I incorporated hill sprints and interval training to maximize my performance.

I completed the July NYC triathlon (Olympic distance), which included braving a swim in the notoriously polluted Hudson River, and stinking for two weeks after, like Kramer on *Seinfeld*. The following November, I ran the NYC marathon with my buddy Popper, who was much faster than me. However, he was kind enough to wait for me at the finish line. Both experiences made me feel euphoric that I had conquered such incredible achievements. Although I reached the pinnacle of my physical fitness journey, I couldn't ignore the newfound aches and pains that had surfaced. Honestly, as proud as I was to have accomplished such a feat, I'm not sure it was worth the long-term effects on my body. Conversely, I have maintained a healthy lifestyle ever since, keeping my weight optimal and walking over seven miles a day.

Turning Hobbies Into Businesses

Amidst transforming my physical health, I continued researching the movie industry, a critical step in decision-making, while also exploring the possibility of turning one of my many hobbies into a legitimate business endeavor. Keeping my legs moving, I sampled two additional ventures—both stretched me beyond my comfort zone in finance and technology.

The first opportunity I sampled came up while playing in a local poker game with a group of fathers in town. The atmosphere was relaxed, with drinks and laughter filling the room, when one of the guys remarked, "Hey, I bet we'd kill it at the World Series of Poker."

"**YES**! Let's do it," I suggested.

We shook hands and made a pact that we'd attend together. The next day, I booked a seat at the tournament, sent in $10K, and then called the other guys to ask them which hotel we should stay in. One by one, they begrudgingly told me their wives wouldn't let them go. It looked like I was going solo.

Unlike my buddies, I didn't need my wife's permission because my marriage was almost over, and we were leading separate lives (including me getting an apartment in NYC), on the verge of divorce, but staying together for the children.

Weeks later, I entered the vibrant poker room at Foxwoods Resort Casino in Connecticut. Over the course of several days, I engaged in intense poker battles, pitting my skills against various players, one of whom was the actor James Woods. The success and *Confidence* I gained from competing at Foxwoods led me to the grand stage of poker: the World Series of Poker in Las Vegas. Playing against some of the best players on the planet, I managed to navigate through intense competition, surviving the early days and making it through the fifth day of the tournament.

On the sixth day, tension ran high as I faced off against a top professional redheaded Australian, who happened to be a mere twenty years old. Cameras were rolling, capturing our every move for live TV. As I was about to attempt the bluff of my life, I went all-in, portraying I had hit the flush on the river. Luck eluded me as the pro took his time and made an unbelievable call, and I lost the hand.

During the break, the redhead approached me and said, "Listen, old man. I don't mean to offend you, but you'll never beat me."

"Why?"

"Are you married?" he asked.

"I am."

"You got kids?"

"I have four."

"Is this your only job?"

"No."

He looked at me with a stern expression. "I play poker twenty-four hours a day. I don't have a girlfriend. I don't have a job. I just travel around and play poker. Think about how many more hands I've played than you. You might beat me occasionally, but I usually see the scenarios in my head and win. If you want to succeed, you'll need to *Focus*, put your family aside, and quit your job. But I don't think you're going to do that."

His words rang true, and from that moment on, I quit playing professional poker.

You Can Call Me Ishmael or Captain Ronnie

The next casual hobby I decided to sample led me on an open-sea voyage. It all began when Faron, my colleague from Adeptra, invited me to Naples, Florida, and asked if I would be interested in starting a charter fishing business. As an avid fisherman, the prospect of turning my beloved pastime into a lucrative enterprise and eventual retirement business sounded irresistible, so I exclaimed, "**YES!**"

Our plan was straightforward yet promising. Faron would captain the boat three weeks each month, and I would captain the vessel for one week a month. In addition to the charter service, we envisioned reeling in profits by selling the bounty of our deep-sea expeditions. However, soon after we got the business running, a devastating hurricane struck, and gas prices soared, cutting into our revenue stream. Furthermore, the monotony of the daily grind began to take its toll on me. The real kicker, though, was dealing with seasick, hungover passengers puking over the side of the boat. Finally, at my wit's end, Faron and I called it quits.

This experience taught me that not every **_Passion_** should be turned into a profession, and sometimes, the call of the sea is best answered with a simple fishing rod in hand.

Heaven Awaits

I called various non-profit organizations, looking for a place to donate the boat. The only person interested was a pastor from the Church of Christ in Texas.

"Y'all got a big boat to donate?" the pastor asked, reiterating what I told him. "Well, we could use that. Let me call you back on my mobile phone."

Strange, I thought, unsure why we couldn't make the deal on the landline. Nonetheless, I gave him my name and phone number, and the pastor called me back a moment later.

"Yeah, we can make a deal. I'll pick up the boat, and you can value it at whatever number you think it's worth. By the way, did you say your last name is Stein? Is that Jewish?"

"**YES**," I responded, wondering why he asked me that.

"You're smart, Ron Stein. You're playing both teams, the Jew team and the Christian. So if you're right, you're right, and if you're wrong, that's okay too, because I'm giving you a card to present to St. Peter to get into heaven."

All I could think of was the song by Norman Greenbaum, a Jewish artist, titled "Spirit in the Sky" with the line "I have a friend in Jesus."

How about that? Not only did I get a hefty tax break from my donation, I also got a ticket to heaven.

High Holy Days Call from Above

One evening, as my six-month internship at Company 3 (more about this later) was coming to a close, a random business opportunity came out of the blue that would take me on an adventure and expose me to a different culture, sparking a beautiful love affair. And I'm not referring to a romantic relationship but rather an intense attraction to a country.

While enjoying Rosh Hashanah dinner with my family, I got a call from Valerie.

"Ron, sorry to bother you on your holiday, but a client of mine in Brazil is in trouble and needs your help. And if you work with him, you'll make a shit ton of money. Better yet, you'll have a chance to rake him over the coals."

I laughed at her unusually crude sarcasm and gave her a firm **YES** to another Valerie-inspired adventure. It was now time to figure out what I said **YES** to.

There's a Lot of Yawning in Brazil

October 2007

"Hello, Ronald," a man with a deep, heavily accented voice greeted me on the other end of the phone. "This is Mauricio, the CIO of Bank of Bradesco in Brazil. I'm calling because I have a major technology issue at the bank that I can't make public, and I need help fixing it ASAP. Valerie told me you're the best guy for the job. Would you be willing to fly to Sao Paulo tomorrow night? Do not worry about expenses. It's on us. We can discuss your large fees when you're here. Just book your ticket and send me the receipts. I'll have a check for you when you arrive."

I had never been to Brazil before, and since I trusted Valerie, I blurted out, "**YES**, Mauricio, no problem. I'll book the next flight out to Sao Paulo."

After ending the call, I dialed my lawyer who asked, "Did you get a contract from this guy?".

"No. He said he'll explain everything and give me a contract when I arrive."

"Ron, don't be an idiot. For starters, you have no idea what they need you for, and you don't even know if it's a job you can do. It's difficult to get paid and take money out of another country, especially in Brazil. I suggest you call this guy back and tell him you're uninterested."

"I appreciate your advice, but I already said YES. So, I'm going."

"Of course you did but please be careful. Brazil is dangerous too. And if it goes awry, don't call me crying."

My lawyer was right. I had no idea what I was getting myself into. Since I'd never been to Brazil, this seemed like an excellent opportunity to check it out. If it didn't pan out, then so be it. This is what saying YES is all about—following my intuition, using **Doubt Management** again, and not letting the noise from the naysayers cloud my thinking.

My Ronaldo Brazilian Second Life Begins

A few days later, I landed in Sao Paulo. Outside baggage claim, a man resembling André the Giant held a sign with my name. He had a boyish face and wore a fitted black T-shirt and jeans. The driver introduced himself as Eduardo while grabbing my luggage. I followed him to the parking lot and did a double take when he stopped in front of a silver-colored sedan riddled with dents, scratches, and a cracked windshield. He placed my luggage in a hidden trap compartment of the trunk. Picking me up in this beat-up car seemed strange. I wanted to call Valerie to ask her what was going on. A pit grew in my stomach, wondering if I was about to get kidnapped.

As if reading my mind, Eduardo interrupted my anxious thoughts. "Don't worry. This car is armored, and the windows are bulletproof," he said, opening the door for me. "Take your suit and tie off and put on a T-shirt and jeans. You can't look wealthy."

"Why? What's going on?" I asked, concerned for my safety.

"If you look like you have money, you will risk getting robbed or flash-napped." (This is where you are snatched out of a car or off the street, driven to an ATM, and forced to take out cash in order to be released.)

Shit. Did I make a mistake coming here?

Once we got on the eight-lane highway, we were in bumper-to-bumper traffic. Every vehicle appeared to be at a standstill. Motorcycles and dirt bikes, making loud roaring noises from their mufflers, weaved in and out of the lines of automobiles. Cyclists slowed down when they drove next to our car, trying to peer through our window. This must be what the driver was talking about. I had never been so thankful for bullet-proof windows.

"Is this typical?" I asked.

"Oh, it is, sir," the driver responded. "But you have nothing to worry about. I have protection if someone tries to shoot at us." He pulled out a handgun from the console and waved it around in his hand. I could feel my heart rate increase.

What did I get myself into? Maybe I should've listened to my lawyer and said NO to coming here.

Eduardo dropped me off in front of the five-star hotel, where I had booked a room. It was a modern, towering structure made of gleaming glass and steel. A uniformed doorman with a cap opened the car door, greeted me warmly, and offered to take my luggage. I assumed Mauricio wanted me to get to work right away.

"I'll be quick," I told Eduardo. "I can drop my bags and check in, and then you can take me to the bank."

"No, no. Don't be silly. Today, you rest and have fun. Go to a nice dinner this evening. Tomorrow, you can start."

I would've thought the situation at the bank was urgent, but I soon discovered that Brazilians are some of the friendliest, most laid-back, and easygoing people. They **Prioritize** play before work, a quality that would resonate more with me later in life.

"What time do you want to pick me up tomorrow? I can be ready as early as 6:30 a.m."

"No, relax, Mr. Ron. I will pick you up at 9:30 in the morning. There's too much traffic before that hour."

I might as well do as the man suggested. After checking in, I dropped my bags in my room and headed to the hotel pool, a beautiful oasis surrounded by palm trees and lush tropical plants. The weather was perfect, with clear blue skies and a gentle breeze that kept the heat from being overwhelming. For the rest of the afternoon, I sat in a lounge chair and drank refreshing caipirinhas, the traditional cocktail made with lime, sugar, and cachaça. That evening, I went to a Brazilian steakhouse (reminiscent of those in the U.S. but on a much grander scale, offering an extensive variety of meats) and indulged in a traditional churrascaria experience, stuffing my face with succulent meats, black beans and rice, and creamy polenta.

Back to the Future

Eduardo picked me up the following morning and drove me to the Bank of Bradesco headquarters. This building was a testament to the city's rich history and culture with its grand architecture and lavish décor. Despite its age, it exuded an air of prestige and authority that made it stand out. The exterior was made of stone and concrete with large arched windows and a formal entranceway.

When I entered the lobby, I admired the intricate moldings and frescoes on the walls, depicting Brazilian history and cultural scenes. A thin, proper, well-dressed man with silver and dark hair greeted me with a handshake. "Welcome to Sao Paulo. I am Mauricio. It's a pleasure to meet you in person."

"Likewise," I said.

On the elevator, Mauricio filled me in on the bank catastrophe. The bank's ATMs all over the country were breaking down at different times of the day, which meant customers couldn't take money out or use their bank cards to make purchases. The issue had been happening randomly for the past six months, and there didn't seem to be a pattern as to why it was occurring. To minimize the risk of getting mugged or flash-napped, most people didn't carry a lot of cash and instead relied upon their ATM bank cards to pay for all essential items like groceries and sundries.

Exiting the elevator on the basement level, Mauricio escorted me down a long corridor. At the end of the hall was a door that led to a fortress-like room that made me feel like I had stepped back in time to the 1970s. The room was huge, with rows of massive, cabinet-style computers occupying most of the space. Machines hummed and whirred with bright lights and flashing indicators. The air was thick with the sound of cooling fans and the unmistakable smell of hot electronics.

"This is a joke, right? It's pretty obvious what your problem is," I announced. "You need new computers. You're running half of the country's banking system, and you're one of the top banks in the world, and this is your computer system?"

"Oh, no. We have a project underway to rebuild our system to make it the most advanced in the world, Mauricio explained. "This kind of project takes a long time in Brazil."

I learned that another characteristic of Brazilians is their tendency to describe everything as the most amazing in the world.

"All right then, let's figure this out. First, tell me about any changes you made in the last six months."

"We change things every day," Mauricio replied.

"Do you test it after you make a change?" I asked.

"No."

How backward was this technology department? I wondered. "Do you keep an electronic log of any changes you made in the last few months?"

Mauricio grabbed a thick paper binder from a desk and handed it to me. I scanned through the pages. "Any of these could be your problem. If you change one thing in the bridge, you don't know where it breaks. You need to make a testing center."

"That's so dumb it is smart!" he replied.

Then a young guy with a ponytail walked into the room, attempting to cover his mouth while yawning.

"Hey, Ricardo, come here." Mauricio waved to the man. "I want to introduce you to Ron."

I shook his hand.

"Ricardo is the team leader of the twelve consultants we hired."

Ricardo yawned again.

"Why are you so tired?" I asked. "Did you have a late night?"

"Let me guess, this is your first time in Brazil?"

I smiled. "Is it that obvious?"

"Well, here in our country, we drink and have sex all night."

"What?" I could feel my eyebrows arching, shocked by what Ricardo had just said.

"That is why we are always happy and never stressed, but an uncontrollable side effect is being tired."

I knew I was going to like it here. I asked, "Are you married?"

"No, but I have several girlfriends. It doesn't matter anyway. Any girl I pick up wants to have sex. The women don't care, they just want sex."

At that moment I had one thought: *I can't believe my lawyer tried talking me out of coming here.* I was beginning to love this country, and since my wife and I were separated at this point (just not announced to others or the kids), I planned to take advantage of our open arrangement. No rush, no panic, lots of women, and always a good time—what more could I ask for?

"It was nice to meet you, Ron. If you'll excuse me, I need to get an espresso."

"Now, I would like to introduce you to the internal team working on the project," Mauricio said.

"A team?" I gave him a confused look.

"Come this way."

I followed him into a spacious office room where about twenty people were shuffling and reading papers on their desks. "What's going on in here?"

"They are trying to fix the problem."

"But what are they doing?" I felt like I was in an episode of *Seinfeld*, and these men and women were a bunch of George Costanzas pretending to work on the Penske file, appearing busy but not making any real progress.

"We don't need this," I said. "Give me your smartest guy, and we'll figure it out between the three of us——Ricardo, the internal expert, and me."

Mauricio pulled a chubby man with a gray beard aside to join our group and left us to work. We sat around a large wooden conference table while I flipped through the pages of their logs, firing off questions. I immediately noticed they had bought and replaced five new computers to modernize the old ones about six months prior. "Who told you to buy this, and what areas of the bank technology do those computers run?" I asked.

"It's IBM," the chubby man said. "And we always have a team of IBM people on standby. Oh, and they manage the ATM network."

"Wait a minute, let me understand this. Did you throw in one new computer after the next and expect it to work with your antiquated machinery? Do you realize that the new and the old don't always speak the same language? Please promise no more changes without testing it first."

Hours later, I called the head of their IBM people, using a phone that looked like it was from the 1980s, and the line kept cutting off. "You need phones that work," I barked.

"No, that's never going to get fixed in this country," Ricardo said. Reclining in his chair; he had been watching my every move.

I responded, "Buddy, why not just buy some phones in America and bring them back here."

We spent two hours on and off the call with IBM. When they informed me that the new machine worked, I told them it might be compatible, but the software was different. Mauricio then took me to look at one of the newer machines in the computer center. They planned to replace all the computers, but until they could, they were using the freebie from IBM, trying to integrate it with the outdated machines. I found this whole situation mind boggling. Hundreds of people were working on the problem, and nobody could figure it out. And yet, based on the timing of the first issue, these five computers seemed to be causing all the issues.

I suggested they replace the new machines with the old ones, reverting to the setup from six months prior, to test the theory. We spent the night working to get them out of the closet, and by morning, we had them up and running. There were no ATM outages for the rest of the week, and the system seemed to function. However, I knew this was a temporary fix because they needed to upgrade their entire system and change the coding. I told them I would develop a three-month detailed plan to correct the long-term issue and find former IBM people from the States who understood the language and knew how to re-code in that ancient language.

Mauricio agreed to the deal, and Ricardo brought in people from his team to assist. He insisted I stay in his apartment and meet his friends to learn how to fit in with their culture, marking the beginning of a friendship that would continue throughout the years, playing a part in my future.

Giving Back—Charity

As it turned out, Ricardo's friend Felipe has a local charity in Rio de Janeiro, Brazil. He invited me to fly down for a few days to check it out before heading back to New York to see my own kids. The charity collaborates with orphanages and assists them in getting computers and access to technology. The organization procures the necessary supplies, hiring local teachers, and implementing a curriculum. This initiative is designed to provide education and vocational training in Rio only. I said **YES** to helping expand the charity's local presence in Rio by donating equipment, money, and time.

Giving back is immensely significant and the ultimate expression of humility and gratitude. It will inevitably return to you many fold—spiritually, mentally, monetarily, and emotionally. Upon my arrival, I was struck by the stark contrast between the immense poverty of the sprawling Favelas and the breathtaking beauty of Rio, with its picturesque beaches.

As I explored the charity's various programs, I bonded with orphans who lived in makeshift homes in the favelas. These innocent and appreciative children were eager for food and knowledge. I played interactive games with the kids and taught them basic digital literacy skills. It was a rewarding experience, yet it also opened my eyes to the perils of Brazil. Gunshots echoed in the background, a horrifying reminder of the ongoing conflict between drug lords and the police.

Witnessing these orphans striving to learn and improve their lives amidst such dangers was disheartening. Overall, providing support for Felipe's charity with visits and securing over a one-hundred-thousand dollars in donations for the charity over the years, continues to bring me immense fulfillment.

In Through the Back Door

The night before my flight back to New York, Felipe and his roommate in Rio Pablo suggested it was time for a well-deserved break and a taste of Rio's exhilarating nightlife. We kicked off the evening with a fantastic dinner featuring grilled meats and caipirinhas at Café de Ipanema, where the famous song "The Girl from Ipanema" was written. We then went to a lounge with neon lights and an eclectic ambiance, and the night ended with an impromptu late-night party. Felipe turned in, but Pablo and I continued with our raucous night in my multi-room hotel suite, where we turned up the music, raided the mini bar, and had an impromptu topless dance party. Things got pretty wild but harmless, with boobs flying everywhere.

The morning after, I woke up with a pounding headache and queasy stomach. I didn't have time to nurse my hangover because I had to make it to the airport, eager to return to New York to see my kids and then kickstart the planning for the project. Remember how Ricardo yawned a lot when I first met him? On the entire drive, I yawned too, something I rarely do, but I had become Brazilian.

Upon reaching the airport, I was abruptly confronted by massive, barking German Shepherds surrounding me, leaving me bewildered and apprehensive. Then, two imposing guards armed with machine guns seized my carry-on bag and demanded that I accompany them. Through a side door in the airport, we ventured into a secure room, my anxiety escalating as I grappled with the sudden turn of events.

"Sit down," the guard with a face full of acne commanded. I sat at the table while the two guards stood, staring at me with their beady eyes. A senior officer walked into the room and sat across from me. He had neatly trimmed facial hair and wore a tailored uniform. "Do you know why you're here?" he asked.

"I have no idea," I responded.

"The dogs smelled drugs in your carry-on, and we tested your laptop and found traces of cocaine," the officer said in a matter-of-fact tone. "You are obviously a drug smuggler. Please tell me which cartel you work for?"

My eyes widened in disbelief, and my voice, edged with frustration, cut through the tense air. "There must be some mistake. I am definitely not a drug dealer, and I've never even used drugs."

"Then how did the cocaine get on your laptop?"

Suddenly, it dawned on me that while partying in my room, I had briefly stepped out to call one of my kids. One of the girls must have used cocaine on the desk where I had my laptop. I tried to explain this to the guard—to no avail. He didn't believe me or just did not care.

"If you consent to a cavity search and we don't find hidden drugs, then I will release you, and you can take the evening flight out of here."

My mouth dropped in shock. *Cavity search—oh boy*. **"YES,"** I said feebly. "But can you make sure it's a small person and not one of those big guards standing there?" I asked, joking but not joking.

For the first time, the officer cracked a smile. The guards escorted me to another room. On top of the folding table in the corner was a box of plastic gloves and a huge jar of Vaseline. The acne-faced guard told me to strip down to my underwear. Another man with a thick black beard and white lab coat entered the room.

"Lower your underwear," he demanded. A cold chill ran up my spine. "Now, bend over the table and put your hands straight forward. And try to relax."

How the hell was I going to relax when another man was about to ram his hand up my asshole? My stomach dropped when I heard the distinctive snap of the latex gloves stretching over his hands. Without warning, a shooting pain ripped me from behind. Obviously, he didn't find anything up there while violating me.

"My associate will perform a second test in case I missed something."

"Missed something? How is that possible? I thought your hand was going to come out of my mouth."

He didn't respond to my joke and left the room. A moment later, another man, also dressed in a white lab coat, entered. While he put on his latex gloves, I asked, "Can you please use one hand and not go up to your elbow?"

This guy didn't utter a word and went ahead with the cavity search—yet again. I thought of Chevy Chase in the movie *Fletch* singing "Moon River." When he finished, I dressed and waited for the senior officer to tell me what would happen next. Upon entering the room, he said, "I am sorry that had to happen. We will release you, but I must warn you to stay away from people doing drugs in Brazil. You should consider yourself lucky."

"Yeah, I get it. Do I at least get a drink or dinner?" The pain I was about to feel in my ass while sitting for the eleven-hour flight home would be a good enough reminder to stay away from people doing drugs.

"Have a safe flight," he said, chuckling.

When I finally landed in New York, I couldn't have been happier to see my kids and sleep in my bed. That said, one minor obstacle would not deter me from returning to Brazil right away to complete the project and help with the charity—and, of course, still have fun.

The Walking Wounded

I didn't think recruiting people willing to jump on board for this project would be tricky, but I was about to discover another obstacle. I called Kristy, the miracle worker, and asked her to find some retired IBM employees versed in the old language. Hours later, she phoned me with bad news. "Ron, I got a list of fifteen retirees from my friend at IBM. But I've got to tell you, this is the most depressing thing I've ever done."

"Why?"

"Because the first eight people are deceased, so I only have a few names of people to contact."

"Thanks, Kristy. Email me their info, and I'll reach out to them."

The first person I called was Murray, an eighty-seven-year-old man who spent his entire career at IBM. He answered my call immediately, and after introducing myself, I explained the situation at the bank.

"Speak up, young woman," he yelled. "I can't hear you. My hearing aid isn't working."

I repeated my spiel.

"What? Eh? What are you saying? Who is this again?"

After screaming into the phone again with no success, I decided Murray wasn't right for the job.

The next person I called on the list thought I was his granddaughter and complained that I never visited him. Eventually, I found two guys from Northern California, Harold and Milton, to join my team and fly to Brazil. Both men were in their mid-eighties, but their minds were sharp.

Jessie was the third guy I found, a six-foot-five Australian living in Maryland, who told me he loved Brazil and couldn't wait to come down there. Familiar with the old language, he was a great project manager with ten years of experience working at a competitor's bank and living in Sao Paulo.

I flew back to Sao Paulo two weeks later and met my recruits. Harold was in a wheelchair, and Milton, hunched over, moved at a snail's pace. But since they would be coding all day, their physical ailments wouldn't interfere with their work.

When I introduced Jessie to them, he looked disturbed and pulled me aside. "Who the fuck are these guys? They look half-dead. I'm a project manager, not a fucking nursing home operator."

Like most Australians, Jessie had no filter. He just said what was on his mind. The four of us spent the rest of the day working, and when we finished, Jessie suggested he and I go out.

"Mate, I know of a great club we should hit. And we can both use a few Brazilian drinks and some relaxation. You in?"

"**YES**, I'm in," I responded, looking forward to a night out. After all, I needed the break. My head was jumbled in coding.

Brazilian Culture and Nightlife

The club, a multi-layered wonder with different levels connected by winding staircases and elevators, was unlike anything I had ever been to. Colorful murals and geometric patterns filled the walls, and the music was a mix of samba and electronic beats. I made my way through the crowd, taking in the sights and sounds of the club. On the first level was a large dance floor with a raised stage where a live band was playing. Men and women were swaying and dancing to the music. The top level had various-shaped swimming pools and hot tubs.

"What kind of club is this?"

"Let go a little, Ron. I promise you, this is nothing like any club you've been to in the States." Jessie continued, "Now, I'm going to make you some new friends."

I went to the bar and grabbed a cocktail. With a drink in hand, I wandered the club, checking out the beautiful women strutting around in slinky dresses and high-heeled shoes that accentuated their legs and natural Brazilian butts. When I turned a corner, I knocked into a woman from the other direction, spilling my drink.

"I'm so sorry," I said. "I didn't see you."

Of all the women milling around, I somehow managed to run into the prettiest one in the club. She had long, shiny black hair that cascaded down her shoulders and bright red lipstick, the same color as her dress.

"No, it was my fault. I didn't see you either," she said in perfect English.

"How about I buy you a drink as an apology?"

"Sure, that would be nice."

"I'm Ron," I told her on the way to the bar.

"Gabriella," she responded. "Is this your first time here?"

"Is it that obvious?"

"It is." Giggling, she threw her head back. "I noticed you when you first walked into the club. You looked lost."

"You could say that. There seems to be a lot of fun going on in this club. Do you come here often?"

"No, I just like to come here when I'm looking for a good time, and I get to meet different people from all over the world. Also, my job is very stressful, so I need to let loose a little."

When we got to the bar, we ordered caipirinhas and talked for the next few hours. I briefed her on what I was doing in Brazil, and she told me she was a nurse at a nearby hospital. Gabriella grew up in a small town outside of Sao Paulo and came from a large family. With every caipirinha we drank, our bodies edged closer to each other.

Finally, she whispered, "Do you want to go somewhere private?"

"That seems fast?" I blurted out looking at her as if she may be a pro.

"No, Ron. I'm not a prostitute." Her wide smile indicated that she wasn't offended by my insinuation. Most American women probably would have slapped me for making that assumption. "I just flirt with guys for fun. And besides, I have a boyfriend. He's out of town for a few days."

"I'm sorry. I shouldn't have thought that about you."

"Don't be sorry. But I do like you."

I was dumbfounded. But, of course, Gabriella's words made me like her even more. "Can I at least take you to dinner?"

"Sure, food would be great." Afterwards, I decided to keep my distance given that I didn't need the trouble, but it was flattering.

During the next several weeks, Jessie yawned the entire time we worked at the bank, and like the time in Rio, I yawned often too. I now understand intimately why so many people in Brazil yawned a lot.

But, for the record, Crocodile Dundee Jessie yawned exponentially more than I did. His stamina with the ladies was astounding. Go, Jessie.

Right before we completed the project, Jessie and I decided to take Harold and Milton to the club for shits and giggles, bringing over women to shake their boobs and ass in their faces. Thankfully, neither of them had a heart attack and died on us, like Blue in the movie *Old School*. The next day, they couldn't stop yawning or wiping the smiles off their faces. Go, Harold. Go, Milton. I was happy I could make their trip to Brazil memorable, and who knows, maybe I helped add a few years to their life. As Kanye said, "What doesn't kill me makes me stronger."

Brazil Forever

My team and I tackled the project together, presenting our achieve-ments to the bank's board of directors. Ricardo's dedication paid off with a promotion in his firm. During our discussions on career growth, he shared his dream of establishing an M&A company to sell Brazilian tech startups globally. (M&A stands for mergers and acquisitions, which are deals where companies combine, or one buys another.)

Saying **YES** to the Bradesco Bank project started my love affair with Brazil's laid-back culture, where leisure time is highly valued, whether it be through music, dance, or simply spending time with friends and family. And despite what you might think, my infatuation with Brazil had nothing to do with the women I got to know intimately. As a New Yorker, I come from a fast-paced pressure cooker where most people are so busy one-upping each other in business that they lose sight of what's essential. Brazil starkly contrasts that life, a place to let go and live life to the fullest—with no strings attached. I took this new attitude back home and incorporated it into my disposition.

After the project ended, I maintained my Brazilian contacts for phil-anthropy, work, and fun, jumping at any new opportunity to take on new projects. I also returned to Rio on many occasions to visit Felipe and help with the charity and recently assisted by donating the funding to open an entire new tech center in a school. Brazil will always be in my heart and play a part in my future.

Bridging Boarders: From Corporate Consulting to Hollywood Hustle

The Brazil project lasted from 2007 to 2009, accumulating plenty of airline miles commuting back and forth from New York. Whenever I returned to the States for a long stretch, I continued to simultaneously plunge headfirst into my movie projects—*Meskada*, *The Kids Are All Right*, and *The Romantics*. Upon completing the Brazilian consulting gig, I realized I needed to ***Focus***, given all the moving parts, and devote myself full-time to my film career to be successful.

Lessons Learned Chapter 10 - DOUBT MANAGEMENT

Embrace the Moment: Managing Doubt in High-Stakes Situations

Doubt, worry, and fear are inevitable, but their power over you is not. The secret to managing these emotions isn't about eliminating them entirely—it's about grounding yourself in the present moment, where clarity and *Confidence* thrive.

In this chapter, I faced multiple moments where doubt could have derailed my progress. Whether it was stepping into the unknown during my first triathlon, tackling the NYC Marathon, or taking in and navigating the cultural and technological complexities of the Brazil project, each scenario tested my resolve. By practicing *Doubt Management*, staying present, and acting decisively, I turned these challenges into triumphs.

Let's Recap:

Meeting the Moment Head-On

When faced with the grueling physical demands of the NYC triathlon, I could have given into self-doubt as the uphill climb and harsh weather pushed my limits. Instead, I *Focused* on each step of the journey—transitioning between swimming, biking, and running—with determination and grit. Similarly, when tasked with resolving the ATM outages for Bradesco Bank in Brazil, I didn't let the scale of the problem or the disorganized team overwhelm me. Instead, I honed in on the core issue, tackled it methodically, and delivered results.

Key Takeaway: Rather than letting fear drive you away from challenges, confront them head-on. *Focusing* on incremental progress allows you to navigate even the toughest moments with *Confidence*.

Using Presence to Navigate Negotiations

On the day of my first triathlon, the chaos and doubt were palpable, from the freezing water to the slippery roads. Yet, by staying present and taking the race one segment at a time, I crossed the finish line, proud of the journey. Similarly, during the Brazil project, when I faced setbacks like outdated technology and resistance from team members, I stayed grounded, worked with what I had, and negotiated creative solutions.

Key Takeaway: Decisions made from a grounded, present state are more effective. By staying in the moment, you can find opportunities others might overlook. *Focus* and achieve clarity under pressure.

Confidence in the Face of Chaos

Confidence doesn't come from avoiding challenges—it comes from meeting them head-on, even when the odds are stacked against you. During the NYC Marathon, when my hamstring cramped, I could have stopped. Instead, I powered through, driven by the determination to finish. Likewise, in Brazil, I built trust and *Confidence* in my team, including older consultants who many doubted could deliver results. This ability to navigate chaos while maintaining *Focus* helped me deliver meaningful outcomes.

Key Takeaway: *Confidence* grows when you meet challenges with a steady, *Focused* mind. A present mindset enables you to tackle unpredictable situations with clarity and resolve.

Chapter 11

Positive Mindset

Becoming a Movie Producer With No Experience Whatsoever

January 2007

As I shared in previous chapters, I engaged in sampling, a process of exploring new endeavors without a full-time commitment. This allowed me to confirm my decision to move forward with film.

Once completed, I decided to move forward with my **YES** to film. I started *Networking* by digging through my Rolodex, loose business cards, and contacts in my Blackberry® (I was a "crackberry" back then, hooked on my Blackberry®, similar to how today's iPhones™ feel like an extension of our hands), and perusing my contacts on the brand-new LinkedIn™ platform, looking for someone to help me break into the movie business. Considering I spent my entire career in financial services and technology, this proved much more complicated than I imagined it would be when I first made the decision to switch my *Focus*.

I may not be smart enough to know the shortest or easiest path, but I've learned to identify the essential steps, draw from my life lessons, and proceed accordingly. Anything becomes possible with the right attitude and a willingness to efficiently and productively tackle tasks. **_Confidence_** plays a crucial role in this process, combined with the practice of **_Doubt Management_**—setting aside all doubts, worries, and fears—and allowing a **_POSITIVE MINDSET_** to guide you.

Finally, one day, it dawned on me that I knew a guy in the field who owned Company 3 (Co3), a post-production business in Manhattan. His name was Marcos, and I met him through my youngest daughter, Erin, who was friends with his son. We had been introduced at a school fundraiser some years back. Most likely, we told each other what we did for a living, and I probably stored it somewhere in my memory bank, but back then, unless someone mentioned tech or finance, I didn't pay too much attention.

I gave him a call completely out of the blue. "Hey, Marcelo, it's Ron Stein, Erin's dad."

We made small talk for a minute, and then I jumped in and told him why I was calling. "I'm interested in investing in the movie industry, but I need to learn the business before I get in too deep. Any chance you'd be willing to help me and give me some pointers?"

Marcelo suggested we meet for a drink at Tequila Sunrise, a local restaurant in Westchester, New York, where he would talk it over with me.

That evening, after ordering, he went right at me. "You're not really thinking about going into this business, are you? Because if so, you're a moron."

"I'm dead serious."

"Let me be straight with you, Ron. I'm swamped and don't have time to teach you. Not to mention, you're going to fail miserably, and you're going to flush a shit ton of money down the drain."

He looked into my eyes and noticed I wasn't fazed by the words he was heaping on my head. "Okay, I'll tell you what, if you insist, I've got a couple of college interns working for me right now, so if you want, you can join my minions and learn the business that way."

"**YES**," I responded enthusiastically, despite having no idea what the internship might entail. "When can I start?"

Working at Co3 would allow me to gain real-life experience, acquire inside knowledge, and ultimately determine if this was the direction I wanted to follow.

"You can start tomorrow, but I've got to warn you, nobody gets into the industry like this, and I can guarantee you'll lose your shirt and probably your pants too," he cautioned. Then he ordered another double of their most expensive tequila and laughed deviously.

"I hear what you're saying, but if I use my other skills, I'll figure out how to be successful and make money in this industry."

"I've got a better plan for us," he said with a smirk. "Let's take your money and head to Vegas, where we can party, gamble, get some hookers, and literally blow it all there. Now, that would be a lot more fun if your goal is to be broke."

I stared back at him with a straight face.

Again, seeing the seriousness in my eyes, he said, "All right, whatever, buddy. Why don't you show me any scripts you're considering, and I'll introduce you to people, but you should expect them to bother you for the rest of your life, sending scripts all the time to get you to invest. Welcome to the movie business, Ron."

"All good. I'm willing to take that risk. Thanks, Marcelo."

Here's my take: It's important to value money without obsessing about it. You must also be willing to invest smartly and take risks to make more money while realizing you can survive with much less in the bank than most people think.

To keep my mind engaged and explore different career options, I typically maintain one main job while taking on one or two additional projects or freelance gigs. So began my post-production internship as my second job while my current full-time career was building my next business: Storis Capital, a technology venture capital firm, with my newest junior partner, Ryan, Bradley Cooper's doppelganger. Allocating blocks of time, a technique I learned from Stephen Covey, the author of *The 7 Habits of Highly Effective People*, enabled me to stay ***Focused*** on both jobs and deploy my ***Time Management*** skills by allocating dedicated blocks of time to each activity.

Before I forget, I must reveal one of my great secrets to success: a **Strong Team**. Partnering with highly motivated, ambitious individuals and giving them a piece of the business is essential. Ryan, of course, fit the bill. We used the apartment on Central Park South in Manhattan I had gotten a year earlier, where I could work and crash whenever I was in the city late at night and couldn't make it home.

Meanwhile, I was still married with four kids, Casey, Kyle, Dylan, and Erin (with a ten-year age difference between my oldest daughter, Casey, and my youngest daughter, Erin), living in Westchester, New York. On the weekends and various weekday nights, I was Super Dad, handling carpooling, coaching five different sports teams, being fun-loving, and taking care of household chores. During the week, I shuffled between meeting clients for Storis Capital and interning at Company 3. The trick to scheduling (and almost everything in life) is having as much control as possible. For my kids' sports and activities, I volunteered to be the coach or league coordinator, taking on a little more work, but for a solid return. I was then responsible for scheduling the games and events, making it easier to be involved with my kids by making sure their schedule aligned with my schedule and travel plans.

Ryan's fiancée, Alexa, an interior designer to the stars and set designer for *Saturday Night Live*, decorated the apartment more like an office. I had never seen the apartment look so good, as I trusted Ryan to handle it. It's essential to delegate whenever possible and not micromanage. I walked through the doors of our oversized one-bedroom abode with an incredible view of Central Park South, filled with minimalist clean-line furniture, black-and-white images of Manhattan on the walls, and a massive U-shaped velvet brown couch in the living room, which looked expensive. Ryan was sitting at the sleek, lacquered desk in the corner facing the window.

"Alexa did an unbelievably amazing job in here," I told him, plopping myself on the plush couch. "How much did this cost us?"

"Nothing," Ryan replied. "Alexa redesigned Matt Damon's house, and he didn't want the couch anymore, so he gave it to her. If this couch could talk, I wonder what stories it would reveal."

"We'd probably learn a lot about the movie world. But now that we have the couch, think about the new stories we're about to make." I looked at the time on my Blackberry®. "Oh, no. I didn't realize it was this late. I need to head over to my internship."

I stood up, about to say goodbye, and Ryan added, "Oh, Ron, I forgot to tell you. I have a connection in the movie business. My cousin, Carmen, is a casting director and works with the director Steven Soderbergh. I spoke to her the other day and told her about you."

"That's great, Ryan. Email me her contact info and I'll call her."

"I've got one more for you. My college roommate's brother is Tony. He works for Warner Independent Pictures in LA. I'll send you his contact info too."

How about that? I thought. I loved my thirty-year-old junior partner connecting me with top movie industry people.

The Intern

I had no idea what to expect on my first day on the job at Co3, located in Midtown Manhattan. However, I was confident that with my extensive business and life management experience, I would become a valuable member of their team in no time. Walking through the studio doors, I called up my **Confidence**, took a deep breath, and thought, *No problem. I got this*.

A young woman, who appeared to be in her mid-twenties, with a round face and short, jet-black hair with a red streak, was seated at a desk in the entranceway. "Can I help you?"

"I'm Ron Stein. I'm here for the internship position."

"You're early. And, wow, you're really old. That's weird. Please don't arrive at this time, as it will make us all look bad and have to do more work than we do already. My name is Debbie, and I'll be your manager while you're here."

Was this a joke? I was probably the same age as this girl's father.

"Each day you get here, I'll give you a list of your duties. Since you have no experience, you'll mostly be getting materials, running errands, stocking the kitchen, delivering film, and filing papers, things of that nature. Do you understand, or do you need me to repeat it so you can write it down? Also, try to dress a little younger. You know, like no button-down shirts, just old T-shirts, and maybe change that hair."

I was tempted to salute my child-like boss or tell this annoying granola ogre who I was, but I nodded in agreement like a good subordinate. Basically, while working here, I would have to shed my professional businessman persona and serve coffee like a servant. Yeah—go, me!

Five other interns were in the same unpaid position as me, and like my new boss, they were all around twenty-one. They didn't interact with me at all. I mean, can you blame them? They probably thought I was a creepy forty-year-old man and a complete loser. But I didn't care. I was there to *Listen and Learn* by absorbing all the critical and relevant information. Most of the work was monotonous, but I did it quickly and efficiently, making my co-interns look bad while they were busy idly chatting with each other about their hangovers.

I worked there a couple of hours a day, sometimes four hours, some-times six. Now and then, I took the overnight shift because that was when processing took place (and my kids were sleeping anyway). My first mentor in business, Bill, always told me that sleep management is essential. He pointed out that if you sleep four hours instead of eight hours per night, then you get an extra day (4 x 7 = 28 hours) of productive awake time per week for life. And he added, "There is plenty of time to sleep when you're dead." This is another component of *Time Management*.

Each night at Co3, the editing and coloring work done on the movies during the day had to be reproduced and backed up on discs. I loaded the discs, and when the disc was full, I changed it and put a new one in. One was consolidation. One was color. One was format. I would sit with these big machines, moving discs all night and turning switches on and off. It wasn't the most exciting work, but I wanted to learn how all the processes worked from the ground up—color, edit, and everything else.

One morning, Marcelo asked for a volunteer to work on edits for another film during the night shift. I raised my hand immediately, eager for the opportunity (I live by the "DFA rule": Down for Anything) and ready for the *Hard Work*. That night, when I walked into the editing room, I nearly did a double-take—sitting at the table was none other than Spike Lee. I introduced myself, and for the next two weeks, we worked together, fine-tuning one of his films. It was an incredible honor to get to know the iconic filmmaker.

Ron Does LA

I called Ryan's movie contacts. Carmen blew me off, while Tony agreed to meet with me in person but said it would have to be in Los Angeles. I hopped on a plane and flew to Los Angeles. Playing the part of a movie guy, I splurged on an expensive suite that opened to a deck to the pool at The Roosevelt Hotel in the heart of Hollywood. I decided to get into my role and act the part. After all, it was the movie business, and perception is reality.

After arriving in town, I hiked in Runyan Canyon at sunset, where I saw the Hollywood sign and, at the top, a panoramic view of LA, and that was when I said to myself, *I want to conquer this town next.* (From that day forward, whenever I return to LA, I go back to Runyan Canyon to reflect on this part of my life.)

Tony met me for lunch at the hotel. We sat outside, sipping cocktails by the pool, surrounded by palm trees, clear blue skies, and California sunshine. I wore my aviator shades. You know, the ones that made me look like someone important, the same aviator shades I wore in Cannes. Tony looked preppy in a lime-colored golf shirt, khaki pants, and trendy plastic-rim glasses, giving him a serious vibe. When the server came over, Tony ordered a spinach salad, and I followed suit. Not my usual go-to, but since the LA lifestyle was healthy, I figured, why not eat some greens?

After giving Tony my spiel about getting into the movie business, he said, "Sorry, honey. I think you're making a huge mistake. You should stick to what you're good at. It's too hard to make it in this business. Not to mention, you don't know anything about it, and quite frankly, you do not appear to have any creativity or taste."

"Many people have been telling me the same thing, so I understand this industry is extremely difficult. I've been taking my time and learning a ton. And I've been reading many scripts different people have given me. What if I get a good one? Would you look at it for me?"

"Ron, I get where you're coming from, but you are absolutely not even qualified to read scripts, let alone figure out if they are quality. Also, I'm swamped and don't have time to look at the lousy scripts you think are good."

"How about if I have other people check out the scripts first, and if I'm about to invest, I'll pay you to check it out before I move forward?"

One of the first lessons I learned in life, and is even more true in Hollywood, was that nobody says no to money—and they are all cash-starved and broke. So, they *fake it till they make it*, or they just fake it even more.

Nodding his head, he said reluctantly, "Fine, I'll do it. Can you send me fifteen-hundred for the first script review in advance, like maybe today?"

What did all these people do with their money? Why was almost everyone broke?

Many of them made much more than I did. Take Tony, for example, a prominent Hollywood executive at Warner Brothers who was credited for picking the hit movie *Slumdog Millionaire* from a script nobody thought would make it. Yet he always seemed broke. Again, the key lies in effective money management and maintaining the discipline to spend within your means and minimize recurring monthly and fixed expenses. When you do this, you don't have to be beholden to anyone for money because money shouldn't drive every decision.

I got the feeling that Tony thought I was a joker and a sucker, but he didn't know me well, and when I was on to something, I did not give up that easily. If anything, the more the naysayers told me I couldn't, the more I wanted to prove I could. After returning from LA, I was on a mission to get some quality scripts. How did I accomplish this? ***Networking***. It's another essential ingredient helpful in achieving success. You never know who the next important person in your life might be, today or twenty years from now.

On the way to the airport, I put my headphones over my ears, listened to Elton John's song "Saturday Night's Alright (For Fighting)" and got super pumped for this next chapter in my life.

Making My First Movies

Upon my return from LA, I was invigorated. First thing Monday morning, I met with Marcelo, and he quickly realized I wasn't giving up and could sense that I could be successful. He went through his emails and invited me to the next few industry parties at Co3. The modern, wide-open space with concrete floors, glass staircases, indoor-outdoor fireplace, roof deck, and steel accents allowed many guests to attend the events, giving me plenty of opportunity to mingle with people, many of whom worked in film and were looking for financing.

"Celine," a woman with shoulder-length blonde hair and a long, pinched nose said to me in a British accent. "It's a pleasure to meet you, Ron." She reached out to shake my hand, looking at me like a spider spotting a juicy fly in her web. "I understand you're looking to invest in film."

Instead of answering, I asked, "Who do you work for?"

"Plum Pictures." She took a sip of her white wine. "I heard from Marcelo that you have plenty of money. Is that true?"

I nodded with ***Confidence***. "I've got lots of scripts to show you if you're interested."

The expression on her face grew more sinister with her shit-eating grin and beady eyes. I could tell she saw a live one in me, believing I was a giant, fully fattened pig, and she was ready to lead me to the slaughterhouse.

"What do you have for me?"

"Well, I've got about seven scripts I'll show you."

Celine and I exchanged contact information, and that was when the floodgates opened. She sent me a wedding comedy and said she had a lock-in at Sundance. However, if I was the last investor, Celine promised to give me a favorable position. She also sent me *The Kids Are All Right*, the same script Marcelo had shown me a few weeks earlier.

I was always the most popular guy at these parties. Everyone saw dollar signs in me, wanting me to hand them large checks for their films and not interested in my involvement, thoughts, brains, etc. Despite my stardom at these shindigs, my co-interns still thought I was a circus freak and had no clue how I knew all these people. Laughing to myself, I watched the purple-haired intern with the nose ring looking in my direction and whispering in the ear of the man-bun intern. Poor kids. Maybe I should tell them a little about myself. Then again, being a man of mystery was probably more fun.

Another guy I met gave me a script for *Meskada*, a low-budget crime short film that was to be filmed in the Catskills. I also met an intelligent, attractive Asian woman, Sasie Sealy, a recent graduate of NYU Film School. Like everyone else, she needed money for her short film *The Elephant Garden* but claimed she didn't need that much. Sasie told me that if I invested, I could be the film's executive producer. She also mentioned she had an in with the Tribeca Film Festival, and if they liked the script, it would debut there. Sasie promised it would be great.

I discussed all the scripts with Marcelo, and he said, "You know, Ron, it doesn't hurt to get a credit. So if you do a short, you'll learn how it's done."

"I have an idea. If you do the post-production for free, I'll get you a credit for the movie."

Marcelo agreed.

I said **YES** to Sasie, and it turned out I was the last guy to invest. The post-production costs of the budget were all I needed to put up, which meant I got the big credit without having to put up any cash. Little did they know I would eventually own the distribution rights to the movie after discovering the power the last investor wielded.

The Elephant Garden was the first of many films I did. It was a low-budget short film (under twenty minutes) shot in North Carolina, a coming-of-age tale about the relationship between two sisters as the older one became interested in boys. Sasie used actors in acting school, looking to get credits. One of the actors, Billy Magnussen, would become a pretty big star on Broadway, movies, and television and Kelly Mack in Walking Dead. Billy and Kelly understood the value of **Working Hard** and taking advantage of a potential opportunity.

I sent Tony the other scripts that interested me: *Meskada*, which he said wasn't worth his time, and *The Kids Are All Right*. The film was about a lesbian couple looking for a sperm donor. In 2007, gay marriage was illegal in California. *The Kids Are All Right* highlighted a controversial topic. Tony had already read the script and told me if I didn't do the film, I would be a moron. However, he heard through the grapevine that I probably wouldn't get a piece of the film because the spots were already filled.

My Big Break, A Casting Call

In the middle of all this, I got a call out of the blue from Carmen. Remember her? She was the casting director for Steven Soderbergh.

"Hey, Ron," Carmen said over the phone. "Steven is producing a movie called *The Girlfriend Experience*, starring the porn star Sasha Grey, who's playing a high-end prostitute paid to pretend she's someone's girlfriend. Steven wants real people in the film to act without a script and wants it filmed in twelve days. Since he's looking for a New York businessman who travels to Vegas a few times a year with friends, I thought you'd be perfect for the role. Are you interested?"

By now, you know how I responded. I said, "**YES**," excited to experiment with acting because it was another form of sampling, and the best way to become an industry expert is to learn every aspect of a business.

"Great. I'll need you to come in for a casting call."

Weeks later, I showed up for the casting call. Sitting in the waiting room on a black metal folding chair, I was surrounded by a few other men who looked about the same age as me, in their forties. I stared at the foam ceiling tiles in the windowless room, waiting my turn. Finally, a woman came out, holding a clipboard, her hair in a messy bun with a pencil stuck in it, and she called me into the room. I was told to stand on the red circle in front of the gray screen. Lights and cameras faced me. She turned the equipment on and asked me to discuss one of my Las Vegas trips.

I had a great story to share but nerves were getting the best of me. Who would have thought the lights and cameras would make this so daunting? The words got caught in my throat, and it took some effort to finally spit them out.

"It's 2006, and I'm heading out to Vegas with some of my pals," I said, trembling.

"Cut," clipboard-woman announced. "Ron, loosen up. You're too stiff."

I tried it again. This time, I got a little further. "I called my friend Travis, a buddy of mine from college, who, at the time, was running the food and beverage department at the Hard Rock Hotel and asked him if he could hook us up while we were there."

"Cut," she yelled again. "Relax."

I took it from the top once more, but every time I spoke, she stopped me. Finally, after the sixth take, she told me I would have one last try. Before the next take, I strolled down the hallway to think, realizing I needed a new approach. An idea popped up in my head, and I came back refreshed, and this time, I visualized myself talking to my friends in a bar.

"The pool parties were all the rage. Everyone wanted to be there. I asked Travis if he could make me look like a star. He told me I should hire a private security guard to follow me around, ensuring I looked like someone important, and he knew just the guy for the job. Travis was the best. He put me in touch with James, a six-foot-ten-inch, three-hundred-eighty-pound black man with a gold front tooth, to pretend to be my security guard. Travis also got me a cabana on Platinum Row, the premier section of the pool. LA Laker Lamar Odom was to the left of us, and on the other side was famous porn star Jenna Jameson with her MMA fighter boyfriend, Tito Ortiz. Thanks to Travis, these high-end cabanas were going for 10K, but it cost me zero dinero.

Feeling more comfortable, I went on. "We could see all the action from our location. It was like having front-row seats to the wildest pool party ever. Music blaring, men wearing colorful bathing suits, skimpy bikini-wearing women dancing, and booze flowing like a waterfall. Travis had twenty bottles of Cristal champagne brought to our cabana to add to my celebrity status. But get this, he told me they recycled the bottles and poured cheaper champagne in them. Of course, everyone thought I was a real baller. James stood in front of the cabana, arms crossed, looking like a badass. James said he needed to check their bodies for weapons if anyone wanted to enter."

My audition continued. "We were a magnet for the ladies, and when I announced they needed to take their tops off if they wanted to come in, they complied with a smile. You can imagine what was happening: I was floating in a sea of breasts—every shape and size, and we were all drinking, gyrating, and spraying the fake Cristal."

"We moved to our two-bedroom suite with a huge living room when the pool party died. We continued imbibing in our alcohol binge, stuffing our faces with room service sliders, buffalo wings, chips and dip, and playing video games like rowdy teenagers."

"That night, we went to a strip club. After getting a lap dance from Cindy, a bleached blonde with heart-shaped lips, she told me she was getting off work soon and asked if she could join us wherever we were going next. Being the gentleman I was, I invited her to party with us at the nightclub in the hotel. James patted her down before she met up with us. After all, we had to ensure she wasn't a con artist or a Russian spy trying to kill us."

I continued, "In case you're wondering, I got into my part, pretending to be someone very important. Cindy promised me she didn't want my money. She was just looking for a good time, and I seemed like the kind of guy who could show her that. Later in the evening, Cindy asked me if I knew how she could tell if a guy was good in bed. I said no, and she told me if they could move their hips well, it was a good sign they knew how to move in bed. She then proceeded to give me an exercise to loosen up my hips. Cindy was just so thoughtful. There was a picture from the pool party of me sandwiched between two ladies with breasts the size of watermelons posted on the website, which I had quickly taken down."

When I finished the story, the clipboard lady yelled, "Cut!" for the last time. Snapping out of my trance, I didn't realize I was still doing the audition. The other four people in the room were laughing.

"That was awesome," one yelled.

"You nailed it," another said.

An important side note for clarity: My wife and I divorced in 2017. We had married young and had four beautiful children together—my greatest pride and joy. In hindsight, we stayed together too long. With my attention on work and co-parenting our kids, the timing to split never felt right. Neither of us was a perfect partner, but we didn't give up that easily and had been attending marriage counseling for years. But after we tried unsuccessfully to work through our issues, my wife and I agreed to have an open-style relationship—the start of which happened to coincide with my Vegas trip in 2006. My NYC apartment was part of the deal.

When I returned to the apartment, Ryan asked, "How'd it go?"

"I have no idea," I responded, grabbing a Diet Coke™ from the refrigerator. "I sucked at first, but when I finally got into the story, I went into a zone." Opening the can, I took a long sip.

"Well, if it makes you feel any better, my cousin emailed me and said they thought you were hilarious and insane. And they loved how honest you were."

"Wow, that's great to hear."

"You ready to go over those investor prospectus documents?"

"Mind if we do it tomorrow? I'm coaching my son's baseball game tonight."

"Damn. Coaching, interning, casting calls. Had I known you would be this busy, I never would've introduced you to my cousin," he said, cracking a small smile.

"I promise I'll finish it before going to bed tonight, and you will have it first thing in the morning."

My Big Break, Getting Discovered

A few hours later, in the middle of coaching my son Dylan's baseball game, my cellphone rang during the top of the fourth inning. I didn't recognize the number, but it was a 310 area code, so I knew it was someone from Los Angeles. I answered the phone since we were comfortably ahead of the other team ten to nothing.

"Ron, it's Steven," the man said on the other end of the line.

"Steven, who?" I asked.

"Steven Soderbergh. I just want to let you know I loved your tape. It was hilarious and real. I want you in the movie. You in or you out?"

"**YES**, I'm in. Absolutely," I replied.

"Batter up!" the umpire yelled.

"Awesome. It sounds like you're busy, so I'll let you go. I'll need two more guys for the other parts. If you have any friends who might be interested, let me know. We can discuss it tomorrow. Call me at this number; it's my cellphone.

Wow. I'd just gotten my first part in a movie with a big-name producer. Not bad for a rookie.

I called my friend Marshall, who, believe it or not, I met on a flight to Vegas. After chatting the entire flight, I invited Marshall to party with me and my buddies at the Hard Rock Hotel, which he agreed to. From that moment on, he and I became good friends. Marshall agreed to act with me in the movie. Soderbergh also asked me to find a friend who could talk about politics, and my buddy, a political consultant who looked like Obama, seemed perfect.

We shot the first scene in a location at an Equinox Fitness Club in New York City. This was the scene where Sasha Grey's boyfriend in the movie, a personal trainer, told his friends he was organizing a trip to Vegas.

Following that scene, Marshall, Obama look-alike, and I were told to meet at Teterboro, the private airport in New Jersey. When we arrived, two G4s were waiting for us. Soderbergh and the crew were on one plane, and we were on the other. Soderbergh told us we needed to keep the scene real. We were instructed to get hammered and drink all the booze while in the air. I took directions well and did as I was told.

Since we had no cameramen traveling with us, I had to film the scene. Soderbergh said I should try to hold the camera steady, and he didn't care if it shook a little. Our role was to bring up stories about sex, politics, and finance—some of my favorite topics. I became the sex-talk guy and shared a wild tale about hooking up with identical twins. Obama look-alike talked about a blackmail scandal in Washington, DC, and slicked-back hair Marshall discussed how he swindled some guy's account. Taking turns, we talked over one another while pounding liquor for the entire three-and-a-half-hour flight, filming it all. It was an experience to remember—at least what we could remember of it because we were bombed.

When we got off the plane, we slurred our words and nearly tripped over our feet, walking off the tarmac while cameras filmed us.

Out of nowhere, I screamed, "Cut," and everyone stopped.

Soderbergh ran up to me, red-faced, and said, through gritted teeth, "I'm the director, you drunk asshole. I'll tell you when to cut. Get back on the plane and do it again."

"I'm very sorry. I just wanted to see if saying cut really worked, and it did."

We went back, tried harder, and did it better the second time, and Soderbergh relaxed.

As we made our way into a stretch limo, five professional hookers, wearing sequined mini dresses revealing a lot of cleavage and ass, greeted us when we hopped into the car. The ladies offered us some champagne but, being the responsible and way-too-inebriated guys that we were, we drank Diet Coke™ instead, trying to sober up a little.

Arriving at the Palms Hotel, we were escorted to the Britney Spears suite, which boasted a bottomless glass Jacuzzi on the balcony with a panoramic view of the strip. Soderbergh filmed the scene this time, holding the camera on his shoulder. Our pink sheet gave instructions on how the night would unfold, and the plan was to flirt, drink some more, and dance with the prostitutes for a few hours. From there, we would be driven to Lavo, a nightclub where Soderbergh rented a few tables.

Ten minutes into the hotel scene, Soderbergh yelled, "Cut! That's a wrap. I'm done filming."

"What do you mean we're done?" the producer, sporting a severe crew cut, asked. "We're supposed to film all night long and have five more scenes to finish."

We all stood frozen, our eyes wide, waiting for direction. Soderbergh's abrupt ending of the scene seemed odd. But who can argue with a creative genius? I was sure he knew what he was doing.

"We're good, but I don't want any more," Soderbergh announced. "I'll tell you what, let's have the wrap party at Lavo. I already paid for it."

Just when I thought the plane ride was a crazy experience, I learned that the levels of insanity could go way up. Lavo was even crazier. The marathon drinking binge continued. I was on the dance floor, holding a brunette's hips while her red strapless dress rode up her ass. Behind me, another prostitute had her arms wrapped around my waist. A mixture of sweat and vanilla-scented perfume filled the space around me.

Out of nowhere, I heard a glass smash against the dance floor. I turned around to see what had happened, and there was chaos. Men were punching each other. Chairs were flying. Women were screaming. Bouncers in black T-shirts and bulging muscles jumped in, trying to break up the fight. It turned out Soderbergh started the fight, and I had no idea why. Maybe he hit on someone's boyfriend or called someone a loser. Either way, we escaped unharmed (with our wallets and no stitches or tattoos).

The following morning, I sat in the hotel café, eating breakfast with the Obama look a-like and Marshall, recapping the night.

"What an insane night we had. This entire movie thing was surreal," Marshall said, taking a piece of bacon. "You're not still planning to go into the movie business, are you?"

Without hesitating, I replied, "**YES**, I am. I'm all-in." I picked up my phone and called the producer of *Meskada.* I said, "I'm ready to move forward. Email me the wiring instructions and tell me where to show up."

Saying **YES** to Soderbergh introduced me to real-life movie making. I was now ready to explore the world of producing.

Call Me Spielberg

January 2009

Through extensive research, including my immersive internship and taking on various projects within the film industry, I discovered that the main factors for becoming a successful Hollywood producer were similar to those in most business endeavors. Saying **YES** to new opportunities enabled me to navigate the complexities of the entertainment world.

The first factor is picking good movies and projects. Choosing scripts is no easy task, and project teams are full of sketchy people. A good script is a diamond in the rough. Once you score one, you must polish and fix it—and the best ones are always taken first and offered to top producers. After that, scripts travel down to the bottom feeder. Luckily, I knew brilliant, insider people, so I was one step ahead with a *Strong Team*.

The second factor is negotiating and getting ready to swim with the sharks. In other words, optimize project management skills to handle the project crew, film the movie on time, stay within budget, recruit top-notch stars, perform quality editing and post-production, gain entry into prestigious film festivals, create effective press and PR, get the movie sold, and ensure a high-profile release. And, of course, have fun along the way.

Sounds easy, right? Ha! Not exactly. When you're ready, you just have to take that leap, handle *Doubt Management*, and get moving.

Popping My Cherry: My First Movie Set

July 2009

Soon after investing in *Meskada* at the lowest level—associate producer—I drove to the Catskills (not LA, funny enough) to check out the set. When I arrived, I stood back and observed the organized chaos. I heard crew members shouting on walkie-talkies.

The director barked orders. "Copy that. Did I make myself clear? Move the camera to the right. Lights to the left. Action. Camera speeds. Get wardrobe. Striking. Can we get a playback?"

Everything was moving, but it seemed to be in slow motion with all the starting and stopping. During a break, I was introduced to Josh, one of the directors. It turned out he had heard about me. His father and I worked in technology consulting years prior when I was at Deutsche Bank.

"My dad says you're brilliant, Ron, and you know a lot about finance. Can you do me a favor and look at our books? Something is off. We're running out of cash even though we're on budget, and I can't put my finger on what's going on."

"Yeah, sure. No problem."

I followed Josh to a trailer, sat at a table, and started flipping through the financial records. When I detected the issue, it wasn't pretty. Galin, the producer who brought me the project, was stealing money and trying to cover it up by making up fake expenses and not properly disclosing the actual budget. This was undoubtedly the problem, but I had a knack for turning issues into opportunities. Since they were out of money, they would need me that much more. And I could renegotiate to improve my title and move up on the waterfall of profit disbursement.

After I informed Josh of what was happening, Galin was kicked off the movie and told to return the money. Otherwise, he was going to jail.

Next, I called Marcelo and filled him in on the situation. "Jump ship immediately, Ron!" he yelled at the top of his lungs.

By following my philosophy of **_Doubt Management_**, I overcame my fear and embraced the **_Confidence_** I needed to pursue my goal. I like to think of the issues we encounter in life as ocean waves. When a big wave comes and you run away from it, it will smash you on your head. If you run into the wave, it will strike you back. The key is to dive under the wave—that's how you get to the other side. Most people would've taken Marcelo's advice and run away. But despite the warning signs, I had a feeling pushing me to move forward. I dove head-first under the wave to save the film. As a newbie in the movie industry, I had a lot to learn. And the best way to do that was by going in with my eyes wide open and figuring it out.

Once I decided to move forward, I told Marcelo my plan. "I think I'm in a great spot. I increased my position in the film, and I'm going to put my kids in the trailer. Will you let us post at Company 3 when we finish filming?"

Now that I was controlling the finances, Marcelo changed his tune. "Okay, but like we did in the *Elephant Garden*, you'll need to give me a credit and a small percentage of the movie." I referred to this as the Marcelo Deal.

"You got it."

As for me, I stepped in and offered the additional investment for the post-production, and in return, I would take Galin's full producer title, get a cameo for me and my kids, and become one of the three full producers. Also, I now sat in first position to get my money back ahead of all the others. They agreed to the deal, and I stayed on set for the remainder of the filming to learn the process and perform my cameo.

Some funny incidents occurred during the filming of *Meskada*. One of the actors, Norman Reedus, had recently returned from rehab in Europe. The director, concerned about Norman's well-being, asked if Norman could stay at my apartment in NYC during breaks from filming. The goal was to keep an eye on him and ensure he didn't suffer a relapse. Imagine my surprise as I was just dipping my toes into the world of movies and suddenly, I had this almost-washed-up actor crashing on my couch. And oh, by the way, as I mentioned earlier, it was Matt Damon's couch. My comings and goings didn't align much with Norman's stay, but when we did chat, he asked for my advice, and I told him the value of *Focusing* on your end goals and saying **YES** to the right opportunities.

Remarkably, Norman stayed on the straight and narrow, and shortly after our time together on set, he scored a role in *The Walking Dead*, ultimately becoming one of the biggest stars on TV. It's a testament to his now-proven clean record and the transformative power of staying true to one's pursuits.

Other amusing situations occurred on set. The first one was with Kellan Lutz, who had just filmed *The Twilight Saga: Breaking Dawn - Part 1* and was doing this film as a favor to the director. During breaks, he would take the heavy sandbags that held equipment in place and use them as weights to do bicep curls non-stop to keep his arms looking ready. I guess it paid off because he was cast as Hercules soon after.

The second incident involved Rachel Nichols. Eager to boost her resume and land a big break, Rachel flirted with anyone she thought could help her career. When she heard I was the producer who saved the movie, she approached me, lifted her shirt to show me her breasts, and said, "If you can help me, you can play with these." While I knew she was half-joking, I also knew better than to fall for it.

I got my first small taste of movie production. And while everyone else lost money from *Meskada*, thanks to the Marcos Deal, I got my initial investment back. In this situation (as in all my life situations), being a quick learner is essential. The third was getting three of my four children (Kyle, Dylan, and Erin; Casey was busy) in the movie and even the trailer (since I controlled post production).

Here I Go Again: Movie #2

August 2009

Right before *Meskada* wrapped up, I got a call from Celine. "A spot just opened up, and you need to invest in *The Kids Are All Right*," she insisted. "This is the last piece. You should take it, Ron, before someone else does."

Even though Marcelo and Tony encouraged, or rather, begged me to do the movie, I hesitated to invest in a film promoting homosexuality and gay marriage. Not that I have anything against gays (or as Seinfeld said, "Not that there is anything wrong with that"). I'm all for gay couples, but back in 2009, I wasn't sure the country was as open-minded as me and most of Hollywood were.

"I'll consider it," I told Celine. "But before I commit, I'll fly out to LA early tomorrow morning for the first day of filming and check out the set."

Arriving in LA the next day, I went straight to the set and was introduced to the entire cast. In the middle of filming, I overheard two producers standing behind me, arguing about something. My ears perked up when one of the producers, who helped fund the movie, wanted to back out because he thought the content was too gay. I wondered what was wrong with that producer and his company. They read the script. Didn't he know what he was getting himself into before he agreed to the film? I, on the other hand, was impressed with the acting. Julianne Moore and Annette Bening, playing a married couple with two kids from a sperm donor, Mark Ruffalo's character, were genuine and authentic. And there was nothing over-the-top about it at all. Light bulbs went off in my head. This last-minute fight was my opportunity to jump in and negotiate hard.

During a break, Mark Ruffalo approached me, and we started chatting. He asked me about my kids and how long I planned to stay in Los

Angeles. I liked Mark. He was warm and friendly, and we compared notes about our similar humble childhoods growing up.

"You seem like a cool guy," Mark said. "I know you're deciding if you should do the movie, but if you don't mind me putting my two cents in, I think you absolutely should do it, and it will be a winner. I just know it in my gut."

"You're right. **YES**, I'll do it." When chances arise, don't overthink, don't hesitate, and *__Act Decisively__*.

"Hey, Celine," I called out, walking toward her while she was in a frantic discussion with the other producers I had overheard earlier.

"Oh, hello, Ron." Her posh English accent made her sound like she was calm royalty, but little did she know I was about to knock her off her throne.

Applying what I learned from *Meskada* and other life experiences, I said, "Here's the thing. You're going to need me more than ever since you lost a significant amount of funding. I'm going to do the movie, but"—Celine rolled her eyes, waiting for the catch—"I want all your ownership percentages. I want to be First Executive Producer. And I want a cameo that makes it into the movie."

I could practically see the smoke coming out of her ears as she lost her composure, which was exactly what I wanted.

"What? That's absurd," she screamed, abandoning her posh demeanor. "I'm not giving you all that."

"Actually, you are." I stood there, glaring at her, folding my arms and holding my breath, essentially acting like a toddler. Mark watched, laughing hysterically, making Celine more furious and a bit scary, like a king cobra about to strike.

She scowled and hissed at me. "You're a huge arsehole, Ron."

"Well, it's better than being a whole ass."

The crew gathered around and laughed when they heard me. "I'll stand here all day if I have to. I have nowhere else to be."

"Fine, you stupid fuck!" she growled.

Mark gave me a high five when Celine stormed away. "I'm meeting up with the crew tonight at a bar. You should come with us. You're definitely not a typical douche-bag producer. I can pick you up if you want."

That evening, Mark, who prefers to spend time with genuine people (rather than obnoxious Hollywood players), took me to a dive bar in LA. Most of the crew was there when we arrived. Mark told everyone what had happened with Celine and me. They loved the story. We all took shots in my honor, celebrating that I outsmarted Celine and got my way. As I had demanded, Celine gave me her ownership percentage of the movie (in addition to my investment percentage) and an onscreen cameo: a dinner table scene with Mark. We were goofing around and cracking each other up, much to the director's frustration and he almost kicked us off the set. After several retakes, Mark and I finally settled down and got serious, *Focusing* on the scene.

Once I wrote the large check and the film funding was completed, Celine's anger toward me melted. I became the big dog, Executive Producer, while she maintained the producer title. Don't worry. It didn't go to my head. Then again, maybe just a little. I got a momentary rush imagining myself as the next Steven Spielberg. But once I returned to Earth, I knew I'd never be a creative genius producing and directing blockbuster films.

Still, it felt good to be part of a movie that won a Golden Globe for Best Motion Picture and was nominated for Best Picture of the Year at the Academy Awards. And by the way, the film's substantial financial success reignited Celine's anger toward me for taking all her percentage. But, hey, that's life in showbiz. We're all good now. Not surprisingly, she seems to suffer from selective amnesia and still reaches out to me for investments in her upcoming projects without any hint of shame.

I got my close encounter (**YES**, pun intended) with Mr. Spielberg when, one afternoon, during a producer meeting, he called the director and asked if his daughter, Sasha, could be in the movie. Nobody would turn down a request from one of the greatest Hollywood directors of all time. We, the producers, agreed, and Sasha was given the role of Waify Girl at the party—even though she wasn't waify at all. Since I have two daughters, I thought I should look out for Sasha.

After she performed her scene, I approached her and said, "You were great. What's your name?"

"You don't know who I am?"

I knew exactly who she was. She was a sweet girl, but I met many people with enormous egos after entering this industry and saw no need to play into them. Therefore, despite her father's celebrity status, I treated her like I would anyone else.

"No, sorry. I don't know who you are. I just got into this line of work."

"I'm Sasha Spielberg."

"Ron Stein, top executive producer." I reached my hand out to shake hers. "It's a pleasure to meet you."

It took roughly thirty days to shoot the entire movie. The director was meticulous, so it was longer than expected. I was there for most of the filming, but honestly, it was anything but exciting. In fact, there's nothing slower and more boring than a movie set. First, it took hours to shoot two lines, and even when it seemed perfect, the lighting needed to be changed. Then, they would re-shoot the scene, and if the camera angles were wrong, they would try again. For anyone who thinks the movie business is glamorous, I've got news for you—it ain't. And...because of my ***Positive Mindset*** I was able to do it without complaining.

Lessons Learned Chapter 12: Embracing a POSITIVE MINDSET

Adopting the Creator Mindset: Shaping Your Reality

It's not enough to tell yourself, "Think Positively." When I hear that, I often roll my eyes too. It's overly simplistic and doesn't address the deeper layers of mindset. To truly embrace a *Positive Mindset*, it's essential to first identify where you currently stand. Are you approaching life as a Victim, a Controller, or a Creator?

Let's Recap:

The Three Mindsets

Victim Mindset: The Victim operates from a *HAVE DO BE* model.
  "If I have the right investors, then I'll be able to expand my business, and then I'll be successful." Victims wait for circumstances to change before they take action or feel fulfilled. In this model, external conditions control your potential, making it ineffective for creating extraordinary results.
  Controller Mindset: The Controller works from a *DO HAVE BE* framework.
  "If I work harder, then I'll have more revenue, and then I'll feel satisfied." While proactive, Controllers *Focus* solely on doing, often at the expense of being. This hustle-driven model creates burnout and dissatisfaction because fulfillment always feels just out of reach.
  Creator Mindset: The Creator redesigns their identity with the *BE DO HAVE* approach.
  In this model, *"If I am confident, resourceful, and creative, I will take inspired action, and success will follow."* The Creator starts by *being*

the person they aspire to become. From that foundation, actions align with values, and the desired results naturally follow.

My experiences in this chapter illustrate the transformative power of the Creator Mindset. As an unpaid intern at Co3, surrounded by young coworkers who doubted me, I chose not to operate as a Victim. Instead of thinking, "If they respect me, then I'll work hard and feel valued," I decided to embody *Confidence* and resourcefulness from the start. By aligning my actions with that identity, I took mundane tasks seriously, completing them with efficiency and a *Positive Mindset*. This approach helped me stand out to mentors like Marcelo, eventually earning opportunities like working with Spike Lee—a chance that was the result of persistence and a willingness to embrace uncertainty.

When faced with skepticism from insiders like Marcelo and Tony, I didn't let doubt dictate my actions. Instead, I leaned into the Creator Mindset, deciding to see myself as a determined and capable movie producer. Whether it was *Networking* through Ryan's contacts, boldly investing in *The Elephant Garden*, or saying **YES** to acting in Steven Soderbergh's film, I let every action reflect the person I aspired to be. These choices not only paved the way for professional success but also reinforced my belief in myself, allowing me to navigate one of the most competitive industries with clarity and purpose.

CHAPTER 12

STRONG TEAM

FOCUS ON FILMS

June 2009

Toward the end of the thirty-day shoot of *The Kids Are All Right*, I received a call to join a new production set on the North Fork of Long Island, New York, titled *The Romantics*. The film featured a star-studded cast, including Katie Holmes, Josh Duhamel, Anna Paquin, Adam Brody, Candice Bergen, Jeremy Strong, Elijah Wood, Malin Akerman, and others.

Meanwhile, the wrap party for *The Kids Are All Right* was to be held on the last day of filming of *The Romantics*. Embracing the moment's energy, I said **YES** to fly out to the wrap party in California and another **YES** to fly back to New York to dive in and fully immerse myself in the film business.

My Cousin Warren

August 2009

The Kids Are All Right celebration took place on the expansive outdoor balcony of a chic Santa Monica restaurant, providing a picturesque ocean view and unlimited food and drinks. The entire cast attended, along with their significant others, many of whom resided in the Hollywood Hills. As soon as I arrived at the restaurant, I was introduced to Annette Bening's husband, Warren Beatty.

I greeted him casually (as I always do when I meet famous people), treating him like I would any other spouse of a coworker. He and I got along well and spent time getting to know each other. We discussed his Madonna days and his insightful philosophy on relationships. Throughout the evening, whenever we separated to grab food or attend to other matters, someone would reintroduce us. Annoyed by these re-introductions, Warren told everyone, including Annette, we were cousins.

Upon hearing this, Annette apologized for not being friendlier to me on set. "I had no idea we were family," she said, giving me a big hug and kiss.

Warren flashed me his trademark wry smirk, accompanied by a wink. This cool experience reminded me to always keep my head up, live in the moment, and enjoy myself.

After **_Working Hard,_** involving many tedious overnights in the studio with Marcelo to complete post-production of *The Romantics* at Co3, Tom Cruise and Katie Holmes hosted a dinner for the cast and crew at their house. Midway through the meal, Cruise pulled me aside and asked to talk to me in private. It was hard to believe that just a few years earlier, I met him in an elevator in Cannes, and now, Tom Cruise wanted to speak to me—alone—at his house in Beverly Hills. Who would have thought?

As we walked to the other side of the pool, I was curious what his pearls of film wisdom would be. Tom looked up at me, practically on his tippy toes, and said, "Don't fuck this movie up, Ron."

It was not exactly the secret revelation to the movie world I hoped for.

Leaning down, I whispered in his ear, "It's too late for that, and you know it. The movie is done, and it's good-ish but not great. You'll need to go to the premiere and tell everyone it is great, or it will look bad for all of us. I'll pump up the first weekend, buy all the seats in the theaters in New York, and try to make it as good as possible. We also need Katie to do interviews."

"Katie won't do interviews if the film sucks," he said.

"She has no choice. This is what being a producer is about. After Katie goes to the festival premiere at Sundance, she needs to do her best acting and make people believe the movie is amazing," I demanded. With my biggest Hollywood fake smile, I put my arm around him and added, "Thanks, brotha, and see you in NYC for the premiere event. It's going to be awesome."

Treating Tom like I would anyone else made him respect me. After that, he would call me over the next few years for several one-on-one dinners whenever he popped into NYC, asking me all kinds of questions about indie film production.

Everything Comes in Threes

October 2009

The Romantics was my third film project in the span of three months. It took a great deal of ***Time Management*** and ***Prioritizing*** to juggle this. Shooting of *The Romantics* had just begun when I arrived on set, and much like my previous experience in the film industry, looming budget constraints threatened to halt progress. As usual, I requested access to the financial records only to uncover another instance of theft. Shocker.

To address the budget issues, I negotiated the Marcos Deal (mentioned in chapter 11), giving Marcos a percentage of the film in exchange for the postproduction work. Simultaneously, I secured my position as one of the overall producers, snagged a cameo, became friendly with Adam Brody (who is a real down-to-earth regular guy) as we connected on a personal level, and aligned myself with the top financier, Michael Benaroya, who had invested millions compared to my modest contribution. This time, I insisted on taking charge of the film's marketing, which included the poster design, managing the film festival, coordinating the premiere event, and orchestrating the opening weekend theater roll-out.

This film marked Katie's first venture into producing, which turned out to be challenging. Producing is more demanding than it appears, and perhaps she should have stayed *Focused* on her acting instead. As a condition of my financial involvement, I stipulated that my investment hinged on two critical events: the cast's attendance at Sundance and the appearance of Tom Cruise, Katie's husband at the time, at the premiere. I understood the value of securing the attendance of the cast, and especially Cruise's. It would guarantee us favorable press coverage, and I told Katie, the executive producer, that she had to make it happen.

A Festivus for the Rest of Us: My First Dance

January 2010

Meanwhile, believe it or not, I had two movies premiering at Sundance Film Festival (a.k.a. The Dance), a feat few producers have achieved. Not only did I have my second full feature, *The Kids Are All Right*, in one of the top movie festivals in the world, but it quickly made the cut. We received the news an hour after the executives viewed it.

To everyone's surprise, *The Romantics* was also accepted. We persuaded the Sundance Film Festival executives to include *The Romantics* movie in the lineup without them having viewed it and assured them that the fantastic cast was willing to attend in person—my idea, thank you. (The truth was, if they had seen it, they might not have accepted it.)

Amidst all the excitement of *The Romantics* getting into Sundance, I encountered a precarious situation when one of the producers from the movie never paid me the hundred-grand I was owed. To help me out, a friend introduced me to his relative, Jonathan, a prominent lawyer from Boston. Jonathan offered to take the case, but rather than payment, he wanted my assistance getting him on a casting call for a film. As usual, he negotiated like a rock star and got me my money, but sadly for him, he bombed the casting call.

I kept my cool when I met Fergie from the Black Eyed Peas, who, at the time, was married to Josh Duhamel. While Josh was talking to reporters at a press release in Park City, Utah, I sat in a holding room for *The Romantics* screening, hanging out with Fergie, an absolute beauty who is surprisingly down-to-earth. She asked me about my children, and when I mentioned that my eldest daughter was a big fan and I bought tickets to her upcoming concert at Mohegan Sun, Fergie texted her agent to give my daughter and her friends backstage passes. I'll admit, I'm a sucker for some of the perks I get in this industry. After all, as I already mentioned, you've got to have fun too.

I thanked Fergie and told her she was awesome. She got up, hugged and kissed me on the cheek, and said, "You're a real person and a great dad."

Quick note: While backstage at the concert six months later, we not only had a private meeting with the entire Black Eyed Peas, Fergie ran up to me in front of my daughter and her friends and gave me another embrace and smooch. And since she broke up with Josh in between, the kiss was on the lips this time.

The Kids movie was the smash hit of the festival, receiving a standing ovation for over five minutes after the premiere. Unfortunately, there was much less interest in *The Romantics*. Following each premiere, we attended massive parties for the cast, producers, and the major players, like HBO, United Artists, Focus Features, Weinstein Company, etc., all looking to purchase featured films.

At *The Kids* party, someone introduced me to John Sloss, the owner of Cinetic Media, a film sales, financing, and distribution company. He was dressed sharply in a cashmere sweater, and his dark hair was sprinkled with strands of gray.

Little did we know at the time, this would lead to a friendly and lucrative relationship. John would later become the sales agent for all my movies. In a few months, I would say **YES** to investing in and getting on his digital distribution company (CRM) startup board.

John, the film sales agent, agreed to let me trail behind him like a puppy dog that night to learn. Suddenly, a big guy with beady brown eyes, a stout figure, and a receding hairline forcefully tapped me on the shoulder. "You're Ron Stein, right?" the man asked.

"That's right," I responded, giving him a curious look. "And you are?"

I knew him but wanted to entertain myself by playing my favorite I-have-no-idea-who-you-are game. This guy already had one of the most enormous egos in Hollywood, if not the world. I was doing him a favor by not letting his large noggin get bigger than it already was.

"I'm *The* Harvey Weinstein. We met before. Aren't you from New York?"

I shook my head. "Sorry, I'm just not placing it. Where did we meet?"

My poker face was so good. Of course I remembered meeting Harvey. How could I forget? About a year ago, I ran into him in the lobby of my apartment building. A few businesses are located on the second floor, and Harvey was coming out of the hair transplant clinic, getting his hair plugs, when we bumped into each other and started chatting.

Ignoring my question, he got right to the point. "I want to buy *The Kids Are All Right*."

"Oh," I responded, deadpan.

"Can you help me?" he asked.

"Sure, anything for *The* Harvey Weinstein."

"What can I do to get it?"

"Well, Harvey, you've got to bid more and offer more money for the promotion budget than the other bidders. That's how it works. The guy who has the highest bid gets the movie."

I sounded like such a big shot, didn't I? I wasn't, but I enjoyed pretending.

"No fucking way. Do you know that I have the power to make *The Kids* enormously successful? If you let me buy it, I can guarantee it will win an Oscar."

"I'll tell you what, I'll talk to John and pitch it for you."

I went over to John and whispered, "Pretend you're interested in what I'm telling you and go along with it. Weinstein wants to purchase the film."

"Not happening," John said. "I don't care if he gives the most money."

John and I gave fake smiles at Harvey while we spoke.

"Weinstein has a reputation for buying movies, and then he dumps them when they don't hit. But, let me guess, he promised you an Oscar."

"He sure did."

"Tell him no."

I walked back to Harvey. "Sorry, man. It's a no-go."

"You're going to regret it. And you can kiss your chances of getting an Oscar goodbye."

Harvey stormed away from me.

John was right. Since the Weinstein Company did not specialize in movies with gay tones, they were not the right fit. Focus Features ended up buying the film, which was a much better choice.

Oh, What a Night

Ari, an entertainment executive, joined me as my guide to all the festival and film events. The parties at Sundance were enjoyable and star-studded but few were over-the-top exciting. At least not how TMZ portrayed them. It was mostly a lot of mingling, meeting people, and making small talk. Ari was the smartest, nicest guy in the world and everyone responded positively to him.

On our last night, Ari and I were trying to figure out what to do, hoping to find some harmless fun. The snow was dumping outside, and massive flakes piled on my head. And just when I thought it would be another lame night, a slimy, greasy-haired marketing dude invited us to a party in Deer Valley at some billionaire's ten-thousand-square-foot ski-in, ski-out mansion. I told him **YES** because, after all, we had to have a good time. Slimy Dude promised me it would be crazy, but the one catch was we had to provide the transportation, and there were no cars to be found anywhere. Then, Asher, a Russian guy with a gleaming, cleanly shaved head sporting a classic Hollywood style with oversized, black-rimmed glasses, shouted, "I have a huge Suburban and can drive all of us."

Off we went, silently praying that Asher wasn't another Jeffrey Dahmer and wouldn't murder us in a remote cabin in the snow. Asher pulled up the long driveway to the chateau-looking house. All the lights were on, but from the outside, it didn't look like much of a party. Slimy Dude told me not to worry, we were still early.

Stepping inside the house, we entered a stunning two-story atrium foyer, which opened to a massive great room with a wall of windows showing off the panoramic mountain vistas glowing under a full moon. Next, we wandered into the enormous kitchen, where we found a catering staff dressed in black pants and black vests over white button-down shirts, arranging hors d'oeuvres on silver platters and shuffling around the kitchen preparing food.

Following the sound of live music, we took the spiral staircase to the recreation room. About twenty gorgeous women, averaging around five-feet nine-inches with voluptuous curves, were prancing in bathing suits and high-heeled shoes. My mouth was agape, and all of us were staring wide-eyed at what appeared to be a fashion show.

"What'd I tell you, guys?" Slimy Dude said, grinning. "Ron, these ladies are here for the after-party, and they all want to meet big stars and big producers. And since you're a producer, they will be all over you." He winked at me. "Expect to hit it big tonight."

I felt like I was standing in the center of a Victoria's Secret Fashion Show, not that I had ever been, but I imagine this is what it would be like. When the ladies finished modeling their swimsuits, they grabbed their bags and undressed in the middle of the room. The women flashed their enormous breasts in our direction, and we gawked at them while they changed into tiny dresses, revealing major cleavage.

"Are you gentlemen here for the party?" a young Cindy Crawford look-alike with a beauty mark on her cheekbone asked.

"We are!" we yelled, like a bunch of high school boys.

Asher chimed in, "You know who this guy is, don't you?"

She shook her head no.

"This is Ron Stein. He's a major producer. He did *The Romantics* and *The Kids Are All Right.*"

"Really? Wow. I saw both of those movies at the premieres. Annette Bening was so good, and so was Mark Ruffalo."

"Yeah, they were all great." My tone was modest. I didn't want to come off as some pompous Hollywood guy.

"Holly, Jamie, come over here," Cindy look-alike called out to two other beauties. "You've got to meet Ron. He's like a major producer."

I wanted to warn her not to get carried away. She was giving me way more credit than I deserved.

The next thing I knew, a few other women crowded around me, asking all kinds of questions. This must be what Hugh Hefner felt like in the Playboy Mansion. All I needed was a red robe to complete my look. The women hung all over me, and eventually, we made our way back toward the foyer and into the great room. I could see a long line of people through the window by the massive double front doors, waiting to give their names to a bouncer so they could enter. Dozens of guests began to fill the house. As the night went on, the party got wilder. People were dancing on the furniture and singing at the tops of their lungs. I was in the thick of it, drinking top-shelf liquor and moving from room to room with my harem of women.

I awoke the next morning in someone else's house on a stranger's couch. I had no idea where I was. Bits and pieces of the night flashed in my mind: dancing, belting out tunes for karaoke, more dancing, and a lot of shots. I tried calling Ari, but he was sleeping back at his hotel and didn't pick up. Next, I called my little bald friend, Asher, and thankfully, he answered the phone.

"What the hell happened last night?" I asked.

"You don't remember?"

"If I did, I wouldn't have asked. I don't even know where I am."

"I know where you are. Hang tight. I'll get the car and pick you up," he said. "And by the way, last night was definitely a night to remember. At least when you do remember."

I heard Asher's laughter echoing through the phone, signaling the start of yet another lifelong friendship.

A Back Door into Tribeca

April 2010

I managed to get *Meskada* into Tribeca using a back door approach—pun intended—with the help of Tony. Reaching out to him to leverage his connections turned out to be a good call. He promised he could make it happen. When Tony called me a few days later to let me know he got the film in, I thanked him and asked how much I owed for the favor.

"Nothing," he said. "I did it for trade, not money." By the way he said it, I assumed his favor involved sex with a man, and that was how the film made it in through the back door.

Working on a shoestring budget of under five-hundred-thousand for *Meskada*, we faced the challenge of not having funds for a festival party. Having ***Listened and Learned*** previously, I thought outside the box and approached an unknown vodka company for sponsorship. Their condition? Kellan Lutz's presence. Naturally, I assured them of his attendance.

With the funds secured from the vodka company, I turned my attention to designing a poster for the film. Placing our biggest star, Kellan Lutz, alongside Grace Gummer, Meryl Streep's daughter, seemed like a strategic move for gaining good press, despite Grace's limited role in the movie, with only a few lines.

On the way to the festival, I received an unexpected call from Grace's mother. "Hey, Ron, it's Meryl Streep."

How about that? A Hollywood queen was calling me. But I was about to discover she wasn't calling to sing my praises.

"Who the fuck do you think you are?" she screamed into the phone. "Who gave you the right to put my daughter on the poster? Why are you exploiting her?"

"Relax, Meryl," I responded as though I were speaking to just any ordinary person. "I put her on the poster because we need all the good PR we can muster."

Meryl huffed and puffed.

"You should watch the film. It's not that bad," I said, then hung up.

I probably should've pushed Meryl to attend the party, but it didn't sound like she was too fond of me. Much to my chagrin, Lutz was too busy filming *Hercules*, so he never made an appearance at the party in NYC. And then the vodka company wasn't too fond of me either. Nonetheless, the party went on, and the cast enjoyed the celebration. I was able to make it up when we did a premiere party at Voyeur, a nightclub in LA, with Kellan and all his friends in attendance six months later.

Premiere of Romantics: They Closed the Streets for Tom Cruise

September 2010

Weeks later, I set up the premiere for *The Romantics* at the rooftop deck of the Gansevoort Hotel in Midtown Manhattan. The hotel gave us the space for free on the condition that Tom Cruise showed up.

To make extra money, I sold sponsorships for the event. I approached major vodka, watch, and other high-end product companies, proposing an exclusive opportunity at the party. For a fee of twenty-five thousand, I told them they could have their brands featured on the step-and-re-peat backdrop, where Tom would be photographed. My plan worked well. I got many bids and made a nice chunk of change.

Even though the movie wasn't good, Tom's appearance helped make the premiere hugely successful. In preparation for his arrival, we noti-fied the media in advance. Barricades were placed to close off streets, managing the enormous crowds of eager fans. Tom exchanged warm greetings and signed autographs as he made his way into the event. Many other celebs, including the rapper Wyclef Jean, showed up. And

get this: Kelsey Grammer couldn't even enter the doors without someone calling my cellphone to ask for my consent.

Time to Hit the Box Office

The Kids Are All Right soared at the box office during its release,
with huge accolades from the press. However, when it came to *The
Romantics*, I first had to determine what was possible and then bent the
rules to ensure that it, too, became a box office hit.

A simple formula was used to accomplish that, measuring the average
per theater. In other words, the movie had to sell out in at least two
different theaters in two different cities to meet the minimum average.
How did I manage to do that? Easy. I *Acted Decisively* and convinced
friends who owned big companies to purchase all the tickets in their
local theaters and distribute them to their employees. The ploy worked
like a charm, transforming *The Romantics* into a weekend sensation and
making it one of the top-five grossing movies.

From there, a theater representative secured screenings in more
than two-hundred-fifty theaters across thirty-seven states the following
week. Unfortunately, the euphoria was short-lived as the movie failed
to resonate with audiences, leading to a swift decline in interest. In
hindsight, a direct-to-digital release would have been a wiser choice.

Meanwhile, *Meskada* lacked the star power and quality for a theatri-
cal release. In a pinch, I reached out to Tony again, urging him to "work
his magic butt." True to form, he convinced the head of Starz to strike a
deal with us. With that, I secured the TV and cable rights, putting a new
spin on what it meant to have a **STRONG TEAM**. Thank you again,
Tony.

Golden Globes and Golden Night

January 2011

The Kids Are All Right achieved tremendous success. Financially, the film, with a budget of just under five million, raked in over eighty million. Critically, it garnered an impressive one hundred-thirty-three award nominations worldwide, securing thirty-three wins. And notably, the film received significant recognition at The Golden Globes and The Oscars, a huge honor that instantly granted me significant credibility in Hollywood.

At the Golden Globes, we were nominated for three awards: Best Motion Picture (Musical or Comedy), Best Actress (Annette Bening and Julianne Moore), and Best Screenplay (Lisa Cholodenko). Held at the Beverly Hills Hilton, The Globes had a more intimate atmosphere, and on-site venues hosted major parties. Despite being the First Executive Producer, only full producers went on stage to collect the trophy. Nevertheless, my role was significant, and congratulations poured in continuously. We lost the Screenplay award, but Annette Bening won Best Actress, delivering a Hollywood-centric speech about gay marriage. The announcement for Best Motion Picture came next, and we emerged victorious, sparking cheers, hugs, and a surreal moment of popping champagne.

After taking pictures, it was time for the parties. There were six major ones, and we had automatic invites for winning. I decided to attend three——Sony, Weinstein, and HBO. First, I went to Sony for a quick hello to my executive friends. Then, I headed to Weinstein for a drink with Harvey, who personally invited me for a toast, recalling our time together at Sundance. Finally, it was off to the biggest party at HBO, where I met up with my friend Jo, a.k.a. HBO-Jo, the head of marketing at HBO and the person who bought the TV and cable rights to *The Kids Are All Right*.

As we approached the venue, the front was packed with an incredible crowd—everyone who was anyone wanted in. I felt lost in the chaotic sea of people until, out of nowhere, a beautiful young lady with her hair in an up-do and dressed in a long sequined gown appeared before me. She informed me that her job was to escort me in as the winner. I was riding high on cloud nine. She guided me to the back entrance, where I encountered a striking figure: a handsome black man dressed in a crisp, expensive white tuxedo with tails and a top hat. Catching sight of me, he insisted that I go in first. I introduced myself and asked for his name——even though I knew it was P. Diddy (the old P. Diddy, that is). Smirking, he revealed himself as Sean and greeted me with a warm hug. Walking in together, we grabbed a drink—just me and P. Diddy. The excitement was palpable, and little did I know, the night's craziness had just begun.

With drinks in hand, my escort led my new buddy P. Diddy and me to a private table featuring bottles of Dom Pérignon and Don Julio 1942 Tequila. Raising our champagne-filled glasses, we toasted. Shortly after, HBO-Jo hugged me while ignoring P. and asked if she could bring over a big fan who had a question. I agreed, and to my surprise, she returned with Tom Hanks. Tom inquired about the backstory and rationale behind investing in independent films with a purpose, given their often-uncertain success. As we delved into the conversation, Tom received a text, mentioning that a few others wanted to meet me—**YES**, me, Ron Stein.

Moments later, I felt a pat on my back, and a shorter man with a perfectly groomed grayish beard embraced me. Steven Spielberg and his wife, Kate Capshaw, expressed gratitude for looking after their daughter, Sasha, on set. Their thanks as parents and fellow filmmakers left me with goosebumps.

The night became a blur, filled with drinks and hugs with some of the hottest Hollywood stars. When Mark Ruffalo spotted me from across the room, he ran up to me. Embracing each other, we jumped up and down. As the party wound down around 2:00 a.m., HBO-Jo informed me that the limo was waiting to take me to a private after-party at the

Chateau Marmont. Upon arrival, paparazzi swarmed the area, but I entered a lounge teeming with celebrities through a private entrance. Norman Reedus approached, thanking me for hosting him in my apartment and congratulating me on my success, and I reciprocated the congratulations. He was accompanied by Paz, who, having indulged too much, needed assistance to leave discreetly out the back door to avoid the paparazzi.

As I was making my way out, I stepped into the elevator, and right before the door was about to close, the stunning escort from the HBO party rushed in. Glancing at me, batting her long eyelashes, she asked if I was having a good time.

"It's the party of a lifetime," I responded.

With a flirtatious smile, she hit the stop button on the elevator. She gazed into my eyes and said, "It's about to get even better."

In an unexpected moment, she kissed me. All the while, Aerosmith's "Love in an Elevator" played in my mind.

After the elevator escapade, I returned to the lobby, intending to leave for home, only to unexpectedly encounter HBO-Jo, who told me we had to leave immediately. We were invited to a private pool party with the cast of *Mad Men*, but there was a catch: the rules would not be revealed beforehand. Without a second thought, I said **YES**. We passed through a gate to find a pool surrounded by towering hedges, with naked people and floating bottles of lit-up Dom Pérignon. Jon Hamm looked at us, shouted for us to strip off our clothes, and jumped in. And so, we did.

It was one of the craziest nights of my life!

The Oscar Goes to... not us :(

February 2011

Undoubtedly, there's no greater achievement in the film industry than receiving a nomination for Movie of the Year. The Oscars arrived, bringing nominations for the major categories––Best Motion Picture of the Year, Best Lead Actress (Annette Bening), Best Supporting Actor

(Mark Ruffalo), and Best Original Screenplay (Lisa Cholodenko). Although it was a cool experience, we didn't secure a win in any of the
four categories.

I congratulated and sympathized with Mark and joined HBO-Jo at
several other parties, albeit in a more subdued atmosphere. The final
gathering, held at a lively dance club, turned out to be enjoyable as I
unexpectedly bumped into Kevin Spacey, and we hung out. To top it
off, I snagged a beautiful hat from some guy, keeping it as a memorable
souvenir. The lesson learned——winning (as we did with the Golden
Globes) truly rocks!

The Sequel: Navigating Another Attempt at Film

March 2011

While still basking in the glow of the soaring success and wild adventures from my initial three movies, the time had come to double down
my efforts and recreate the magic. Blinded by my previous success, I had
difficulty determining what was possible. When I eventually realized
that my earlier victories had somewhat spoiled me and that timing
was everything, it hit hard and hurt a lot, but, of course, hindsight is
twenty-twenty.

The Kids Are All Right, the only one of my films that turned a profit—an achievement akin to winning the lottery with odds of one in
a million each year—proved that the stars and moon must have been
aligned in our favor. Independent film-making presents a myriad of
challenges, and when things go awry, financial losses are inevitable,
which happened with *Meskada* and *The Romantics*.

That said, we often tend to forget the pain we have endured, which
explains why people return to Vegas after a losing streak and women
give birth to more than one child. Nevertheless, fueled by fierce determination and a willingness to reset, I created a path toward my second
round, firmly committed to *Work Hard*. Despite the uncertainty of what

lay ahead, I *Acted Decisively* and pursued my goals with unwavering *Focus*, determined to discover my next successful projects.

Go Digital

Before taking the plunge into other movies, I was smart enough to hedge my bets and sampled another angle. The only companies guaranteed to make money in the movie industry were the ones that service films, regardless of whether they are good, bad, successful, or horrible failures.

I thought about the line Mr. McGuire said to Benjamin (played by Dustin Hoffman) in the movie *The Graduate*, "I want to say one word to you. Just one word," but instead of "plastics," I replaced it with "digital."

John Sloss was starting a digital distribution company, CRM. He and I had lunch together, and I told him that, given my core strengths and past experience in technology, I could add value to his company by overseeing the software and reporting components. He agreed and asked me to make a minimal investment and join his small board of directors in charge of IT, including Todd Wagner, Mark Cuban's former business partner. Saying **YES** to John turned out to be financially lucrative, beating every movie I made combined by a significant margin. More on that soon.

Porn Again

When *The Kids Are All Right's* marketing team promoted the film in Cannes for the remaining international markets, I headed there with Ari, hoping to catch the wave again and research potential film opportunities. While there, I was inundated with meetings searching for new scripts, but nothing seemed worthwhile. On another note, I had a chance to reconnect with familiar faces and made plans to collaborate on the film *Margin Call*, acting as an advisor to kick-start the project when I was back in NYC.

Exhausted from the meetings and tired of listening to sleazy producers pushing crappy projects, I was tempted to decline the invitation

when my close group of friends, including lawyers, bankers, and producers, invited me to join them at a party. This group became some of
my closest friends with whom I would stay with in LA. David and Tif,
with whom I spend holidays with, even built a studio apartment in their
Hollywood Hills home for me to stay. And remember, you must also
have fun, and you never know what will happen in life which is short,
so naturally, I said **YES**.

We walked for what seemed like miles until we reached the biggest
yacht in the harbor, where the billionaire Ron Burkle hosted a private
get-together. Aboard the extravagant yacht, we spent the evening playing with twelve Russian escorts and reenacting the *Saturday Night Live*
synchronized swimming skit in the sleek full-size glass pool on top of
one of the decks. It was one of the funniest moments of my life. We
laughed so hard we cried. Afterward, a Mercedes van picked us up and
drove us to an exclusive club. Upon arrival, the manager greeted us at
the door and led us to Leonardo (Leo) DiCaprio's private table.

Right before I sat, Leo, red-faced with anger, looked me straight in
the eye and said, "Who the fuck are you? I don't like guys in my booth."

"I'm Ron," I responded as usual, not even acknowledging who he was.
"Who are you? And why are you so afraid of the competition?"

Bursting into fits of laughter, Leo offered me a shot of tequila, and we
partied the night away until sunrise.

Another funny incident occurred the following evening after Ari and
I returned to our hotel around 2:00 a.m., weary from a long day of
meetings and drinking alcohol. We were finally ready to hit the pillows.
Entering the lobby elevator, I hit the seventh-floor button. The doors
closed, and then suddenly, the walls shook violently, and the lights
flashed. We were nearly thrown onto the floor by an earthquake-like
jerking motion as the elevator plunged downward for what seemed an
eternity. The absence of a lower floor button in the elevator added to
our unease.

Ari looked at me, his face ashen, and said, "You did it now, Ron. Your
contract ran out. Satan is calling you to hell, and you're dragging me
with you. Not cool!"

Finally, the doors opened, and if Ari was right and we were in hell, it sure looked like a great place. Bodies swayed and twirled to the loud, rhythmic music in the nightclub setting. Stepping inside the action, a well-dressed Frenchman in a skin-tight white suit and a perfectly trimmed dark beard approached us and said, "You're finally here. We've been waiting for you forever."

Ari and I glanced at each other, scared shitless. *What was going on?*

I scanned the room, looking for an exit, but instead of escaping, my favorite word popped out of my mouth, "**YES**! I'm here."

Beckoning us to follow him, he said, "Your VIP table is all set and paid for. But please forgive me. I had to put the talent at your table because I had nowhere else to seat them. Not to worry, though––I will kick them out, so they won't disturb you."

I noticed Tyga, Kylie Jenner, and their entourage seated there. "No, don't be ridiculous. They're welcome to stay as my guests."

"As you wish, sir," the man informed us. "If you need anything else, please do not hesitate to find me."

Since the manager had obviously mistaken me for someone else, it only made sense to play along. If the real person showed up, Ari and I would make a run for it. Until then, I had no choice but to let the games resume.

"Thanks for allowing us to stay here," Tyga said, reaching out to shake my hand. He wore a sleek black leather coat with intricate gold accents and a thick layer of gold chains around his neck.

"Who are you?" I asked, indulging in my pretend game of not knowing who they were.

His eyes widened in disbelief. "I'm Tyga, and this is Kylie."

"Can you spell that for me?" My poker face was too good.

"T-Y-G-A."

I shook his hand. "Nice to meet you, Tigger."

Doubling over in laughter, he hugged me, and then we toasted each other and downed the refreshing Cristal.

Ari was acting as my bodyguard while a gorgeous and voluptuous woman kept trying to come in the VIP section to meet me.

"Ron, meet Lexy. You two are perfect for each other." He whispered in my ear that he knew her from Los Angeles. She had been in "short movies" and was now a model.

I kissed her hand and then led her to the dance floor when Tyga excused himself from the table to perform on stage. Ari excused himself and went to his room upstairs. Sexy Lexy and I danced all night, taking countless shots of alcohol between songs. The rest of the night was somewhat foggy, and the following morning, I woke up to the blaring sunlight in my eyes with Lexy sprawled out next to me. A case of mistaken identity and a good-time **YES** made the evening extremely memorable.

Second Wave of Films

May 2011 to March 2012

Back in NYC, I began working as an advisor on *Margin Call,* enabling me to stay close to home and spend more time with my kids. With my experience, I ensured the movie included a realistic portrayal of Wall Street.

When Kevin Spacey, whom I had met at the Oscars and was one of the lead characters, asked, "Hey, Ronnie, what's a fucking margin call anyway?" I chuckled while realizing I had to start with teaching him the basics. I taught Kevin about financial markets and investing, covering everything from stocks and bonds to eventually what a margin call was, which occurs when a broker requires an investor to deposit more money or securities to cover potential losses on investments bought on borrowed funds.

Now I had to continue searching for the next opportunity by *Net-working* and reaching out to my contacts for leads. With each new project that came my way, I *Acted Decisively* and committed myself to its success.

The next film project emerged when I was introduced to an Italian production team working on the coming-of-age film *Someday This Pain*

Will Be Useful to You, starring Lucy Liu, Ellen Burstyn, Aubrey Plaza, Stephen Lang, Peter Gallagher, and Marcia Gay Harden. The film was shooting in Central Park, a short walk from my NYC office/apartment. Elda Ferri, an Italian grandmother figure and Oscar-winning producer of *Life is Beautiful*, was on the production team. While visiting the set, I soon discovered they were facing some financial issues (not surprising) and pointed them out to her. Grateful for the insight, Elda invited me to join as a full producer and eventually become the Italian government-approved North American co-production company.

Additionally, I received a call out of the blue from a couple I had met at one of the Golden Globe parties: a billionaire businessman and his fiancée. They expressed interest in producing a B-horror film called *Darkroom*. The billionaire funded most of the movie, and once again, I facilitated the Marcelo Deal, limiting my financial exposure and maximizing any returns. The film was shot in a sprawling mansion, ivy hugging the weathered stone, on a quiet lane in Long Island, New York. One memorable moment during filming involved blowing up a car with actual dynamite, adding an exciting touch to my production experience.

While on set one morning, handling paperwork before the crew arrived, a guy in a leather jacket and dark shades rode up on a motorcycle. The man had a compact build and a receding hairline. Approaching me, he mentioned he was instructed to speak with me for permission to check out the property, as he was interested in renting it for his birthday party. Extending my hand, I introduced myself and asked for his name.

Smiling, he said, "I'm Billy." He left out his last name, Joel, which, of course, I immediately recognized, but as usual, I pretended not to. "The Piano Man" and I spent the next hour casually strolling around the property, sipping coffee and exchanging friendly conversation.

Following that project, Marcelo introduced me to the production team of an art film, *Billy Bates*, a story centered around the experiences inside the mind of a street artist, Burton Machen. Part of the team included Al Pacino's daughter Julie, her first-ever venture into production. Given the film's financial constraints, Marcelo suggested I assist them with the Marcelo Deal. I agreed to help and collaborate with them in

New York and, to some extent, in Toronto, to complete the remaining filming and handle post-production work.

One afternoon, I received a shocking phone call. The caller bluntly stated, "You better be paying for everything!"

I recognized the voice but still asked, "Who is this?"

His response confirmed my suspicion—it was Al Pacino. "Pleasure to meet you, Al. But I'm not following. Can you clarify what you mean by everything?"

"Yeah, well, Julie needs rent money, and you need to cover it."

"Hate to break it to you, Al, but Julie is your daughter, not one of mine. That means, as her father, you're responsible for financially supporting her. Her rent is not part of the film's budget."

Al persisted, emphasizing his celebrity status, to which I responded, "Why don't you sit down with Julie for a genuine father-daughter conversation about her career and finances? Trust me. You'll thank me later."

With that, the call ended.

Amidst everything, I received a call from Milena Canonero, the four-time Academy Award-winning costume designer and producer on *Someday This Pain Will Be Useful to You*. Milena proposed the idea of co-directing a music video. I enthusiastically said, "**YES**." We spent a day filming in Central Park and two other locations in New York City in September, featuring the music of the Italian superstar Elisa, a fantastic experience.

Subsequently, I had to ***Focus*** on the post-production work for *Someday This Pain Will Be Useful to You*. However, there was no Marcelo Deal to assist this time because the Italians were obligated to do the editing and post in Rome, Italy, in line with their financing from Rai, a TV and film conglomerate. Throughout the fall, I enjoyed traveling back and forth to Rome, a delightful experience, aiding them in post-production. They even provided me with an office with a stunning view overlooking the Colosseum.

While in Rome, I was treated as part of the family, enjoying Sunday afternoon dinners with Elda, who prepared a fantastic meal. I couldn't get enough of her delicious homemade gravy. Her entire family, including all the exes and lovers, showed up, but unlike most Americans, they all got along. We ate, laughed, and watched fútbol on TV. Unfortunately, despite our efforts, the movie's outcome was merely okay, proving too bland for most film-goers.

Not Just Another Bachelor Party in Vegas

When I returned from Rome, Ari asked me to be in his wedding party. We celebrated his bachelor party at Caesars Palace in Las Vegas, and after a raucous night, I awoke the following morning and had a life-imitates-art moment. I thought I was dreaming as we began reenacting a scene from *The Hangover*. Barely awake, I heard a noise but couldn't muster the strength to open my right eyelid. When I finally cleared my eyes, a banana hammock with a huge black bulge was staring at me. Attempting to get my vision straight, I looked again at the startling image before me and then up at the man's rich ebony complexion with a patch of white on his face.

"Hi, I'm George," the bald man said, resembling a young George Foreman.

"I'm Ron. Can you put some pants on, please?" I asked, turning my head away from his beef stick. "And why does your face have white?"

"I sneezed," he replied casually, then pranced around the hotel suite—still naked.

Repeating the exact line from *The Hangover*, I asked again, "Would you please put some pants on? I feel weird having to ask you twice."

After he dressed, we had breakfast together, talking nonstop as we got to know each other. From that day on, we became great friends with an outrageous story about how we met.

Off to Miami Beach

The next challenge lay in trying to make these films successful, and I no longer had the help of Tony's lips or ass to secure entry into festivals. He and I parted ways after he told me he already went above and beyond for me. This should have been a major sign that things were going astray when I no longer had my ***Strong Team*** to rely on.

I had to pivot and shift to the second tier of festivals. *Darkroom* was posted in New York with Marcelo's company, but lingering issues couldn't be rectified since it was the director's debut film. Consequently, the movie didn't make it to festivals or a traditional release——it went straight to digital on CRM.

On a brighter note, I secured a spot for *Someday This Pain Will Be Useful to You* at the Miami Film Festival, leveraging its impressive pedigree and cast. Off I went to Miami Beach, ready to promote my ass off and try to pull off a miracle while having fun in the sun.

<u>Lessons Learned From Chapter 12 The Power of a STRONG TEAM</u>

The strength of your team often determines the success of any ambitious endeavor.

This chapter illustrates how collaboration, adaptability, and clear communication are vital in overcoming challenges and achieving goals.

Let's Recap:

Assemble Diverse Talent

Collaborating with a range of experts ensures that every aspect of a project is addressed. For *The Romantics*, I worked with financier Michael Benaroya, negotiated the "Marcelo Deal" to handle post-production, and managed marketing efforts while Katie Holmes tackled her production responsibilities. By assembling a team with complementary skills, we covered every critical component of the production process.

Key Takeaway: Build a team with complementary talents but also unique perspectives to effectively address the diverse needs of your project.

Establish Clear Roles and Responsibilities

Defining roles and responsibilities was crucial to maintaining accountability and streamlining decision-making. On *The Romantics*, I *Focused* on marketing and festival logistics, Marcelo handled post-production, and Katie ensured the cast's attendance at Sundance. This clarity prevented overlaps and confusion, enabling the team to move forward cohesively.

Key Takeaway: Define and delegate roles strategically to maintain efficiency and avoid unnecessary overlap.

Foster Collaboration and Communication

Effective teamwork relies on trust and transparency. When I uncovered theft in *The Romantics'* financial records, addressing the issue directly with the team fostered trust and ensured that we could refocus on the project's success. Open dialogue allowed us to maintain resilience in the face of setbacks.

Key Takeaway: Open communication builds trust and fosters resilience, helping the team navigate challenges together.

Reward and Recognize Contributions

Acknowledging the efforts of your team motivates them and strengthens morale. Ensuring that the cast attended Sundance and the premiere of *The Romantics* highlighted the value of their contributions, boosting publicity and building a sense of shared accomplishment.

Key Takeaway: Celebrate individual and collective achievements to maintain morale and momentum.

Adapt and Overcome Challenges Together

Flexibility and problem-solving were essential when budget constraints threatened progress. By negotiating the Marcelo Deal and organizing strategic ticket purchases to boost *The Romantics'* opening weekend box office performance, I demonstrated the power of creative solutions in overcoming hurdles.

Key Takeaway: Collaborate creatively to find solutions and adapt to changing circumstances.

Invest in Relationships

Strong professional relationships open doors for future success. My connection with John Sloss at Sundance led to multiple distribution opportunities, including the successful sale of *The Kids Are All Right*. These partnerships became a foundation for long-term collaboration.

Key Takeaway: Build lasting relationships with collaborators and partners to enable long-term success.

CHAPTER 13

PUTTING THE PRINCIPLES TOGETHER

REAL ESTATE EMPIRE

March 2012

A Bald Guy Buys Me a Drink

The bright, sweltering sun beat on me, and beads of sweat trickled down my forehead. The sand felt like hot coals on my feet as I weaved through the maze of lounge chairs. Needing a break from the heat and crowds, I went to the Bleau Bar in the Fontainebleau Hotel lobby, where I was staying during the Miami Film Festival.

Entering the bar, I was greeted by a cool and inviting atmosphere, a perfect escape from the chaos outside. The floor-to-ceiling windows offered stunning views of the ocean and the hotel's lush gardens. The bar had a spacious and comfortable seating area with plush cushions and armchairs in white leather. I sat at the bar and ordered a cocktail from the bartender, a slender woman with a blonde pixie haircut.

"How's your day going?" she asked, handing me a tequila on the rocks.

I took a sip of the refreshing drink. "It's good now," I said, relishing in the peace and lulled by the soft music playing in the background.

My calm state was interrupted when three men strolled into the bar, cackling loudly. Leading the way was a short, bald guy wearing an expensive Italian-made suit tailored to fit his large frame and big belly, exuding a commanding presence. Behind him stood two muscular bodyguards with broad shoulders, their faces obscured by dark sunglasses, adding to their intimidating appearance.

"Hi, Mr. L. How are you today?" the bartender asked, her blonde hair catching the light.

"Never better." His voice was deep and loud.

Suddenly, a tall, brown-haired, good-looking man in a gray suit made a beeline for the bartender, delivering instructions to her in a hushed tone. The bartender nodded attentively throughout their conversation.

Out of nowhere, Bald Man pointed at me and shouted from across the bar. "Hey, who are you?"

"Ron," I replied. Not wanting to engage with him, I quickly finished my drink and stood up to leave.

"What are you drinking, Ron?"

"I was drinking tequila, but I'm about to leave."

Bald Man looked at the bartender. "Get Ron the best tequila on the house," he demanded.

"Thank you, but I'm good." Repeating myself, I added, "I'm leaving in a minute, and I can afford to buy my own drinks."

His face flushed red with rage, his features contorted in fury as he erupted, "Nobody says no to me!"

"Frankie," called an attractive woman heading toward Bald Man. She was wearing a floral print short dress that barely covered her ass, paired with the highest heels I'd ever seen. "I want to go shopping in Bal Harbor."

Bald Man pivoted from me, his eyes fixating on the woman. Ignoring my presence, he reached into his pocket and withdrew a thick wad of cash, which he pressed into her palm. In response, she leaned in for a swift kiss on his lips.

This was my time to make a break for it. I got off the chair, attempting to slip from the bar unnoticed, when the man in the gray suit appeared and asked, "Are you enjoying your stay at the hotel?"

"It's been great. The staff is so friendly and attentive."

"That's what I like to hear. I'm Ricky, the room manager here at the hotel." He reached his hand out to shake mine. "Please let me know if I can do anything to make your stay more enjoyable."

"Thank you. I'm Ron Stein." I gave him a firm handshake.

Ricky leaned over and whispered, "There is something you can do for me. Please let Mr. L. buy you a drink. He's a really big, important client here. Trust me, you don't want to upset him anyway. And it would be a great personal favor to me."

When the woman left, Bald Man demanded, "You ready for that drink now?"

"**YES**," I replied. I said **YES** to him—not because I had to but because I wanted to help Ricky, who appeared to be a genuinely nice guy in a jam. Not to mention, I needed Ricky for my safety. After all, I watched enough mob movies to know the type of person I was dealing with.

Bald Man sat in the chair beside me, and his two subordinates sat on the other side of the bar. The bartender handed us our drinks. "What are you doing in Miami Beach?" Bald Man asked.

"I came down for the film festival."

"You in the industry?" His gold pinkie ring tapped the side of the glass when he picked up his tequila.

"I'm a producer."

Bald Man raised his eyebrow. "A producer, huh? What movies have you produced?"

"Did you see the movies *The Kids Are All Right* or *The Romantics*?"

"Nope. But I'll watch them, especially now that I know you." Bald Man took another sip of his drink. "You know, I got a few stories that would make a great movie."

I heard that line just about every time I told people I was a producer.

"Really?" I said, pretending to be interested.

Bald Man leaned in close and lowered his voice. "Let's just say I know how to make things happen. I've been around a long time, and I've seen it all. If you're looking for a story with a little bit of everything and a lot of action, I'm your man, but I can't say too much in here. If you're interested, we can discuss it in the future. I'll give you my card."

He pulled one out of his pocket and handed it to me. I read his business card. Construction in New Jersey—go figure.

Bald Man and I continued chatting for the next hour. He reminded me of a miniature Tony Soprano, the fictional character from *The Sopranos*. When we finished our drinks, he patted me and said, "You're a good guy, Ronnie. I like you." He threw a few hundred-dollar bills on the bar. "Stay in touch," he said, standing up.

"Will do. And thanks for the drinks."

Whitney Houston Suite

I waited a few minutes for him and the group to leave. Then, I thanked the bartender and left the Fontainebleau to meet the film folks for dinner and prep for the upcoming premiere. When I got back to my hotel room later that night, there was an envelope taped to the outside of my door with a room card and a note inside, telling me to go to the Whitney Houston Suite on the top floor.

What was going on? After this long, strange day, all I wanted to do was get some sleep before the big day tomorrow.

Arriving at the suite on the top floor, I found another note welcoming me to my new room. Upon entering the spacious suite, I was blown away by the massive balcony that offered spectacular views of the pool and crystal blue ocean. The hotel staff had moved all my things, pressed my clothes, and laid my toiletries out in the bathroom just the way I had them in the old room. There was a bottle of champagne chilling in a bucket of ice on the marble coffee table in the living room. An envelope with my name on the outside was on top of a folded napkin. I opened the envelope and read the card. It was from Ricky, thanking me for saying **YES** to Mr. L.

Ricky and The Fontainebleau

How about that? Ricky did me right.

I got free drinks from a mob boss and a major upgrade in the hotel. I slept well that night. The next day, I found Ricky in the lobby and insisted he let me take him to dinner as a thank you.

Ricky and I dined at a cozy little Italian restaurant in Miami, filled with the aroma of freshly baked bread and pasta. We were seated in a booth at the back of the restaurant and discovered we had a lot in common. Talking to Ricky was like meeting a long-lost cousin.

While we ate, I told Ricky about how I got into the movie business, and he listened intently. He had a background in film production but never pursued it after he landed his first job in hospitality and never looked back. Instead, we bonded over our shared interest for storytelling.

"I'm glad you agreed to let Mr. L. buy you a drink. He's not used to people saying no to him. As the hotel's general manager, I meet many crazy people. High-maintenance celebrities, athletes, musicians, and over-the-top wealthy guests demand the most insane things. A socialite once requested that a staff member dress up as a Roman emperor and wanted us to carry him around the hotel on a throne. Another famous guest insisted that her room get painted pink before her arrival, and then we had to fill it with hundreds of pink roses, pink cupcakes, and pink candy for her three-year-old daughter's birthday celebration. Celebrities often have odd needs. I could probably write a book about all our wacky guests staying at the hotel."

"Instead of a book, how about a TV series? Behind-the-scenes stories of the guests, the staff, and guys like Mr. L. would make for a fascinating show."

A grin spread across Ricky's face. "That's a brilliant idea. Let's do it."

"If you're serious, I will try to make this happen."

"I'm in," Ricky said. He lifted his glass of wine and made a toast. "To the Fontainebleau."

"To the Fontainebleau, a show about the eccentric, sexy, and pretentious asshole guests at a luxurious Miami hotel and the hotel staff." We drank to a brilliant concept for a TV series.

When I returned to New York, I started developing a plan for the show, and then I contacted my friend, HBO-Jo. She loved the idea and told me to devise an engaging logline, a sentence or two summarizing the concept, that she would run by the executives to see if they were interested.

Working tirelessly writing and rewriting a logline, I finally settled on this: *From the glitz and glamour of the Miami nightlife to the scandals and secrets of the elite guests, The Fontainebleau follows the staff of a luxurious hotel as they navigate the wild and unpredictable world of the rich and famous.*

I also created a presentation outlining my ideas for the primetime, hour-long comedy-drama. It highlighted the events of the pilot and the first few episodes, describing the characters and their arcs.

Before sending my detailed pitch to HBO-Jo, I wanted to ensure we had enough material to make an engaging, original series. I took my time preparing my presentation, flew down to Miami occasionally, and stayed at the Fontainebleau. Ricky always hooked me up with upgrades and discounted rates on rooms. He and I spent hours brainstorming and taking notes on potential storylines. I also met with a lawyer about getting the rights to use the hotel name.

Out of nowhere, I received a phone call, and a man with a recognizable voice yelled, "Who the fuck do you think you are?"

"Who is this?" I asked.

"It's James," he said.

Following my usual MO, I inquired, "James, who?"

"James Caan. You better listen up. There's no way in hell you're doing this Fontainebleau TV show bullshit. The owner doesn't want it, and neither do I. Do you understand?"

"I understand. But I hate to break it to you, I am going forward with this. I'm not afraid of you or anyone else. I believe in this project. And I believe in Ricky."

"Wow, okay, then. I guess that shit works. You know what? You seem cool, so if you do go ahead, can I get a juicy role in it?"

"Abso-fucking-lutely," I responded. "Great talking to you, Jimmy. I'll be in touch."

Roughly three months later, I got a call from Ricky when I was putting the final touches on my presentation. "Ron, I'm really sorry, but the hotel owner informed me you are not allowed to have the rights to do the project, and he decided he is not going to give them to you. I certainly don't want to jeopardize the hotel or compromise our guests' privacy."

"You're joking, right?" I knew he wasn't. "No problem. I understand but am disappointed," I assured him, adding that I would kill the project because I would never want anything to get in the way of our friendship.

The hotel owner's reasoning didn't sit well with me. It was a bad case of fearful thinking and failing to use **Doubt Management**. I know all about apprehension and insecurity. It always finds a way to sneak up on me like a slithery snake before every new business venture. If I tried to fight the fear, it would beat me. Instead, I feel it. I hear it. I acknowledge its presence. And I permit it to pass through me. Most importantly, I never let it stop me from stepping toward with **Confidence** or taking a risk. If, and when, those worrisome thoughts creep up on me, I ask myself, *What's the worst that can happen?* I might fail. But so what? If I don't experience and grow from my downfall, I'll never know what winning is.

On paper, my dot-com business was an epic failure. We lost a shit ton of money, but it wasn't a failure. I learned. I grew. And I gained new skills. Fear is the dragon slayer, the killer of dreams—if you let it. It has the power to hold you back from living to your potential, when you allow yourself to become a victim of it. What many of us don't realize is that fear is a choice. You can listen to the irrational voice in your head. Or you can replace your fear with faith and believe that everything you are **Passionate** about will work out in the end for your highest good.

I have no regrets about the time and energy I put into trying to get our TV show off the ground. Saying **YES** to having a drink with the bald guy led me to develop a new lifelong friendship with Ricky. And for that, I'm appreciative and grateful.

At the end of the day, our accomplishments and successes will never mean as much as the relationships we foster with our *Network*. Ricky is a stand-up guy who would drop anything if I needed him and vice versa. Maybe one day, Ricky will decide to follow through with our TV show concept after he leaves the hotel. Then again, perhaps he won't. Whatever happens, I'll support him on his journey while I continue mine.

Denouement

November 2012 to January 2016

Every play, book, movie, or show has its ending. In my case, the film industry's chapter concluded. Even though I spent over three more years working in it, the entire experience felt like a blink of an eye.

Someday This Pain Will Be Useful to You fizzled at the Miami Festival, but I met an incredible and stunning Kiwi TV writer with tattoos and piercings everywhere. We had a long-distance relationship. She nick-named me Apollo, and I gave her the name Artemis.

Despite more excitement at the Rome Festival, including a hot date with an age-appropriate famous Italian TV and movie actress, we didn't fare better financially. With no release or additional foreign sales, we had to go digital in the U.S. (thank you, CRM).

Next, we headed to the Toronto International Film Festival (TIFF) for *Billy Bates*, grateful to Al Pacino, who pulled some strings. The inexperience of the production team and the unique content didn't result in a high-quality movie, but we had a well-received festival showing. Al Pacino showed up and beelined in my direction when he saw me. After a tight embrace, he thanked me for giving him sound advice and said his relationship with his daughter had never been better.

At TIFF, I attended the *Margin Call* showing, after-party, and a small private gathering in Kevin Spacey's suite. Leaving the suite's private elevator, a young, good-looking man dropped the woman's hand he had been holding and told us he decided to take Kevin up on his offer to spend the night. I had never seen a man flip directions and switch teams so easily. But, hey, I guess he couldn't resist.

Billy Bates also did not fare well and ended up with a straight-to-digital CRM deal. On another note, I negotiated a similar deal for *Darkroom*, which, unfortunately, didn't get accepted into any festivals. Thankfully, CRM came to the rescue, and investing in John Sloss's digital company was paying off in spades.

In 2014, I received a call from the Italians about a Holocaust movie called *Anita B.*, based on the true story of survivor Edith Bruck, a young girl rebuilding her life in post-war Italy after her liberation from Auschwitz. They had already filmed it in Czechoslovakia, paid for by the Italian government reparation funds and Rai. However, they needed a North American co-production company to help finish post-production and manage the movie's release. Saying **YES** to that took me on another excursion to Rome and then to Israel for a special ten-day, father-son trip with Dylan. *Anita B.* was accepted as an official movie at Yad Vashem and was screened on January 27, Holocaust Remembrance Day. It was a moving experience for me and Dylan.

Anita B. marked the conclusion of my filmmaking escapade. Upon my return to New York, an unexpected turn of events unfolded. I was summoned to an emergency board meeting for CRM. We had received a lucrative offer to be acquired by Gunpowder & Sky, a media conglomerate owned by the billionaire mogul Peter Chernin. Recognizing the opportunity, we unanimously decided to accept the offer. My role in technology assistance played a significant part in sealing the deal, and I was handsomely rewarded—more than tenfold compared to *The Kids Are All Right*, which was my only financially successful film.

My last involvement in the film world occurred in January 2016 at the Sundance Film Festival. I treated it as my farewell tour and indulged in some serious partying. On the final day, in the afternoon, I was approached by a panicking friend, the head of the Creative Coalition, begging me to be the Master of Ceremonies (MC) at her Coalition

Awards ceremony that evening. A bit too inebriated, I hesitated, but when she insisted, a loud **YES** escaped my mouth. Attempting to sober up, I drank coffee, had a cold shower, and borrowed a tux from the man who backed out. Miraculously, I pulled myself together. To avoid stumbling too much, she gave me a typed speech, and I presented the last award of the evening to none other than Spike Lee. Ignoring the rest of the scripted speech, I explained to the audience that, ironically, I worked on one of Spike Lee's movies as an intern for one of my first film projects at Company 3. He came up on stage and gave me a massive hug. Spike and I hung out after the event, and during toasts, I announced my retirement, a fitting end to my cinematic journey.

The End of the Film Industry

Just before the credits of a film, "The End" appears on the screen, signaling the conclusion of the movie. Similarly, it was time to embrace my version of "The End" in the movie-making business. Reflecting on the past six years, filled with both exhilarating and challenging moments, I recognized the intensity and time-consuming nature of the work. Despite being rich in knowledge, film production was a financial net zero. Although, according to film finance experts, that should be considered a major success. As previously stated, I only made money on *The Kids Are All Right* (which paid for all the other movies), and CRM was financially lucrative.

However, the experience allowed me to achieve various goals, from creating lasting films with my name on them to earning awards during my brief fifteen minutes of fame. Sharing these reflections with Ari, he acknowledged that in his career, only a few producers could claim such accolades, considering it an enormous achievement (and you made some amazing friends/relationships). All in all, a huge success!

My story didn't end there. Approaching fifty, I had to contemplate a move into a new business area that promised increased financial success, allowing for a more comfortable life as I got older. It was time to look, think, and switch again——maybe from B to C (back to consulting once more), all while keeping my *Listen and Learn* skills on.

Are You Calling Me an Idiot?

2016

Out of nowhere came the next major career shift—yet again. My subsequent business venture, real estate, emerged unexpectedly. It resulted from my openness, *Positivity*, and readiness to say **YES** despite challenging circumstances.

It all began during the dot-com boom when Mitchell and I tried to get U-Connections off the ground. One afternoon, a friend of Mitchell's called him and mentioned that a two-family house had just hit the market in a desirable area in West Hartford. When Mitchell hung up the phone, he asked me if I'd be interested in investing in the property. The plan was to fix it, rent it out, and eventually flip it. It sounded smart, so I wrote a check and let Mitchell do the rest. Saying **YES** to Mitchell served as a strategic move, resulting in a favorable return. From that day forward, I became a silent partner in flipping houses—single and small multi-family units—well before flipping houses became the thing to do.

After our dot-com business crashed, and Mitchell and I were in the middle of growing MPI, he suggested we continue investing in real estate. I checked with my accountant at Marcum, Monte, who confirmed that the tax advantages were solid, and with my financial advisor, Lisa, who noted it was an excellent way to diversify my investment portfolio. With their endorsements, I decided to proceed. Given our extensive U-Connections research on college life, particularly the shortage of student housing, we targeted real estate around college campuses as it made the most sense.

Research, Research, Research

Mitchell asked his Cornell buddies at McKinsey & Co to help us with in-depth research. After their thorough and detailed analysis, we picked schools within a two-hundred-fifty-mile radius of Manhattan. The University of Albany fit all the criteria: the cost of real estate was relatively inexpensive, there was a high demand for more student housing, and it was easy to access from New York City by train for Mitchell to oversee the properties and not miss too much consulting work.

Albany was a no-brainer. I still didn't know much about real estate investing since I was hands-off with West Hartford, so I put all my trust and faith in Mitchell and followed the advice he gave me. After all, since he made us money on the first property, I assumed he knew what he was doing. When the time was right, we decided to sell the few West Hartford properties we owned and transfer the funds and profits for use in Albany. We had just finished reading about Donald Trump's real estate investing. Trump said real estate is for wealth building and that ninety-five percent of the wealthiest people in the world used real estate to get there. He also said to avoid legally paying taxes, take as little profit as possible, and reinvest. Think what you may of Trump, but he does understand real estate.

While ***Prioritizing*** working on MPI at night, Mitchell would show me properties and financial models and ask for my opinion. Since I had never been to Albany and didn't know much about the area, I always responded by saying, "That property looks like shit, but what do I know?"

Mitchell made most of the decisions. My only suggestion was that everything we buy should be clustered because the closer the properties were to each other, the easier it would be to manage and operate them.

Being Hands-On Is Important

Over the years, we continued investing in real estate in Albany, adding more off-campus student housing units to our portfolio. While we grew, other than looking at photos of properties, writing checks here and there, and adding some input, I wasn't that involved. While all this was happening, I was consulting, working, and raising my kids, which meant I didn't have much time or energy to put into real estate. I'd only been to Albany once to check out the properties we owned.

About a decade later, the shit hit the fan. After I sold MPI, Mitchell got married and had kids. His wife convinced him that he deserved more and that I had ripped him off from the sale of MPI.

Humans are storytellers. We often tell ourselves stories, even when they're untrue, and eventually convince ourselves that these narratives reflect reality, shaping our subsequent actions. The problem is we don't see the entire picture and leave out essential parts of a story to make us believe what we want.

This is what happened with Mitchell and his wife. Their false story painted me as the greedy villain, conveniently omitting the crucial fact that Mitchell had amassed a significant sum of money at a young age from MPI, which enabled him to jumpstart his investment career. What they failed to include in their story was that I was the one who scraped together every dollar I had to form the company, as Mitchell lacked the capital to contribute. Additionally, I dedicated myself to working full-time at MPI while he only worked nights. Taking on all the financial risk, I naturally received the majority of the profits when I sold the company. Egged on by his new wife, Mitchell conveniently overlooked these details. Unbeknownst to me, he had been plotting to get back at me, mistakenly believing I had cheated him.

I used to receive my real estate returns annually from a Certified Public Accountant in Albany, which showed about one to two percent profit each year. Mitchell would call to inform me that everything was going smoothly, that the properties were appreciating, that we were making modest profits, and we were paying off our loans gradually. I recognized this as a long-term investment, and since I wasn't experiencing any losses, I didn't feel compelled to become deeply involved. Regrettably, I would later uncover a shocking truth. Nothing was as it appeared. In reality, we were generating a six-figure annual income, but I never received a dime because Mitchell had embezzled the money.

A simple mistake within the CPA's office led me to discover the truth. The accountant we used was in on the scam and falsified the annual documents he sent me. However, a new assistant working in the office inadvertently mailed me the accurate returns. Strange, I thought to myself while reading the documents. The return showed we were making lots of money that I had never heard of before. I called the accountant to find out what was happening, but he refused to answer my questions and said I needed to bring it up with Mitchell. Realizing something was fishy, I called the accountant's boss to get some info from him, but he claimed their firm did nothing wrong and that all their reports were based on the input Mitchell had given them. He told me it was between Mitchell and me if I had an issue.

Scrutinizing the documents that showed a loss, I noticed a repeating pattern with many repairs. The same toilet, for example, would get fixed numerous times at high labor costs instead of replacing it, which would have been much cheaper. Also, it was clear that almost all the expensive repairs were not being made, and the funds went directly to Mitchell. I called the property manager to ask what was happening and if he had receipts for supplies. He told me he couldn't talk to me until after he spoke to Mitchell.

Once I put the pieces of the puzzle together, I knew Mitchell was scamming me. Of course, he denied it when I confronted him. I threatened to go after him with criminal charges, which would've been an enormous headache. Instead of going down that path, I decided the easiest thing to do was to break up the partnership, settle with him, and get out of real estate by splitting the properties and moving on. Most of our investments were in Albany, with one larger one in Saratoga Springs.

A Chance Encounter

It was time to do my research and due diligence and drive to Albany to assess the properties. I left the city after a business meeting, dressed in a suit, and drove north. Pulling in front of the biggest building we owned, located off the highway, I got out of my car and stood momentarily, feeling my blood pressure rising at what I saw. The two-hundred-fifty-thousand-dollar air-conditioner replacement unit supposedly purchased was not there, and the property was in complete shambles, with garbage and rats everywhere. I had been scammed. I walked out to the front of the property, took a deep breath, looked up at the sky, and closed my eyes, trying to think of a solution to this troubling situation. Just then, a man with a thick head of silver hair drove by in a red Mercedes convertible, and when he noticed me standing there, he U-turned and headed in my direction.

"You're not from here, are you?" he yelled out his window.

I opened my eyes, looked at him, and said, "Nope. I live in Manhattan."

"Me too. I'm heading back to the city right now. Do you own this property?"

"I do."

"I want to buy it. I'll offer you double what it's worth. In cash."

My eyes narrowed in disbelief. *Was this guy for real?*

"I've got to get back on the road. Can I take you to lunch on Monday in NYC at Avra?"

"Sure." I wouldn't turn down a free lunch at my favorite upscale Greek restaurant. Not to mention, if this guy was for real, I would make a sizable profit from the sale. Mitchell and I originally bought it with the intention of fixing it up and making high-end apartments, but obviously, that never happened.

Mr. Mercedes flashed his expensive Rolex when he handed me his business card. "I'll explain everything over lunch. Then, if you like what I tell you, sell me the building, and I'll teach you what you need to know about real estate in Albany."

What were the odds that something like this would happen? A real estate investor, who appeared to be well off, happened to be driving by at the exact moment I was looking at the building and offered to pay a premium for what most would deem a shitty investment? I took it as a sign that I met Mr. Mercedes for a reason. I now had to determine what was possible.

On Monday, I had lunch with Mr. Mercedes at Avra to *Listen and Learn*. Sitting in a corner booth, we shared an expensive bottle of white wine and polished off a plate of crispy zucchini and eggplant chips dipped in tzatziki sauce, a crab cake appetizer, and grilled branzino for our main course. While we ate, Mr. Mercedes lectured me on how real estate funds make money. He told me I should start on a smaller scale and not sell my other bad properties because I would owe a lot in taxes. He also alluded to Donald Trump and how he made his fortune in real estate. I left lunch with a new outlook on how to build wealth, a deal on the table to sell Mr. Mercedes the building he wanted, and a revised plan for which I could have *Passion* to invest the money I made from this sale into development and build a residential apartment building in Albany.

Instead of getting out of real estate, I *Acted Decisively* and said **YES** to diving in headfirst. But now, without Mitchell, implementing better *Time Management*, and with my eyes wide open, I was eager to learn firsthand.

Up, Up, and Away

I went to Albany again the following weekend, surveying all the other properties and finding a new, local *Strong Team* to help. Finally, after an extensive *Networking* and interview process, I hired a property manager, a young go-getter named Pete. I also contacted Paul, a highly reputable real estate attorney in Albany whose name was given to me by our previous lawyer before he died. Pete and I drove around looking at all the properties I owned. Following the advice of Mr. Mercedes, I wanted Pete's input on which ones I should keep, which I should clean up and sell, and which would lead to my first development project.

The Saratoga Springs building doubled in value on paper because the land supposedly had space to develop. However, when I discovered the difficulties of starting construction projects due to the city's constraints on available building zoning, I knew I'd have a better chance in Albany. Pete suggested taking several of my run-down two-family houses in a row and developing a boutique-style small building that would service the Albany Medical Center staff across the street from the hospital. Since these properties were in a low-income, dangerous neighborhood, nobody wanted to redevelop them. It was a risk, but it was the differentiator that made this project work.

Outsmarting The Fox

Now that I understood the portfolio of properties, Pete provided a detailed analysis of them, including costs to repair, potential market value today and in the future, etc. It was time to meet with Mitchell to break up the partnership and divide up the properties. He had no idea I had been to Albany or that I had done so much preparation. I also found out he hadn't been up there for several years, so clearly, he had been lying about his monthly visits. I was ready to play poker. And remember, I'm a good poker player.

During poker games, I often joke that if someone thinks I'm lying or exaggerating, I'm likely telling the truth, and if they believe I'm telling the truth, I'm probably not. I played Mitchell like an amateur poker player going up against the pros at the World Series of Poker, using my favorite technique: reverse psychology. It had worked wonders with my children when they were younger and proved equally successful with Mitchell. I made him believe I wanted Saratoga Springs because it was our best building, driving the price up. My feigned interest led to a heated argument between us. Finally, I pretended to break down. To add extra drama, I leveraged my movie experience, conjured fake tears, and told him I was done fighting and just wanted it to end. He could have

Saratoga Springs while I kept all the crap in Albany, which was severely undervalued due to the condition he had left them in. Once we had an agreement drawn up and signed, Mitchell left my life forever, and I was off to become a developer in Albany.

Re-urbanization and Creating My Opportunity Zones

2017

Months later, after we were finished dividing the real estate and the sale was finalized with Mr. Mercedes, I returned to Albany to create a game plan and establish achievable milestones for the new development project. Pete helped me sell off almost all the properties except the few near Albany Medical Center. The proceeds from these would be used to pay for the start of the development, the initial equity needed. Thanks to reinvesting the funds, I was able to avoid paying taxes altogether. I also used a reputable third-party CBRE to value my properties to avoid any potential issues down the road and knowing the banks would accept them.

Three of the properties I owned were not contiguous. Two were beside each other, and an empty house stood in the middle, next to my third lot. I purchased the home for cheap. With four lots together, I assumed it was big enough to build an apartment building. I went to a local architect, had a drawing rendered, and submitted plans to the city for permits, but the asshole who worked in planning kept giving me roadblocks. He seemed to derive pleasure from exerting what little power he possessed.

I also took this hurdle as a time to research Opportunity Zones (the newest idea in real estate). Unfortunately, it was not prevalent in Albany, New York, so I was not eligible. That said, I went into deep thought and explored how to overcome these obstacles. I looked at all the components of Opportunity Zones and decided to create my own by working with the mayor of Albany, development groups for tax breaks, treasurer, etc.

I discussed the situation with Paul, my lawyer.

"This is going to be tough," he warned. "The area you want to fix up is in the hood, and since this is your first project, the approvals for these government breaks are really tough and strenuous. Also, you'll need a bank to finance the loan. I suggest you contact my friend Marge from Pioneer Bank to see if she'd be willing to provide it."

Remember, dear reader, I'm a believer in saying **YES**, while remaining *Positive*, so it only fuels my hunger when I'm told I can't do something. I had every intention of getting my building finished, even if it meant doing it unconventionally. It was time to ***Act Decisively*** and seize the moment by crafting a comprehensive plan with a clear timeline and essential checkpoints.

The first step was to go to the Capital to get approvals. Then, off I went to the bank with my rendering of the ten-unit building, the calculated cost of the project in my head, and a proposal for the bank. Little did I know I would face a slew of new challenges.

What Doesn't Kill You Makes You Stronger

Inside the bank, a teller directed me toward the loan department. A plump middle-aged woman with short brown hair was sitting at her desk. A nameplate in the front read "Marge, Loan Officer." She looked up from her computer and greeted me with a wide grin, displaying a crooked front tooth. I introduced myself and mentioned that my lawyer, Paul, suggested I see her.

She instructed me to sit in the chair across from her. "A friend of Paul's is a friend of mine. Now, how can I help you, Mr. Stein?"

I explained that I was here to inquire about a loan for a redevelopment project. I handed Marge my business plan and financial projections, and she began reviewing them. Looking through my proposal, she appeared to frown and shake her head. I knew this wasn't a good sign.

"You're from downstate, right?" she asked and started belly laughing.

I was confused. *Why was she laughing? What was so bad about being from downstate?*

If anything, I was from the city, and city folks tend to think they're better than country folks. And yet she was laughing at me like I was a clown or something.

"Is it that obvious?" I asked.

"Well, yeah. You clearly don't know what you're doing. Nobody is going to finance this garbage. I'm only telling you the truth because you know Paul."

Marge continued to look through my proposal and pointed out several issues with my plan. Finally, she explained that the location of the building was not desirable and that my projected rents were not high enough to make the loan viable.

Despite her objections, I asked Marge, "For shits and giggles, just tell me more of the important points that would make a model work for you."

I *Listened and Learned* as she explained that the project appeared too risky since I was a first-time developer and that I needed to get to the next stage, but that would never happen. It would require too much money and time. Instead, she suggested finding a more desirable location, increasing projected rents, obtaining additional collateral assets, and considering finding a partner.

Everyone Is a Virgin Once

2018 to 2019

Instead of denying or getting angry, I thought about it for a while and realized Marge was right. I needed to devise a new plan. I thanked her for her time and left the bank disappointed but determined to make the project happen. I had no intention of letting a few roadblocks get in my way.

After leaving the bank, I called the architect and told him we needed changes. I also looked at purchasing more lots. I knew I was taking a significant risk, so I developed a new theory: Put the money in now and get the building site work done, foundation poured, and wood framing completed. Then, I would go to the bank with equity already in the project, which would give me a better shot at securing a bigger loan.

My architect put me in touch with a builder named Carl who had been working for one of the more prominent builders in Albany and left to start his own company. He already had a crew and was eager to begin. So we started building.

Everyone thought I was nuts doing it like this. Paul told me I was an idiot and that nobody goes into real estate like that. Even Carl, who had already started construction, expressed concern that what I was doing was very risky. Carl lived in a perpetual state of fear and was afraid he wouldn't get paid if I ran out of money and couldn't get a loan, so he had a lot on the line too. He reminded me of this several times a day.

Marge suggested I get an official property appraisal before returning to the bank. I contacted CBRE to schedule a site visit. Manny, a young guy with dark circles under his eyes like a raccoon, arrived.

Like everyone else, he thought I was crazy. "Explain something to me. Why haven't you secured a bank loan?"

"Since I'm a virgin at this, no bank would trust me. So, I decided to take initiative and have you value the property."

"But you're already framed," he said, tilting his head in confusion.

No shit, I wanted to say to raccoon eyes, but I bit my tongue.

"You're crazy. You have a lot of money in this already."

Obviously, I did.

"What if you don't finish?"

"That's what you're here for," I said. "I need an appraisal to get a bank to fund the project."

"Okay, but I've never done it like this before."

Manny appraised the framed structure higher than nine million dollars, which I took to three local banks. One of the banks said **YES** immediately and gave me a credit letter. When the loan closed, I transitioned from being a virgin to becoming a bonafide real estate developer.

Like Potato Chips

Remember how I got burned with Mitchell? Everyone was ripping me off, including the property manager. Ever hear the expression "Burn me once, shame on you, burn me twice, shame on me?" Well, I was not going to get burned a second time. I needed to be knee-deep in the hoopla. While the building was under construction, I was hands-on and asked to be included in the weekly meetings with the subs, electrician, and concrete workers.

They kept telling me not to attend because I wouldn't understand and couldn't add value. They were wrong. I was there to **Listen and Learn** and add a fresh perspective. There was a lot of bickering during the first meeting, and nobody could agree. Finally, I whistled to get everyone's attention. "What if I get you the space across the street?"

"But those properties aren't for sale," someone said.

"Yeah, but if I can get them, we'll save a month with storage." The next day, I negotiated a lease to own the lots, enabling me to use them immediately. As a result, we saved three-hundred-thousand dollars, and the lots cost me two-hundred-thousand.

Pete suggested I buy the rest of the lots and build another building. It was a great idea because we already had the construction crew. Four years after meeting Mr. Mercedes, I was officially a successful real estate developer. Once the first building was completed, Pete leased the units out. The bank was happy. I was happy. And the money rolled in. From there, I started construction on my second building across the street and continued to look for more deals. I bought a few smaller properties to fix up, including a historic 1870 building from Vince at Albany Medical, using Pete as my right-hand man, and continued building my portfolio.

A Three-Hour Tour

One morning, while I was in Albany working on my real estate projects, I caught up with Kristy, whom I spoke with every morning on the phone.

During our conversation, I mentioned to her that Kyle, my son with special needs (who shares the same birthday as her son, Luke), was eager to give back, and I had been searching for a suitable charity for him to contribute to. Kristy suggested I contact The Ronald McDonald House, an organization providing a "home away from home" for families traveling long distances seeking medical treatment for their children in Rochester, New York, where she lived.

Taking her advice, Kyle and I headed west to Rochester, an easy three-hour drive from Albany. The welcoming staff embraced our willingness to get involved. Since then, Kyle and I have spent meaningful time there—cooking dinners, organizing family gift packs during the holidays, and raising over seventy-five thousand in donations. In recognition of our support, a room at the facility was named after Kyle. It has been an incredibly rewarding experience.

Unexpectedly, Rochester, a city that had never been on my radar, became a place where I formed a deep connection. Kristy, her husband, John, formerly Wall Street now turned high-level State Trooper, and their entire clan, including their son, Luke, as well as other relatives, such as Timmy, Mel, Jay, Morgan, Sue, and the gang, have become my extended Western New York family. Saying **YES** to the three-hour drive gave Kyle and I a greater sense of purpose and an opportunity for us to find a second "home away from home" in Rochester with Kristy and her loved ones, enjoying holidays and meals together whenever I was in town.

COVID-19 Hits—Double Down Focus on Real Estate

2020 to 2022

As I traveled back from LA after visiting my friends from film, including Ari, David and Tif, Asher, Norm, and George and the gang, in February 2020, COVID-19 struck. I watched the news on the live TV screen in Delta's first class, taking advantage of the perks as a Diamond member, having learned early on the importance of maximizing airline, hotel, and other reward programs due to my frequent travels.

Ironically, New Rochelle became the Tristate area's Ground Zero; the first case emerged in a neighborhood where I had been renting a house with my son Kyle and our dog, Brooklyn, less than a mile from where my two high school children Dylan and Erin lived. Meanwhile, Casey lived in NYC and was already navigating the real world, having flown out of the nest.

A weird side note: I got our dog, Brooklyn, from Marcelo, of all people, who asked me to watch his Bluetick Coonhound for a long weekend while he went to LA for business. That long weekend turned into something more permanent, as he never returned and moved to LA. This unexpected situation, however, was a blessing because Brooklyn became a service dog for my son and an emotional support dog for me.

The COVID-19 pandemic presented new business challenges. With the high costs of supplies and construction, everything became more expensive. Despite this, I refused to succumb to fear and instead employed *Doubt Management* and spent those two years *Focusing* on growing my real estate investments in Albany.

Just Like Donald Said

November 2022

During the COVID-19 restrictions, *Focusing* on real estate made sense due to the outdoor nature of work. I decided to go all-in, investing everything I had. Additionally, with many renters unable to pay rent, developers were facing cash shortages. Moving ahead, I purchased land at discounted prices, hired workers at lower rates—taking advantage of the limited job market—and surged ahead full steam.

I spent the majority of my time in Albany and even had a bright, pretty girlfriend, Nora, for a while, until she ended our relationship and resumed dating women. As the COVID-19 crisis subsided and 2022 neared its end, I lifted my head and took inventory of my real estate.

Following Trump's advice, my real estate portfolio had grown exponentially, and so had my wealth (not cash, as that is different).

My **Focus** had paid off, and I seized the opportunity in the thriving real estate market, increasing my ownership to two-hundred units in the New York State Capital Region. I was nominated for Developer of the Year in 2022 and secured the second-place position. This situation shows that if you remain **Focused**, determined, and **Work Hard**, you will increase your odds of success.

However, the tide was turning swiftly. Interest rates began to soar, thanks to Biden's spending policies, and this marked a significant shift in the real estate landscape. The Opportunity Zones I had created for myself were closing as material costs, labor shortages, and capital prices all escalated. The real estate game I had grown accustomed to had come to an end.

What was next? I wondered. Dazed and confused about my future, I had just turned fifty-five and had one year left before becoming an empty nester. Life Volume II was ending.

It was time to start planning my Life Volume III.

THE WRAP UP

September 2022

While writing this last chapter, I considered myself untethered for future planning. Essentially, we all contend with constraints that shape the boundaries of our lives. These are guidelines, or rules, we adhere to and they are often non-negotiable. While not inherently negative, limiting them as much as possible fosters flexibility.

In my case, the imminent departure of my youngest daughter, Erin, for college marked the beginning of my journey as an empty-nester, the start of Life Volume III.

Life Volume III: Sunset Period encompasses the retirement, empty nest stage, and living out the rest of our days. This marks a reflective period in our lives where accumulated experiences guide us through the remaining time.

It's Show Time

"Other than that, how was the play, Mrs. Lincoln?"

Planning an entire Life Volume is daunting, and no small order for anyone. While navigating crossroads during Life Volume I: Becoming an Adult (my high school and college years) and Life Volume II: Post-College (my various life choices and careers), I developed *Ronnie's Steps to*

Success, a systematic approach utilizing my life lessons that have helped me achieve goals.

Before starting Life Volume III, I needed to employ these techniques again. I will walk you through my thought process, allowing you to *Listen and Learn* how I apply *Ronnie's Steps to Success* in easy READY. SET. GO. format. Then you may apply them to your situation, whether it is a simple new endeavor or an entire reset, or Life Volume planning. Below is a highlight, and you will find more details (catch you up to today) in the workbook:

ownyoursuccessnow.com/workbook.

READY. SET. GO.

When I stepped into what I call *Life Volume III*, I made a bold decision: life isn't winding down...it's just getting started. With that mindset, I created my own personal methodology: READY. SET. GO. to guide me through reinvention with clarity, confidence, and purpose.

READY

I began by defining my overarching goal: Giving Back.

- To society, through this book, and a future charity.

- To my kids, through life lessons and support.

- And to myself, through legacy, joy, and meaningful relationships.

I asked myself what truly matters and used that clarity to explore where I wanted to head in my professional life, where I live, and personal relationships. I evaluated my constraints, finances, family, health, and began mapping realistic, aligned options for my next chapter.

SET

To gain inspiration and insight, I embarked on what I call my Reconnection Tour. I visited twelve cities and reconnected with old friends to hear about their lives, lessons, and aspirations. What I discovered was comforting: No one has it all figured out. Doubt is universal but manageable.

Through these conversations, I started researching and testing key choices.

- Professional Direction: I began pivoting from real estate into new ventures like AI consulting and M&A deals in Brazil. I ran small pilot projects to see what fit.

- Location: After testing five cities (LA, Charleston, Austin, Miami, and Nashville), I chose Miami, a city that checked nearly all my boxes: sunshine, community, opportunity, and joy. We see how this works out.

- Personal Life: I experimented with new activities like pickleball and rollerblading, reflected on my relationships, and decided I was seeking depth, fun, and future partnership, but not necessarily traditional marriage. Also, get a new Redbone Coonhound puppy (Daisy Duke).

GO

With my vision and research in hand, I took action. I moved to Miami, refined my business strategy, and leaned into a new rhythm of life, balancing travel, legacy projects, and my own well-being.

Today, I continue consulting, preparing for my future charity, and embracing each day with **YES** energy, whether that's watching the sunrise, working out, dating, or hopping on my Vespa for a ride to pickleball.

It's not perfect, but it's progress. It's purposeful. And it's mine.

Conclusion

Through the READY. SET. GO. method, I've learned that reinvention isn't a one-time leap, it's a thoughtful process of realignment. It's about trusting your intuition, trying new things, and surrounding yourself with the right people.

My ultimate message?

Say **YES**. Trust the process. Own your success.

To get started, download the workbook at:

ownyoursuccessnow.com/workbook.

ACKNOWLEDGEMENTS

To everyone whose path has crossed mine—teachers, mentors, team-mates, colleagues, relationships, friends—much appreciation for the life lessons. Especially for those whose positive support, wisdom, and presence have shaped me in ways too vast to fit on these pages.

With deep gratitude, I thank you all.

Some special shout-outs (please do not be offended if I missed you—see above).

To My:

Brother from another mother: Tommy Ara (wife Lina and Bella and Cam)—my consiglieri and travel buddy.

Advisor, therapist, #1 employee, and trusted friend: Kristy Nin-fo—there every day for me.

Proofreaders and close friends: Stephen Fitzpatrick, Jeff Popper, and Edwin Ashley, M.D.—thank you for your time, effort, and taking my numerous calls.

Technology guru and longtime friend: Tom Zschach (wife Tanya and brother Andy)—always up for a discussion and work through a problem.

#1 case study and social media helper: Renee Phillips—proving the book works.

Community shout-outs: LA, Miami Beach, NYC, Albany, Brazil, Boston, Toronto, Rochester (Bills Mafia), and now Charleston—love all my peeps.

Creative collaborators: Photographers Dan Marino (Daniel Marino Studio), Web Designer Sev Sanders, and Publicist Jennifer 'JLo' Lopez (JLPR Media)—my support network.

Wellness connector: Myk (Modern OM)—who discovered me at Kathy's breath-work party and made introduction to the publishers.

Publishers: Jennifer Grace and Raven Petty (Raven + Grace Press)—thank you for organizing my thoughts, embracing my questions, believing in me, and helping create a book I'm proud of.

Ron Stein

The spark for this book was lit over brunch near Central Park, where friends, curious about my career pivots, asked how I managed to reinvent myself so many times.

One of them said, "You should write a book. Then, when people ask, just tell them to read it."

I said "YES!" and here we are.

Ron Stein is a transformational business leader, entrepreneur, and author. His career spans Wall Street, consulting, finance, film production, real estate development, and motivational leadership. His mission is simple: to empower others to say "YES!" to opportunity and own their success.

Born in Manhattan and lived across New York (from Long Island to Westchester to upstate), Ron earned a Bachelor of Science in Finance and Economics from the University of Delaware and an MBA from NYU's Stern School of Business. He has also completed executive programs at INSEAD, Wharton, and Harvard because, apparently, sleep is optional for Ron.

Ron's ventures have earned recognition across industries. His films have appeared at Sundance and Tribeca and received Golden Globe and Oscar nominations; his tech firm was named IT Firm of the Year; and his real estate projects earned Developer of the Year honors.

He has helped countless individuals and organizations transform their paths, lectured at universities, and taught courses.

Now based in Charleston, South Carolina, after a few years in Miami Beach, Ron's plan is to focus on motivating and coaching others through career transitions—especially in today's fast-moving, AI-driven world.

So "Say **YES**! to Own Your Success" now at ownyoursuccessnow.com.

Take control. "Own It!"

www.ingramcontent.com/pod-product-compliance
Lightning Source LLC
Chambersburg PA
CBHW051612120626
46551CB00014B/1758